POSTSCRIPT

Though this book was completed some time ago, a succession of adversities has prevented publication until now. The reader should therefore view it as a discussion of the subject up to 1967.

At first sight this would seem to be a grave if not fatal disadvantage, since the music is so influenced by rapid changes of fashion, and particularly since the book deals hardly at all with the new "progressive pop". I have however found it necessary to make few changes, since the method of approach, that of the academic music critic, is well tried.

Furthermore, I believe that "progressive pop" has already become a separate form, which can be excluded quite logically on the criteria already given. It has only briefly been a mass music; that the nature of mass taste remains much the same is shown by the continuing popularity of Tom Jones and Herman's Hermits, and by the rise of the Reggae. Moreover "progressive music" is no longer functional—its audience goes to listen attentively, not to dance. Most important, unlike all previous popular music, it concerns itself with musical development, and not with the statement and repetition of a theme.

These considerations combined with professional experience in the field have convinced me of the importance of this new music, and that it requires a separate study, which is in course of preparation.

Edward Lee
Cambridge, May 1970

experience or impression rather than careful sociological investigation has been the basis of my argument. I can sympathise, as there are many ideas which I, myself, wish to go on to examine far more closely. To have done so in this book would, however, have postponed completion indefinitely, and I have long felt that there was an urgent need for a work of this kind, since, to the best of my knowledge, no writer has covered the area dealt with in Part Two in any detail. No man can be an expert in everything, and previous authors on popular music have clearly felt more able to offer something of value when discussing earlier periods; my indebtedness to these writers will be clear both from the text and from the bibliography. Nevertheless, I too have been obliged to leave gaps: naturally, I shall be glad to receive from readers any points of information or constructive criticism which may help to fill them.

Edward Lee
Cambridge

to be generally agreed that in earlier centuries a more distinct stratification of society, with consequent cultural divisions, can be shown to have existed. Moreover, differences might logically be expected between the two types of art, since the one depended on the patronage of a small number of persons of a very limited social range, and the other upon a much broader cross-section of the community, with much less leisure or means to study and enjoy the more complex forms of art.

It may be argued that the upper classes have enjoyed and played popular music, a view supported by the popularity of "Greensleeves" in the sixteenth century or of the Beatles in the twentieth. But the vital consideration, from my point of view, is that these classes did not call such popular music into existence in the way that the Tudor court did with much of Skelton's work.

3. The music under consideration will not be of the type which, though usually easily recognised, has not yet been adequately labelled, i.e. what Stravinsky calls "composer's music", and which has been variously named "symphonic", "serious", "classical", "art", "conservatory" or "straight" music.

The characteristic features of this music are minority appeal, influence of individual patrons (these may take the form of a body such as the Arts Council) and an interest in extended composition which involves the development rather than the repetition of the original material.

It will be seen that the selection of these criteria automatically involves the consideration of "folk music", but also dictates that equal attention be given (especially in the present century) to types of music which would be rigorously excluded by many lovers of traditional song as being commercially produced and not authentic manifestations of popular culture. It may be that such differences cannot be argued, because they are dependent ultimately on deeply held personal preferences. It is certainly necessary for me to declare my own strong interest in and even affection for "commercial popular music". But I believe that some rational claims may be made for my point of view, because my interest in this book is primarily in an aspect of social life rather than in value judgements, though these are perhaps inevitable. Moreover, I feel that a more comprehensive picture is obtained by taking what are admittedly easier criteria to apply. It may also perhaps be argued that in this way one is less likely to fall into an unbalanced viewpoint, as is sometimes found when an investigator starts out with a strongly held aesthetic or socio-political belief.

In conclusion, I must anticipate the complaint of the reader who finds that he wishes a topic had been pursued further, particularly where personal

Preface

The aims of this book are to present the main facts about the history of popular music in England in one volume, and to discuss the nature of popular music in this century from a technical and aesthetic viewpoint.

It is therefore divided into two parts, historical and modern, either of which can be read separately, though clearly a knowledge of one will enrich understanding of the other. The book is not technical in aim—it does not, for instance, teach the reader how to compose or perform popular music—but musical illustrations and analyses are included, since an understanding of the techniques of the music can only be an advantage.

I have found it necessary to limit myself to the consideration of English popular music, especially in the historical section, though the increasingly international quality of modern life means that what is said about the modern period largely applies to the whole of Great Britain. The Celtic cultures are very different both in mythology and underlying philosophy from the culture of the English peoples and require a specialised knowledge which I lack.

The term "popular music" may be defined in several ways, but for the purposes of this book I have taken the standpoint that it has three main characteristics:

1. It must be popular in a strictly numerical sense, i.e., it is the music which is most frequently listened to by the majority of the population.

2. It is not the music of the court, the aristocracy, the episcopal churches, or of the richer middle class.

Such a distinction is not made on the basis of political or social theories of inter-class hostility; in fact, I tend to feel that historians and sociologists have shown such generalisations to have only a limited validity. But it seems

Illustrations

Contents

To Bill and Ann Hamilton

© 1970 by Edward Lee
First published 1970 by
Barrie and Jenkins (Barrie Books Ltd)
2 Clement's Inn, London WC2
Printed in Great Britain by
Western Printing Services Ltd, Bristol

EDWARD LEE

Music
of the People

A STUDY OF POPULAR MUSIC IN
GREAT BRITAIN

BARRIE & JENKINS
LONDON

THE MAIDEN'S DILEMMA,
OR
"WHICH IS THE MAN".

As Sung by Miss Leslie,

IN

"THE WATERMAN,"

Written by
C. DIBDIN.

The Music by
J. GRAY.

Ent. Sta. Hall.   Price 2/-

LONDON,
Charles Jeffery's, 21, Soho Square.
EDINBURGH,
Paterson & Sons, 27, George Street.

L'Enfant, Printer, 18, Rathbone Pl.

MUSIC OF THE PEOPLE

Acknowledgements

This book could hardly exist without frequent quotation from songs. Unfortunately, it has not been possible to discover whether copyright is applicable to all the Victorian songs quoted, and if so, to whom, but I hope that if there have been any oversights, owners will at this point accept grateful thanks. In particular, I would like to thank: Messrs Campbell Connolly for "Ain't It Grand To Be Blooming Well Dead?", "Christmas in Killarney", "I Ain't Got Nobody", "I'm Flying High", "My Very Good Friend the Milkman"; Messrs Francis, Day and Hunter for "It Happened In Monterey", "Lovely Lady", "Wonderful Love", "You Don't Have To Tell Me, I Know", "Laugh Clown Laugh", "That is Love"; Messrs Jewel Music for "Little Red Rooster"; Messrs Northern Music for "Anna", "I Love Only You", "I Saw Her Standing There", "Love Me Do", "Misery", "Please Please Me"; Messrs Victoria Music for "That Old Black Magic", "Tangerine"; Messrs Williamson Ltd, for "You'll Never Walk Alone"; Messrs Lawrence Wright Ltd, for "Basin Street Blues", "I Can't Give You Anything But Love", "On The Sunny Side Of The Street", "Memories Of You", "Mistakes", "Burlington Bertie"; Messrs Chappell Ltd, for "All The Things You Are", "Body And Soul", "How High The Moon", "Moonlight In Vermont"; Messrs Robbins for "Laura"; Messrs Mills Music for Ewan MacColl's "Four Loom Weavers" and "Twenty One Years"; Messrs J. G. Windows Ltd, for C. E. Catchside-Warrington's "Weshin' Day"; Messrs Ascherberg, Hopwood and Crew Ltd, for "We Don't Want To Fight"; Messrs Feldman Ltd, for "Father, Dear Father, Come Home With Me Now", "Martha", "The Husbands' Boat"; Messrs Keith Prowse Ltd, for "My Beastly Eyeglass"; Messrs Joseph Williams Ltd, for "Under The Weeping Willer".

I owe a great deal to *Victorian Song: from Dive to Drawing Room* by Maurice Willson Disher, and I have also drawn upon the labours of Reginald Nettel in his *Seven Centuries of Popular Song* (Dent), A. L. Lloyd in *Come All Ye Bold Miners* (Lawrence and Wishart), and Christopher Pulling in his *They Were Singing* (Harrap). I would like to thank the publishers for permission to quote from the following books: Messrs Barrie and Rockliff, *Music in a New Found Land* by Wilfrid Mellers; Messrs Dent, *Anglo-Saxon Poetry* ed. R. K. Gordon, and *Seven Centuries of Popular Song* by Reginald Nettel; Messrs Dobson, *Music and Society* by Wilfrid Mellers; The English Folk Dance and Song Society, various editions of *English Dance and Song* and the Society's journal; Messrs Evans Bros., *The Wakefield Mystery Plays* by Martial Rose; Messrs Faber and Faber, *The Seafarer*, from *Personae* by Ezra Pound, *Conversations with Igor Stravinsky* by Igor Stravinsky and Robert Craft, *Concerning Jazz* an article by Douglas Hague (ed. Sinclair Traill); Messrs Harrap, *They Were Singing* by Christopher Pulling; Messrs Hodder and Stoughton, *The Story of the Jubilee Singers* ed. Theodore Seward; "The Opposition to Jazz in the United States" (*Jazz Monthly*, vol. 4, no. 4, 1958) by Neil Leonard; Messrs MacGibbon and Kee, *The Reluctant Art* by Benny Green; Messrs Methuen, *English Folk Song: Some Conclusions* by Cecil Sharp, *Poetry and Music in the Early Tudor Court* by John Stevens; "Sixties" by Wilfrid Mellers (*New Statesman*, 24 February 1967); Oxford University Press, *Music in the Five Towns* by Reginald Nettle; *Lark Rise* by Flora Thompson, *Chopi Music* by Hugh Tracey; "Town Waits" by J. C. Bridge (*Proceedings of the Royal Musical Association*, 1928); Messrs Secker and Warburg, *Jazz: its Evolution and Essence* by André Hodeir; Workers' Music Association, *The Singing Englishman* by A. L. Lloyd.

I am indebted to the following for permission to reproduce the illustrations: The Fitzwilliam Museum (*Auditus* by A. Bosse, *Humming Birds* by G. Cruikshank, *Farmer Giles* by J. Gillray, *The Enraged Musician* by W. Hogarth, *That Old Fashioned Mother of Mine* by W. R. Sickert); The English Folk Dance and Song Society (Traditional Dancers—photograph from Sir Benjamin Stone's collection—early photograph of the Padstow Hobby; Barry Herbert (late photograph of the Padstow Hobby); The Hulton Picture Library (Bill Haley, Jitterbug, Tango); Popperfoto (Dance Hall scene, The Love Affair; Apple, The Beatles).

Finally, I offer my grateful thanks to the following, who have made this book possible: Mrs Irène Armitage and Dr Alan Bush of the Workers' Music Association, for their thoughtful comments; William Ashton, for much help in the past with popular melodies and chords; the staff of the English Folk Dance and Song Society at Cecil Sharp House for their assistance; the Librarian of the University Library, Cambridge, for much help; Chris Hatton, for the first guidance on a serious approach to the subject; Pete Lay, of the Soulstirrers, for the opportunity to experience beat music at first hand; Graham Phillips, for information about aspects of Welsh music; Dave Turner, for much advice and insight into folk music; John Simpson, for reading the manuscript, and Elizabeth Simpson and Virginia Valdambrini for typing it; Robert Arnold for the first idea, and for hours of discussion; John Bannister and John Blake for much informed discussion; David Baxter, Theo Garson, Bill and Ann Hamilton, Norman Hearn, my wife, Jenny Lee, Mr and Mrs A. E. Lee, and Col. and Mrs G. L. S. Vaughan for unfailing support during some very difficult times. I owe a special debt, because of their intimate involvement with the book, to: Adrian Kendon for constant support, advice and records; James Payne for constant standards of musical taste and excellence; Malcolm Lowe for unremitting attention to detail and for the unpublished notes which have largely formed my ideas about an approach to the analysis of rhythm; Malcolm Cormack and his wife Lynn for an ever open ear and the bulk of the work in obtaining and preparing illustrations; David Sharp for much advice and more patience; and to Frances Wyllie who never refused help in the last and most tedious stages of preparation.

Part One

The History of English Popular Music

The English could lay claim to the best-looking, most musical, and to the best tables of any people.
ERASMUS, *Encomium Moriae*

I Before the Conquest

cyninges thegn,
guma gilphlaeden. gidda gemyndig.[1]

Though the earliest period of British history for which we have any written record is the Roman-British (AD 43–410), little is known of the indigenous culture. We have a few popular fragments from Rome (not British in origin), such as a marching song of Caesar's legions:

urbani servate uxores, moechum calvum adducimus.[2]

We know a little about the music of the Church, and we have the twelfth-century testimony of Giraldus Cambrensis that the Celts sang in parts

quot videas capita, tot audias carmina discrimina vocum varia.[3]

To the dispute about the meaning of this phrase—most likely denoting a form of organum, or singing in fourths and fifths—we may offer, for the sake of argument, the idea that it referred to the form of singing found among some primitive peoples which is known as heterophony, the simultaneous free interpretation of the same melody by several people. Giraldus himself points out the likelihood of Scandinavian influence in the post-Roman period.

The evidence being this slight, perhaps the most valuable thing we can observe is the way in which the music, like the Celtic language, was almost entirely obliterated by the Anglo-Saxon invaders (some dozen or so words remained). The idea that the culture of centuries can be swept away in a few years is, as we shall see later, an important one.

[1] The king's thegn, a proud man, mindful of songs.
[2] Citizens, guard your wives, we bring the baldheaded adulterer.
[3] You may hear as many distinct and varied songs from the voices as there are heads.

Our knowledge of Anglo-Saxon music is equally scanty, but we do know that it was accompanied on the harp, both from internal evidence, such as the line from *Beowulf*:

thaer waes hearpan sweg, swutel sang scopes.[1]

and also from archaeology; a harp from the Sutton Hoo ship burial of AD 654 can be seen in the British Museum. It has six short strings and a largish sound-box; these would suggest a sound halfway between the Spanish guitar and the ukulele.

The researches of Professor Milman Parry among Serbian folk singers are generally accepted as being relevant in pattern though not in detail to Old English poetry.[2] In particular, he noted that Serbs use a form of chant, rather than more strikingly wrought melodies.

About the verse, of which we have a substantial amount, much more is known. In the first place it is typically Teutonic in that each line was divided by a caesura into half-lines of two stresses each, these being linked by alliteration, as in the line:

hlude bi hearpan // hleothor swinsade.

Rhyme was not a feature of this poetry. The natural break, and its consequent suitability for antiphony, may account for the use, on occasions, of two singers:

thonne with Scilling sciren reorde
for uncrum sigedrythne song ahofan
hlude bi hearpan, hleothor swinsade.[3]

There has been some misunderstanding of the nature of the gatherings at which these songs were performed. A. L. Lloyd, in his book *The Singing Englishman*, says:

The Anglo-Saxon military class had its heroic pagan epics, and the clerical class—missionaries, monks, priests—had their Latinized lyrical poems on Christian themes. But what the third class had, the farm

[1] In that place were was the sound of the harp, the clear song of the minstrel.
[2] *Serbo-Croatian Folk Songs*, collected by Milman Parry, ed., A. B. Lord, contributions by B. Bartók and G. Herzog (Columbia University Studies in Musicology, New York, 1951).
[3] When Scilling and I with clear voice raised up a song for our victorious lord, the story sounded loud and cheerfully to the harp.

workers, we hardly know beyond a few magical charms for the swarming of bees, the curing of sick cattle, or the securing of at least a crop a man would not starve on.

Such a statement is open to question in several ways. It is true, for instance, that some of the extant poetry deals with Christian topics (*Elene*) and some shows a pagan influence (*Beowulf*). But the exact relationship of these elements is very complex and although outside the scope of this book, it should be noted that the last pagan area, Sussex, was converted in 680, some two hundred years before the writing down of much of the poetry we have. Moreover, the Church was by no means in a self-imposed isolation: Aldhelm, Bishop of Sherborne from 715, used to put religious lyrics to popular songs, and sang these to people returning from church to make them more aware of the Christian message. This imaginative move is the first recorded instance of such an approach, which was not repeated until the thirteenth century. It is also erroneous to suggest that the verse was Latinised: indeed, a striking factor of Old English was its resistance to any but Teutonic (especially Norse) influence. Latin had no serious effect on the language until well into the Middle Ages.

Charms do exist and are clearly popular in origin, but they are very far from being divorced from the heroic poetry; they differ only in variety of vocabulary and strictness of treatment of the alliteration and metre.

However, there is more convincing evidence as to the genuine popularity of the traditional poetry, and to the consequent unity of culture in this period. Milman Parry's researches show a situation very similar to that manifested in the account by Bede of the life of Caedmon, a cowherd. From this it is clear that regular communal feasts in the lord's hall, followed by the improvisation of songs by all present, were a feature of Anglo-Saxon life:

> Then in banquets, when it was decided, for entertainment's sake that they should all sing in turn to the harp, when he saw the harp approach him, he get up in shame from the gathering and went home.

Later, Caedmon received Divine inspiration, and "whatever he learned of holy teaching, through scribes, after a small while he adorned with poetic language of the utmost sweetness and inspiration, and nearly always created in English poetic form". These "pious songs" were imitated by others. One of them ("Caedmon's Hymn") survives and is completely traditional in nature.

The feasibility of such improvisations is again corroborated by Milman

Parry, who discovered that the Serbian poems consisted entirely of stock phrases, or formulaic patterns. The American scholar F. M. Magoun, followed this lead and showed that at least seventy per cent of Old English poetry was similarly formulaic. If we compare

Unferth mathelode, Ecglafes bearn[1]

with

Beowulf mathelode, bearn Ecgtheowes[2]

which occurs a few lines later, it will illustrate the point.

Such a discovery forces one to rethink one's attitudes to poetry, since our view today is still very much that of the Romantics, in that we value freedom of ideas and originality of expression. Formulaic poetry is not concerned with these, nor even Dryden's conception that good poets produce

What oft was thought, but ne'er so well expressed.

Poetic value for Anglo-Saxons lay not in the discovery of individual phrases, but in the selection and arrangement of traditional ones. The poet was concerned with *cumulative* effect, in which the individual phrase may well be alterable or dispensable. This suggests that we may have to reconsider our attitudes to statements of the type which pop singer Paul Jones made recently, that "lyrics can always be altered". Such a comment must imply a total condemnation in any poetic system in which the most valued text is that which is most highly wrought (as in T. S. Eliot's work) and that which is "organic", in Aristotle's sense that nothing can be added or taken away without detriment. But this is not so in a system in which suitability to occasion and skill in arrangement of traditional material is considered more important. This conception takes on extra significance to the lover of literature when it is realised that a similar theory has recently been advanced about the poetry of Wyatt.[3] It should however be added that some scholars of Old English have suggested a theory in which every formulaic phrase is experienced as having overtones of the other contexts in which it appears. A tension is thus felt to arise between these overtones and the usage in question. The quality of a poet will be shown in his skill in managing these tensions, and in his use of the juxtaposition of formulae to obtain contrast.

[1] Unferth spoke, the son of Ecglaf.
[2] Beowulf spoke, the son of Ecgtheow.
[3] H. A. Mason: *Humanism and Poetry—the Early Tudor Period*, 1959.

Such a theory implies a need for very detailed knowledge, and the reader—especially if confronted also with a language barrier—may feel that acquaintance with the period is beyond him. This, I think, would be unfortunate, since the very difference in the nature of the period is what is so fascinating about it. The different poetic values, and different nature of poetic vision from that of later ages is, as I hope I have shown, provocative. A. L. Lloyd believes that we can confidently look forward to a time when society is so altered that there is no longer any special distinction between the composer and the rest of his fellow men, when cultured music and popular music become one and the same. This idea becomes the more stimulating when we realise that it is not merely a Utopian prophecy, but that such a condition did at one time obtain.

Fortunately, the Old English need not be a barrier to acquaintance with these early lyrics. There are available translations by competent scholars and to some extent the inevitable loss which occurs in the more literal translation can be made good by turning to freer renderings. Ezra Pound's version of *The Seafarer* is perhaps the most well known of these. We find that Old English poetry is full of clashes of accent:

> Waeron fet mine forste gebunden

and Pound's

> Frost froze the land, hail fell on the earth then

reflects this, as well as catching the sense of bleakness which at times exerted a definite attraction on the Old English poets (the poet speaks of "huilpan sweg"—the sound of the curlew, and of "maew singende"—the singing gull).

On the other hand, it is a prose version which more nearly reflects the simple dignity which can arise in popular song from genuine experience: "Then the hard night watch was often my duty, when [the ship] tosses by the cliffs. Afflicted with cold, my feet were fettered by frost, by icy bonds."

But Pound's virtue is his ability to catch something of the Old English heroic spirit, and also of the remoteness which its specialised diction gave. Admittedly he omits the Christian elements of the original but the following lines reflect closely a spirit which vanished only after the Conquest:

> And for this, every earl whatever, for those speaking after—
> Laud of the living, boasteth some last word,
> Frame on the fair earth 'gainst foes his malice,
> Daring ado. . . .
> So that all men shall honour him after

> And his laud beyond them remain 'mid the English,
> Aye, for ever, a lasting life's-blast,
> Delight 'mid the doughty.

This vision of the loyal soldier/servant and the proud, heroic and generous leader was for the Anglo-Saxons so comprehensive that it even stamped itself on the divine: thus Satan, in the *Fall of the Angels*, is conceived of as a disloyal thegn of God, his bountiful chieftain.

Again, this view was a communal one; the sentiments were deeply held, and their expression in well-composed poetry was even demanded by the community:

> From time to time the King's thegn, a proud man, mindful of songs who remembered very many of the old traditions, picked out words well linked together; the man again began to recite with skill the journey of Beowulf, and cunningly to create a suitable story and to vary the words.

It would be pleasing to think that such a unity of culture could again exist. But the truth seems to be that such cultures can only exist in societies in a fairly elementary state of development, in which the duties and rewards are equally experienced by all the members. Our own society is too fragmented, and began to become so fairly soon after this poetry was written down. After the Norman Conquest, epic tales were still told in ballads, but the listener is entertained rather than addressed as one who is closely identified in reality with the problems examined by the poet. It is significant that in the later Middle Ages, as the functions of the soldier and the peasant became separated elements in society, the interest turned to fantasy and magic, and away from such monsters as Grendel, which though unreal possessed deep symbolic qualities. Interest turned away from the relationship of the individual to the community, in which personal feelings were bypassed and superior powers were amorphous, to the feelings of the individual towards woman—both in her physical form as a lover, and in her sublimated religious role, as the Virgin Mary.

2 The Medieval Period

Is it not fine to dance and sing
When the bells of death do ring.
ANON

The idea that medieval people were either brave knights, beautiful damsels (whose problems in life came from dragons and the occasional evil baron), or faithful retainers who sang "Sumer is ycumen in" loudly, spontaneously, and in four parts, has never been very convincing to scholars. Similarly, literature has long since passed the point at which the more subtly Romantic conceptions of Scott could be regarded as central in importance. Contemporary manuscripts show us the ostentation of noble banquets, and the transmutation of this feeling for display which produced the splendour of Gothic architecture; we find also the extremes of fantasy which meant that for a royal Maying of 1515 there were "certain bowers purposely filled with singing birds" in the woods near Greenwich. On the other hand, we discover in the tradition of reformist sermons the appalling poverty pitied by Langland. Perhaps this aspect of medieval life is better known because of its relevance to the theses of modern radical thought. A contemporary sermon illustrates the point:

> The poor man will not have bread to eat, except perhaps a handful of rye or barley: his poor wife will lie in and they will have four or six little ones about the hearth or the oven, which perchance will be warm; they will ask for bread, they will scream, mad with hunger. The poor mother will have but a little salted bread to put to their mouths.
> (Gerson, *Vivat Rex*)

Such extremes of material condition might be expected to result in a division of culture, if only for financial reasons. Thus the minstrels and the nobility had a large variety of instruments at their disposal—shawm, rebec, crwth, portative organ and trumpet were but a few. At this time the idea of combining instruments into an orchestra was first developed, and on occasion very large numbers were gathered together. It is probable that Chaucer was inspired by such a performance when he wrote, in *The Parlement of Foules*:

> Of instruments of strenges in acord
> Herde I so pleye a ravyshyng swetnesse
> That God, that makere is of al and lord
> Ne herde nevere beter, as I gesse.

Such instrumentalists were used in the houses of noblemen on all musical occasions, including as an accompaniment to dancing. For the nobility, dancing was highly formalised and was seen as a vital part of the whole complex of social relationships. A nobleman had to learn to dance, partly as a form of self-expression within the whole framework of the code of courtly love, but also in order to know how to conduct himself in this, as in other situations, in a manner which both became his station and showed his awareness of the social standing of others. Typical of the kind of ensemble which played on such occasions was that recorded in the *Duke of Northumberland's Household Book*:

> Item, Mynstralls in Household iii, *viz.* a taberett, a luyte, and a rebec.

For out of doors, and for noisier occasions, two shawms and a sackbut were preferred. Unlike the dances, the music seems to have been informal and mostly improvised, since most of the music which survives consists of lines of semibreves which probably acted as a rough guide and a basis for improvisation, rather as chord symbols are at present used in jazz.

From this evidence we can deduce that the music must have been governed by strict, widely known conventions, but we can say little more. Accounts of the accompaniment of troubadour songs suggest a style using many thirds and possibly contrapuntal. Harmonisation in thirds and the use of the Ionian mode (major scale) seem to have been the most distinctive features of the popular style: such music as we have which is of known popular influence (such as the songs of the Goliards, or wandering scholars) is most frequently in this idiom, and the Church was constantly advising musicians to avoid such modern, dissonant and uncultured sounds in favour of the older organum with its use of fourths and fifths.

Some idea of the more courtly type of dance music may be obtained from the following:

It is one of the most popular dances of the time, an estampie, and was played
in a lively fashion, probably on two stringed instruments. The repetitions are
likely to have been typical of popular music, but the fact that the piece is
clearly conceived for two instruments in this case (as is shown by the re-
appearance of a theme from the lower voice, transposed, in the upper voice)
indicates the work of a composer and musically literate person.

Such things were not for the peasantry though; in fact it is unlikely that
the majority were ever present at such a performance. A lack of leisure and
money permitted them to own only the simplest and cheapest instruments.
Apart from the occasional rebec, the most complex, and possibly the most
popular, since contemporary writers so frequently associate it with the common people, was the bagpipe. Representations of working men playing the
instrument are to be found in several places—most notably, carved in Win-
chester Cathedral, and in an illuminated manuscript (the *Beauchamp Psalter*)
dated 1372. Perhaps the most well-known performer was Chaucer's Miller:

> A bagpipe wel koude he blowe and sowne.[1]

Mostly, the rural population could only sing, and dance to their singing;
and not always meeting with official approval:

> Karolles, wrastlings, or sumer games,
> Whoso ever haunteth any swich shames
> In cherche, other in cherchyerd,
> Of sacrilege he may be aferd:
> Of enterludes of singing,
> Or tabor bete or other pypinge—
> Whyle the prest stondeth at masse.

The quotation comes from Richard Rolle, but in this he was only one voice
in a continuous stream of attacks by the Church, which thought such entertainments to be conducive to sin—contemporary accounts seeming to suggest
that this opinion was not entirely unjustified. Moreover, dancing was too
closely associated with paganism and the old Nature religion to be acceptable.

Nevertheless, the dance remained popular, and there are many records and
pictures of people enjoying dancing. By far the most important form this
produced was the carole; in fact, something like ninety per cent of the extant
lyrics of the late fifteenth century were in this form. Some authorities suggest
that it was performed in a chain, in much the same fashion as people now

---

[1] *The Canterbury Tales*, Prologue, line 565.

dance the Conga. The dancers are thought to have divided into chorus and leader, and while he sang the verse of the song, they took three steps to the left. Everyone then marked time while the chorus responded with the burden or refrain. Another and perhaps more widely held view is that the carole was a round dance (*viz.* the Chaucer quotation below) in which the chorus danced in a circle round the leader. The link between the carole and the dance disappeared in the later Middle Ages, but at the time of Chaucer the union still existed:

> And after that they wenten in compas
> Daunsynge about this flour an esy pas,
> And songen, as it were in carole wyse,
> This balade, which that I shal yow devyse.[1]

It is an interesting paradox that this most popular form may well have taken its origins from the songs of the leaders of the religious processions, and taken their antiphonal form from the Litany.

The word carole, which as used here should not be confused with its later more limited meaning of a Christmas song, referred to a song of a definite form, dealing with a wide variety of topics. It was a lyric in that it dealt with a personal emotion connected with love, a festival, or a religious occurrence. It had no fixed number of lines or metric feet, though in any given piece the form was fixed, as it had to be if it were to act as the lyric of a song whose melody was repeated many times. As we saw above, its main feature was a verse, followed by a burden or chorus, in which all joined. As the form became divorced from the dance, and then from the music, it became a more complicated and sophisticated literary vehicle.

An example of the carole is given below. It is a story of unrequited love, told in a manner typical of the period. The idea that the lover cannot sleep was a convention of the time, as was the opening ("As I rode out one fine morning"), but the simple technique by which the forlorn maid is introduced is effective enough.

> Als I me rode this endre dai
> O mi playinge
> Seih I hwar a litel mai
> Bigan to singge:
> The clot him clingge
> Wai es him: louve-longinge
> Sal libben ai.

[1] Prologue to *The Legend of Good Women*, line 199f.

Nou sprinkes the sprai
Al for loue icche am so seek
That slepen I ne mai

Son icche herde that mirie note
Thider I drogh
I fonde hire in an herber swot
Under a bogh
With ioie inogh
Son I asked: thou mirie mai
Hwi sinkestou ai?
Nou sprinkes the sprai etc.

Than answerede that maiden swete
Midde words fewe:
Mi lemman me haues bihot
Of loue trewe
He changes anewe.
Y if I mai, it shal him rewe
Bi this dai
Nou sprinkes the sprai etc.[1]

It is likely that such a song was composed after the form had been adopted by the writers of songs which were only to be listened to rather than danced to, but the following one was probably quite close to the original dance form, although its subject-matter and the inclusion of a Latin burden indicate that it was composed by an educated man.

There is no rose of such vertu
As is the one that bore Jesu
Alleluia, Alleluia.

For in this rose conteined was
Heaven and earth in litel space
Res miranda, Rea res miranda.

[1] When I rode out yesterday, for my disport, I saw where a young maiden began to sing: "May the clay cling to him [in death] Unhappy is the one who must always live in love-longing". Now springs the spray; all for love I am so sick that I cannot sleep. As soon as I heard that pleasant song, I drew close. I found her in a sweet arbour, under a bough, to my delight. At once I asked: "Thou merry maid, why dost thou always sing?" Now springs the spray etc. Then that sweet maiden answered in a few words: "My lover promised me true love: but he is changing again. If I can do anything he shall rue it today." Now springs the spray etc.

By that rose we may well see
There be one God in persons three
Pares forma, pares forma.

The angels sung the shepherds to
Gloria in excelcis Deo
Gaudeamus, gaudeamus.

Leave we all this worldly mirth
And follow we this joyful birth
Transeamus, transeamus.

Popular culture also gave rise to another important form, using the pattern of verse and chorus; this was the ballad. It differed from the carole in several ways: its form and content were different, and it remained a popular form for much longer. It dealt with a narrative, usually of a legendary or fabulous nature, into which very little description and less of the personal element were introduced. Its language was more stylised than that of the carole, and possibly more simple. Stock phrases abounded, a fact which, in the light of what has been said about Old English poetry, suggests a similar oral-formulaic tradition, which would enable unlettered storytellers to improvise. In fact, the ballads were not written down until much later. A great deal was done in the eighteenth century at the time when the experience of the "authentic" simple products of men close to nature was popular. Unfortunately, much of the value of this is lost to us, since the collectors and editors of the time felt compelled by their aesthetic ideas to "polish" the verses and to refine the style and content. We can therefore never be sure, without considerable research, whether what we have is a genuinely popular product. This polishing process is usually, from our point of view, more irritating than the other fashion, which was to compose "folk songs", when no real ones were readily available. Though confusing to contemporaries (for example, the Ossian poems), they are usually easily detected.

The ballad is also distinguished from the carole by its metrical form, which is more rigid. The stanza has four lines, either all tetrameters, or alternate tetrameters and trimeters. Most important, the ballad had an internal refrain, giving a pattern of line and response, as follows:

She laid her back against the thorn
Fine flowers in the valley
And there she has her sweet babe born
And the green leaves they grow rarely.

This remained the pattern as long as the form was a communal one; but as the ballad became more and more a vehicle for one person, these refrains gave way to two new lines, which enabled the story to progress more smoothly and quickly.

Many examples of the ballad exist; some of them, such as the Robin Hood ballads and "Sir Patrick Spens", are very well known, but they are too lengthy to quote here. For a fuller understanding of them, the reader should refer to the works by Greene and Child mentioned in the Bibliography at the end of this book.

There was another form, similar to the ballad in style and content. This was the metrical romance, of which the best-known examples are perhaps "Havelock the Dane" and "King Horn". Like the ballad, they are concerned with legend and are in a simple style, full of stock phrases. They are, however, unlike the ballad in that they have no refrain. They are generally longer, and are thus unlikely to have been a musical form. It is also probable that they were an important part of the repertoire of the travelling minstrels, whose work was always aimed mainly at the richer audiences.

These types of poem are very clearly divorced from the Old English tradition—their very names indicate French influence. It is believed that French syllabic metres were taken over and given a stressed basis. Thus the Old French octosyllabic line with stressed fourth and eighth syllables, in the hands of poets used to a four-stress alliterative line became an iambic tetrameter. The Old English forms did not, however, die out at once, but only a few fragments, mostly of inferior quality, are left to indicate a continuous tradition through the Worcester Manuscript pieces to the first version of Layamon's *Brut*, of 1205. Though written by clerics in minor orders, they do show an awareness of Old English poetry, both in form and content. Lines such as

> Other we sculle daede beon, ne muye we hine quic iseon[1]

and

> And we wreken wurhlice ure wine-maies[2]

might come straight from *Beowulf*. In much the same way, the following simile has all the rigour and harshness found in the Teutonic poets:

[1] We must either be dead, or not see him alive.
[2] And we must avenge worthily our pledged companions.

> And he gon to rusien swa the runie wulf
> Thenne he cumeth of holte, bihonged mid snawe,
> And thenceth to biten swilc deor swa him liketh.[1]

Indirect evidence shows that the tradition continued after this point; alliterative forms are used in works of known popularity (for example, the York Miracle Plays) and in courtly versions of popular forms, such as the satirical "Blacksmith's" poem and "Lenten is come with love to toune". But of the popular lyrics proper nothing seems to have been written down.

The change in climate seems to have taken place in the first half of the thirteenth century, since a revised version of Layamon's work (made fifty years later) shows considerable French influence. It is well known that the tradition had, however, a late flowering, when it was adopted by poets of the West Midlands—especially Langland and the anonymous author of *Sir Gawain and the Green Knight*—during the Alliterative Revival. This interest seems to have been stimulated by the desire of various noblemen in the area, especially the Earls of Hereford and Lancaster, to foster forms of thought and art which were opposed to those of the court, with its close imitations of the French. The poetry, though highly cultivated, shows strong evidence of a formulaic approach—a recent analysis comes to conclusions similar to those of Magoun about the Anglo-Saxons—but the Revival ended as suddenly as it arose, when the political situation changed at the end of the fourteenth century. From that point onwards, alliteration gave way completely and finally to a fixed metrical pattern and to rhyme as the basis of popular and courtly verse.

Though the towns were as yet small and relatively unimportant, because the economy of the nation was predominantly agricultural, some differences between urban and rural popular culture were already apparent. In particular, the towns permitted the development of a musical craft parallel to that of the cooper or goldsmith, in the form of "companies" of waits and minstrels.

The first use of the term "wait" is found in an early thirteenth-century manuscript in which Alexander Neckham, Abbot of Cirencester, says: "Assint etiam excubiae vigiles (veytes) cornibus suis strepitum et clangorum facientes."[2] However, the first reference to a link between waits and a town corporation dates from 1408, when Richard Isaacs, in his *Memorials of the*

---

[1] And he began to advance like the hungry wolf when he comes from the wood, covered with snow, and thinks to savage any beast he likes.
[2] Let there also be watchmen (waytes) on guard, making a loud noise and din with their horns.

City of Exeter, says that "the musical weightes were first received and enter-tained in this city". This example was followed by Coventry in 1423 and Norwich in 1433, among others.

The duties of the waits were very varied. Firstly, there was their original function, as musical nightwatchmen:

> The word "waite" signifies watching and still the late form remains of their going about the City with their musick from Hallowmas to Christmas playing under ye windows of all good citizens and bidding them good morrow by name. . . . They divide the City into four parts— to the one part one night, to another ye next and so go over ye whole in four times, viz., Monday, Tuesday, Thursday and Saturday mornings from midnight to about daylight, and then begin again and in Xmas time they go about daily to receive some benevolence of the Citizens for ye same.

This duty still had a practical basis, but had clearly become largely cere-monial, a matter of civic ritual. Their duties became increasingly associated with civic festivals: they were "the musicians of the city who attend ye mayor and Aldermen in principal Festivals to and from Church at public feasts". Similarly, another duty was to welcome important visitors—in 1474, Prince Edward visiting Coventry was welcomed "with Mynstrallcy of the Wayts of the Citie".

They also seem to have originated the idea of public concerts: in Norwich, an account of 1552 states that

> This day it is agreed by this house that the waytes of this Citie shall have liberty and licens every saturday at night and other holly days at night, betwixt this and Michaelmas next comyng to come to the Guyldhall and upon the nether leades of the same Hall next to the Consail House, shall betwixte the hours of 6 and 8 of the clok at night, blow and play upon their instruments the space of half an houre, to the rejoicing and comfort of the hearers thereof.

As official servants of the Town Council they were paid a small fee, usually some pence apiece, and were entitled to wear a livery which could be very decorative—the waits of Stamford wore scarlet cloaks trimmed with gold lace and a silver badge. Their coming was announced by a special tune (sometimes referred to by modern writers as a "signature tune"; an unfortun-ate term, in that its rather vulgar associations do not suggest the element of dignity with which such a tune would have been associated). The tune is more fairly regarded as a musical equivalent of the coat of arms, the right to use which was proudly and jealously held. An example of such a tune follows:

Ex. 2

York Waits' Tune

To their own tune, the Lincoln waits, at least, sang suitably respectable comments in return for benefices received:

> The aungells with myrthe the schepperdes did obay,
> When they sang Gloria in Excelsis in tunes mysticall. . . .

Thus the waits come

> To give the people warning to have all things perfitly
> For they that do not, breaketh Mr. Mayor's commandment
> And according to the order, punysshed must they be.

The exact relationship between the waits and the types of minstrel is not always clear: in certain cases, especially on great occasions when large numbers of musicians were needed, they may have been united, but mostly their roles were different. The majority of the minstrels were hired servants in great houses, and were thought of primarily as entertainers; making music was only one of their duties. There is mention of a servant of the Marquis of Exeter who "can play well with a harp, sing, juggle and other proper conceits and make pastymes", and the Abbey at Glastonbury kept a minstrel, an idiot and a French poet for the entertainment of visitors. Such servants, like the waits, wore livery, but were exempted from the Acts of Apparel which forbade people to wear clothes above their station, presumably to facilitate the use of costume and fancy dress.

In the boroughs, Companies of Minstrels were formed, and in 1469 Edward IV issued a minstrels' Charter of Incorporation which gave members power to "examine the pretentions of all who exercised the minstrel's profession, to regulate, govern and punish". Such rights were jealously guarded: there is a petition of 1502 by minstrels who were not members of such a Company pleading that they were being prevented from earning a living by those who were.

In this, the minstrels had the attitudes of any other craftsmen with their own Guild, with its duties and privileges, and for them life was comparatively good. For the wandering minstrel, however, life was very different, and the popular conception of the minstrel as an Alan-a-Dale figure is far from the truth. The itinerant musician, like the actor, was under constant attack from authority. A statute of 1572 states that

> All fencers, bearwards, common players in interludes and minstrels, not belonging to any baron of the realm or towards any other honourable personage of greater degree . . . which . . . shall wander abroad and have not licence of two justices of the peace . . . shall be judged rogues, vagabonds and sturdy beggars.

Their punishment could involve the brutality shown towards criminals—a statute of Henry VIII orders that a minstrel shall be "tied to the end of a cart, naked, and be beaten with whips throughout the same market town until his body be bloody by reason of such whipping".

Not a little of such harshness sprang from the Church's view that minstrels were purveyors of filth and sin; in Langland's eyes, for instance, they are "Iudas chylderen" since "Qui turpiloquium loquitur is luciferes hyne" (who speaks filth is the servant of Lucifer). The power of music as an incitement to lust is a commonplace of medieval thought; thus, in Skelton's play, *Magnifycence*, Folly says:

> So in their ear I sing them a song
> And make them so long to muse
> That some of them runneth straight to the stews.

Another feature of the musical life of the towns was drama. This may seem strange to us because, since the development of opera and such lighter but similar forms as the operetta and the musical, drama has been largely severed from music. At the same time, drama has become a minority pursuit and only the musical really influences popular taste. To the medieval man, however, declamatory and musical techniques were equally valuable as materials in a dramatic performance, which was itself very much a communal event. The reason for this lies in the origins of drama in the West. It grew out of the Easter services of the Church, and when drama became dissociated from the purely religious, after the Edict of 1210 which forbade the clergy to take part in dramatic performances, dramatists learned a great deal from mummers' plays and the morris dance. Thus, the style, and even the place and time of presentation, became so fixed as to be part of the ritual of the year. By an order of the Council of Vienne in 1311, Corpus Christi day was declared a feast day, making it ideal for drama; people were on holiday, the weather was likely to be good, and the hours of daylight were the longest of the year. The latter was both a practical consideration, and also avoided any difficulty with the authorities over the curfew regulations; only the waits were allowed to perform after dark.

When the responsibility for the plays devolved into secular hands, their production was taken over by the guilds. As the plays were still primarily demonstrations of religious faith and devotion, the producers took their duties very seriously. Each guild was allotted a play which was felt to be suitable. Thus in York, the Shipwrights were responsible for the scene showing the building of Noah's Ark, the Mariners for the voyage, the Gold-beaters for the journey of the Three Kings, the Vintners for the miracle of turning water into wine, and the Bakers for the Last Supper. We should not be too ready to scoff at such literal-mindedness, since it arose from the medieval conception of the universe as being a manifestation of the Divine harmony. The good workman could earn his salvation by accepting willingly his role in life, and by performing his task to the best of his capabilities. In this way, he was working to the greater glory of God.

Nevertheless, money also was vital if the production was to be of the best possible quality, and the York Council levied a rate which varied between 1d and 4d. The need for rehearsal was also stressed, and an order of the York Council for 1415 reads:

> And all maner of craftsmen that bringeth furthe ther pageantez in order and course by good players, well arrayed and openly spekyng upon payn of lesyng of Cs to be paide to the chambre without any pardon. And that every player that shall play be redy in his pagiaunt at convenyant tyme, that is to say, at the myd houre betweene iiijth and vth of the cloke in the mornynge, and then all other pageantz fast followyng, ilk one after other as ther course is without tarieng. Sub pena facienda camere vis viiid.

The "pagiaunt" mentioned was the movable stage which was described in a well-known account of the Chester Plays of 1594 by Archbishop Rogers:

> Every company had his pagiaunt or part, which pageants were a high scaffold with two rooms, a higher and a lower, upon four wheels. In the lower they apparelled themselves, and in the higher room they played, being all open on the top, that all beholders might hear and see them. The place where they played them was in every street. They began first at the abbey gates, and when the first pageant was played, it was wheeled to the high cross before the mayor, and so to every street; and so every street had a pageant playing before them at one time, till all the pageants for the day appointed were played.

The plays were quite spectacular in performance; for among the accounts for properties and costumes we even find (in Coventry): "item pd for halfe a yard of rede sea vjd".

Music was, of course, vital to such performances, as the accounts of the York Plays show:

Item payd to ye mynstrells		xx	d
Item payd to ye mynstrells of ye Corpus Christi playe	iii s	iv	d
Item payde for ye Corpus Christi playe and wrytynge ye speches fo it	iii s	viij	d
Item payd for ye Baner for ye mynstrells	vi s	viij	d

The fullest musical resources of the town would have been needed as there were forty-eight plays to perform. The social nature of the occasion and the need for sustenance by the participants during the strain of rehearsal and production was not forgotten as is shown by the entry:

for ix galons of Ale   xviij d.

The minstrel was a highly rated performer, as we can see from the payments for the Coventry play of 1490:

Imprimis to God   ij s
Item to the devyll and to Judas   xviij d
Item to the mynstrell   xiiij   d

After careful research, Noah Greenberg suggests, in his acting edition of the French *Play of Daniel*, that the musicians should play a trumpet, rebec, recorders, a vielle, bells, a psaltery, a harp and a portative organ. Such instruments were probably played off the main set, since no illustrations of the musicians are extant. On the other hand, the Skinners' play (York, 1415) is described as follows:

> Jesus upon an ass with its foal, xii Apostles following Jesus, six rich and six poor men, eight boys with branches of palms, singing "Benedictus" etc., and Zaccheus climbing into a sycamore tree.

Which suggests that it was common to have songs sung on the stage.

Needless to say, the plays were of universal appeal, and in the best sense popular. They were a meeting point for both music and literature; we find the juxtaposition of slapstick and deeply serious verse, popular song, and religious chant. A "Gloria" is sung in *Mak the Sheep Stealer*, and in the same play there is a part-song. Appearing in the Coventry Cycle is a beautiful popular religious lyric, which is still widely sung under the title of the "Coventry Carol", and the cycle ends with the souls of mankind entering Heaven at the Judgement with the lines:

> Therefore full boldly may we sing
> As we mount up thus
> Make we all mirth and loving
> With Te Deum Laudamus.

The Towneley *First Shepherds' Play* will best illustrate some of these ideas. The shepherds are typical medieval rustics, in the way that Shakespeare's Athenians are typically Elizabethan English workmen. They are sitting in

the fields on the first Christmas morning. After drinking, they begin a round
of songs in a way reminiscent of the Caedmon story:

> Second Shepherd: Bot hark
> Who so can best sing
> Shall have the begynnyng.

Songs are then sung, but the words and music are omitted. The First Shepherd then draws things to a conclusion:

> We have done oure parte: and songyn right weylle
> I drynke for my parte

(perhaps intending a pun on the musical term "part").
   The Angel appears, to announce the Nativity:

> Herkyn, hyrdes, awake: gif lovyng ye shalle,
> He is borne for youre sake; lorde perpetualle
> He is comen to take: and rawnson you alle
> Youre sorowe to slake: kyng emperialle
> He behestys;
> That chyld is borne
> At Bethelem this morne
> Ye shall fynde hym beforne
> Betwix two bestys.

This lyric immediately tells us that its composer was a man both of education
and poetic skill, since its stanza form is far too complex to be a pure folk
poem. Furthermore, the signs of conscious art are confirmed by the presence
of "aureate" vocabulary—the use of words of Latin origin to beautify the
language, such as "lorde *perpetualle*" and "kynge *emperialle*"; a style popular
among the poets of the fifteenth century. There are also fairly clear indica-
tions that the music also was written by a cultured composer, since the First
Shepherd says:

> A, Godys dere dominus, what was that sang?
> It was wonder curiose, with smalle notes emang.

In other words, it was highly ornate, in the style of the fifteenth-century
English Church composers. The Second Shepherd is more explicit:

> Now, by God that me boght: it was a mery song
> I dar say that he broghte foure and twenty to a longe.

A "longe" was equivalent at that period to a modern semibreve, and lasted for 4 beats at approximately MM. 60–80. The music was therefore likely to have offered an opportunity for a display of virtuosity, and again emphasises the closeness of the "artistic" and the popular, since it is commended by the Third Shepherd, whose views are probably representative of those of a contemporary audience:

> It was a mery gle: sich hard I never none.

It was in the context of such a universal art that some of the best-known and, from a modern viewpoint, most successful songs and lyrics of the period were composed. We have already seen the lyric "There is no rose of swich vertu", which was of this type, but it is worth looking at others, both as a guide to what the genuinely popular may have been like, and for their intrinsic merit. Typical both in style and background is the secular conductus "Edi beo thu".

Ex. 3

Edi beo thu

swe - te   le - ve - di | her   mi   bene   And | ren___ of me___ yif | thi___ wille is.

(Blessed be thou, Queen of Heaven, comfort of men and joy of angels, spotless mother and pure maiden—there is no other such a one in the world. It is easy to see that of all women thou hast preeminence. My sweet lady hear my prayer and pity me, if it is thy will.)

This appears to have been written by a man in minor orders, probably a chaplain or a schoolmaster, at Llanthony Priory, Gloucestershire, in the thirteenth century. Musically, its popular origin or influence is indicated by the use of the Ionian (major) mode, and the frequent occurrence of harmonies of the third tends to reinforce the impression (though this was a feature even of the Church style, in England). In the lyric, the use of the vernacular and the general tenor of the words marks it out as not being liturgical. Although not so clearly couched in terms usually associated with the love lyric, phrases such as "Mi swete levedi" tend to have this kind of association for us.

It was probably in similar circumstances that the next example was composed.

Ex. 4

Worldes blis ne last no throwe

World-es___ blis ne last no___ thro_ we, _ Hit wit ant___ wend a___

wey a___ non___ The len - gur that hich___ hit i___

kno - we, _ The lasse ic.___ find - e___ pris ther___ on.___ For al hit___

is i___ meynd wyd___ kar - e___ Mid sor - e - we; ant wid___ u - vel___

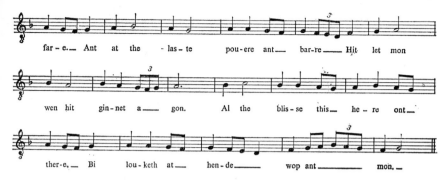

far - e.__ Ant   at   the   - las - te   pou-ere ant__ bar-re____ Hit   let   mon

wen   hit   gin - net   a____ gon.   Al   the   blis - se   this__ he - re   ont__

ther-e, __ Bi   lou - keth   at __   hen - de____   wop ant_____ mon. __

(The world's joy lasts no time at all: it departs and fades away at once.
The longer I know it, the less value I find in it, for it is all mixed with sorrow
and misfortune, and at the last, when it begins to pass away, it leaves a man
poor and naked. All the joy both here and there, is finally encompassed by
weeping and lamentation.)

In this song there is only a melody line, so that we do not have the clear
indication of the work of a composer, which the second part in the previous
piece gives. On the other hand, the general quality of both song and lyric
would suggest a cultured writer. Also, in this case, the song is in a transposed
form of the Dorian mode, and not in the Ionian, giving it the sound which is
more usually associated with antiquity. It should be borne in mind, however,
that this "folky" sound was only typical of a part of the popular products of
earlier times, and that its difference from the standard major-minor idiom
has endowed it, for us, with a particular attraction and delicate charm which
can obscure the real position which it held at the time at which it was produced. We should not allow the undoubted beauty of such songs to blind us
to the fact that the major/minor system of composition grew steadily in
importance, and that modal composition ceased to be a living force in popular
composition early (some would suggest in the seventeenth century), and was
certainly becoming widely regarded as archaic even earlier. It was these
trends which permitted the reintroduction of the influence of the "serious"
musician in the eighteenth century, an influence which was eventually to
swamp the communal tradition.

The lyric is attractive, but is not as unusual as it might at first sight appear
to someone unfamiliar with medieval literature. The sentiments expressed
are, in fact, typical of the age, and are part of a tradition of first-rate works
which expressed the transitoriness of earthly things. Parallels of the "All the

world's a stage" type among Elizabethan authors will spring quickly to mind.

A song which is worth quoting because of its sheer power, as well as its historical interest and because it is quite well known, is the "Agincourt Song".

Ex. 5

Agincourt Song

The author is unknown, as is the case with so many secular songs of the period. Again, it could be genuinely popular, or could be in a popular style, but the work of a minor cleric. It is almost certain, however, that this work was sung on the occasion of Henry V's triumphant return to England after the war. This was a time of mass rejoicing and was celebrated with all the pageantry of which medieval man was capable. Of particular interest to us is that Henry was welcomed by "12 apostles syngyng" and "angels syngyng Nowell Nowell": the angels were boys wearing feathers and flinging down gold coins and boughs of laurel, whilst "patriarchs" sent a flight of sparrows and other birds fluttering round the king as he passed.

No reference to this side of medieval art would be complete without a mention of "Sumer is icumen in". This pleasant round is so well written that it is still sung by amateurs, without any sense of its being a piece of merely historical interest.

Once again, this is because of its "modernity" in the sense that it uses the major mode, and because the technique of the part writing is accepted by most scholars as being in advance of its time (c. 1280). This latter fact alone would be sufficient to indicate its source, though the simple delight in the coming of summer ("bloweth med") and its direct but effective expression ("bucke verteth") could have come from any class of society.

Ex. 6 *(a)*

Sumer is icumen in

Grow-eth sed and blow-eth med and springth the wud – e nu.

hlu – de sing cu – cu.   Gro – weth sed and blo – weth med. and

Sum – er is – i cum – en in,___ hlu – de sing cu – cu.

Sum – er is – i cum – en in___

sing cu – cu   sing cu – cu nu___

sing cu – cu nu___ sing cu – cu

(Summer has come, loudly sings cuckoo. Now is the seed growing, and the meadow flowering, and the forest springing to life. Sing cuckoo. The ewe bleats after the lamb, the cow lows after the calf; the bullock leaps, the buck breaks wind. Merrily sing cuckoo, cuckoo, cuckoo, well dost thou sing cuckoo. Never cease now.)

There is a widely held belief that there was at this time a popular contrapuntal tradition. Perhaps the most careful consideration of this conviction is to be found in John Stevens' *Music and Poetry in the Early Tudor Court*; it is to this work that I am indebted for many of my ideas.

The main evidence for the existence of a popular contrapuntal tradition is necessarily, in the absence of written records, indirect. We have already read of the account of Giraldus Cambrensis, seen the existence of a courtly dance style of the type illustrated by the estampie (p. 11), and also of a style of contrapuntal writing, exemplified by "Sumer is icumen in", which was radically different from that of the Church. We also know that the kind of music written for the Mass by composers such as Dunstable and Taverner was intricately contrapuntal. The courtly music of the Tudor age was polyphonic, and its last flowering in the seventeenth century produced, among other works, many rounds and catches, which we know to have been very popular. Furthermore, though counterpoint is now frequently taught in a very analytical fashion, it is certain that the human mind can learn in a much more instinctive fashion to create lines suitable for quite strict contrapuntal treatment (Peter Maxwell Davies has said that he cultivates this faculty in order to strengthen his writing). It is also known that in some cultures—that of Albania, for instance—counterpoint is improvised, usually in a free style. A modern and relevant example of this is to be found in New Orleans jazz.

This evidence would suggest that a popular contrapuntal tradition might have existed, and that there is no theoretical opposition to the idea that a formal training in composition is a necessary prerequisite of a contrapuntal style. But it has to be admitted that it is a style which tends to indicate careful workmanship and training; certainly the medieval Church composer had to go through a course of long and detailed study. Similarly, even the free counterpoint of the New Orleans style needs, to be really successful, a fair degree of prearrangement and group practice, *viz.* the records of Louis Armstrong's Hot Five. A simpler explanation of the various references in contemporary works to popular part-singing would therefore be more convincing.

I believe that John Stevens offers such an explanation. While not denying the possibility of the existence of a certain number of popularly created rounds, he points to the technique of fauxbourdon used by later English composers. Simply put, this may be described as harmonisation in consecutive first inversions, or as singing in sixths and thirds.

Ex. 8

Example of fauxbourdon from Dunstable 'Quam Pulchra Es'

This would mean that provided the singer knew the tune, and could find his starting note, it would be a fairly simple matter to improvise a suitable part above or below the theme. Three persons could thus improvise part music together fairly easily, and quite acceptably. Such a theory is made more acceptable by the known preference of medieval English Church composers for the "dissonances" of the third and sixth, rather than the more traditional fourths and fifths. This could have been inspired by a popular habit, derived ultimately from Norse culture. The "St Magnus Hymn" of the Orkney Islands is a written sample of the Norse popular style which used piled-up thirds. Such influence might reasonably be expected, in view of the considerable Norse effect upon the language, especially in the North and Midlands.

It will be noted that this argument assumes fairly free interaction between Church and popular musicians. This is an idea which, today, we may find difficult to accept. Despite the recent attempts to use "beat" music in services, it is difficult for us to imagine the successful use of such material in the most excellent religious music. However, composers of the time did draw freely upon such sources for tenor parts for their Masses and motets. In fact, tunes well known in their time, such as "Bele Isabelos", and even tunes based on street cries, such as the Parisian "Frese Nouvelle", were so much utilised by the Church composers that in 1322 Pope John XXII was obliged to issue a famous Bull denouncing the practice, together with the use of the more extreme modern technical devices. Nonetheless, the trend continued, and 150 years and more later the French composer Dufay found the tune "Se la face ay pale" to be suitable as the basis of his greatest Mass, and the Englishman Taverner constructed one of his finest works out of the melody "Western Wynde". Perhaps an important contributory factor was that the Church had not always been opposed to popular music. For instance, Franciscans, under Jacapone di Todi, used dance forms to create a form of religious song called the "Lauda", in much the same manner as Aldhelm must have done six centuries before. This particular attempt at the popularisation of religion reached England in 1224. Possibly the most well-known example of the interaction between Church and secular influences is "Angelus ad Virginem", which Chaucer put into the mouth of Nicholas in "The Miller's Tale":

Ex. 8

Angelus ad Virginem

- num. Ce - li ter - re - que Dom - mi - num con___
ci - pi - es et pa - ri - es___ in - ta___ cta, sa -
- lu - tem ho - mi - num tu___ por - ta ce___ li
fa - - cta me - da - ia cri - mi - num.

This chapter, like the last, has included several ideas which are alien to modern thought on art. Firstly, we saw the organisation of secular musicians into guilds, analogous to those uniting members of other crafts. For them, music was a proudly possessed skill, which came from long and secret training during an apprenticeship in the strict sense of the word. Music thus held a position which it has now lost. The musician was accepted as an equal member of the community: he was not seen as a romantic, isolated figure, but conversely he was not the object of philistinism. His craftsmanship was viewed with the same mixture of admiration and acceptance as was that of the goldsmith or the weaver. It was also as familiar, a point not often enough noted with regard to our own century. Nowadays, the average person rarely comes across the musician at work (at practice), as distinct from being on show. Thus, misconceptions as to the nature of his craft arise. It might well be that if people could live in closer contact with the practical work of musicians, the consequent familiarity with their needs, aims and procedures would largely eliminate the need for liberalisation through musical appreciation.

This chapter would also appear to indicate a universality of art similar to that of the Old English period. In fact, this was only partially so. The music of the aristocracy had a deep intellectual and philosophical basis. For instance, though the Henry VIII Manuscript in the British Museum was made at the end of the period, it still contains "puzzle canons" in which the performer had first to construe a Latin tag, which gave directions about the assembly of the various parts and the completion of the work. Similarly, style was not the spontaneous thing it was in popular song, but the result of careful "garnishing" or ornamentation of the essential theme according to rule—a musical equivalent to the poetic "rules of rhetoric": we may compare this love of ornament with the elaborate character of Gothic architecture.

These ideas sprang from the conception of music which saw it as a branch of philosophy of the type created by Boethius in his *De Institutione Musica*. For this reason Sir Thomas Elyot, in his *The Boke of the Governour*, recommends the study of music, "for the better attaynynge of the knowledge of a publike weale". Boethius' central thesis may be expressed in the words of Gibbons: "It is proportion that beautifies everything, this whole universe consists of it, and musicke is measured by it." Music reflects the Divine harmony which ultimately pervades the universe: in the words of Tinctoris:

> Musica Deum delectat
> musica animas beatificat.[1]

Clearly, this implies study and a state of mind far removed from the secular music which Skelton sees as driving men to the stews.

Nevertheless, the interaction which did take place resulted, as I see it, in the enrichment of both aspects of the art. Take the popular element from Chaucer or Langland and we would have matter of little more than historical interest. To literature, the closeness of popular culture added a simplicity (not implying *naïveté*), a directness and a lucidity which later artists tended to lose. Certainly, the modern artist seems to be able to approach the popular only through pastiche and at the expense of a total rejection of tradition, a situation hardly likely to produce healthy or great art. Similarly, to the music of both types there was added a sweetness and purity, which I would like to feel is not merely a historical illusion, or the mistaken response of an affected taste for modal quaintnesses. The serious musician of today seems only likely to produce banality if he attempts to do the same.

[1] Music delights God and ennobles the soul.

3 Tudors, Stuarts and the Commonwealth

1st Drawer: and see if thou canst find out
Sneak's noise; Mistress Tearsheet would fain
hear some music.
Henry IV, ACT II, sc. iv

Much detailed study has been made of the period which we are about to examine, and many reprints of songs of the time exist. In fact, it is perhaps for this reason that it is often referred to as a "Golden Age" of folk music. Very early on, Erasmus in his *Encomium Moriae* made an observation of a type which is to be found again and again, when he stated that "the English could lay claim to be the best looking, most musical, and to the best tables of any people". The idea that the English were musically a highly cultured people so flourished that in 1597, Thomas Morley, in a famous passage in the Preface to his *Plaine and Easie Introduction to Practical Musicke*, described the position of Philomathes as follows:

> But supper being ended, and Musicke books, according to the custome, being brought to the table: the mistresse of the house presented me with a part, earnestly requesting me to sing. But when after manie excuses, I protested unfainedly that I could not, everyone began to wonder. Yea, some whispered to others, demaunding how I was brought up.

We may be tempted to credit Morley merely with being a good salesman, but we should remember that thirty-seven years later, in 1634, Henry Peacham, in his book *The Compleate Gentleman*, said:

> I desire no more in you than to sing your part sure, and at the first sight withall to play the same upon your violl or in the exercise of the lute, privately to your selfe.

Certainly Charles I appears to have followed this advice, since he played the bass viol, and he bought a violin from Cremona in 1632. In doing so, he was keeping up a royal tradition of music, because Elizabeth I was a fair player of the virginals and her father, Henry VIII, was both a competent singer and composer. All these facts point to a state of affairs among the nobility in which the ideals of the Renaissance, as embodied in Castiglione's *The Courtier*, were not merely given lip service, but were acted upon. It was such ideals that caused John Playford to write, in the Preface to his *Dancing Master* of 1651:

> The art of Dancing . . . is a commendable and rare quality fit for young Gentlemen, if opportunely used. . . . Excellent for recreation, after more serious studies, making the body active and strong, gracefull in deportment and in a quality very much beseeming a gentleman.

It should be borne in mind, however, that musical activities were to be engaged in privately. Sir Thomas Elyot warns that:

> a gentilman, plainge or singinge in a commune audience appaireth his estimation: the people forgettinge reverance, when they behold him in the similitude of a common servant or minstrell.

However, these sources tell us more about the habits of the wealthy classes, whose music is by definition not the subject of this book. Lower on the social scale, and at the end of our period, we find that Samuel Pepys says, "I ventured with good success upon things at first sight" and tells us, in his diary for 8 April 1668:

> To Drumbleby's and did there talk a great deal about pipes, and did buy a recorder which I do intend to learn to play on, the sound of it being of all sounds in the world most pleasing to me.

This was typical of Pepys, whose accomplishments were varied. When Charles II returned to England in 1660, Pepys was in one of the ships that went to meet him, and at the suggestion of the Admiral, and with the help of the lieutenant's cittern, and two candlesticks with coins in them to act as cymbals "made barber's music, with which my Lord was well pleased".

Pepys was typical of the middle class, from whom there was a steady demand for domestic music of the sort written by John Jenkins, or collected by individuals into albums, such as *Elizabeth Rogers, hir Virginal Booke*. This demand was partially due to the steady increase in the size, status and wealth of the middle classes (for instance, social historians estimate that by 1688 there were about 64,000 merchants in Britain). Such people wished to enjoy their leisure and to imitate the gentry, whose preserve music and similar pursuits had largely been until this period. Perhaps there was also a little of the motive which Roger North suggests, while talking of the Commonwealth period, in his *Memoires of Musicke*: "Many chose rather to fidle at home, then to goe out and be knockt on the head abroad."

However, we are still a long way from the common people of whom, in this period, as in the previous ones we have examined, comparatively little is known. Being illiterate, they left no records of their own, and few contemporary writers found the fight for subsistence on an average wage of sevenpence or so a day a matter of interest. They tend to appear as Clowns in Shakespeare, and as idealised shepherds in the courtly writers. As a consequence, we have again to generalise from quite a small amount of information.

It is known that the traditional instruments continued to be used. The pipe and tabor were still played, as were the bagpipes—"Strange fellows", says Solanio in *The Merchant of Venice* (I, i), will "laugh like parrots at a bagpipe". All festivals continued to be an occasion for song, May Day remaining one of the most popular—it may be remembered that in *A Midsummer Night's Dream*, it is thought an unnatural state when in summer

> No night is now with hymn or carol blest
>
> (II, ii)

and Theseus assumes of the lovers that

> No doubt they rose up early to observe
> The rite of May.
>
> (IV, ii)

Perhaps we should temper our tendency to allow the idyllic creation of the great artist to obscure reality with the comment of Phillip Stubbs (admittedly a Puritan):

> On the eve of Maie ... of fortie, three score or a hundred maydes goyng to the wood overnight, there have the third parte of them returned home again undefiled.

A Midsummer Night's Dream also gives us a momentary insight into one of the most simple forms of rustic music, when to Titania's question,

> What, wilt thou hear some music my sweet love?

Bottom replies,

> I have a reasonable good ear in music; let us have the tongs and the
> bones.
>
> (IV, i)

The taverns, which had been full of the sound of rebec and gittern in the
time of Chaucer (Absolom in the *Miller's Tale* was said to perform there),
were now filled with the newer (and louder) sound of the fiddle, if Grosson's
complaint in his *School of Abuse* (1587) is any guide.

Pepys' allusion to "barber's music" draws our attention to another important popular instrument, the cittern, which was a kind of four-stringed
guitar, and was the poor man's substitute for the more expensive and
sonorous lute. It was customary for a barber's shop to have a cittern available
for the customers to entertain themselves upon while they waited; the custom
survived in parts of the United States until late in the last century. There are
many references to the phenomenon in contemporary plays, such as that in
Ben Jonson's *Epicoene* (1609) to a garrulous wife who had been recommended
by a barber:

> That cursed barber! I have married his cittern

(*i.e.* it was always sounding).

Naturally, dancing remained popular, and though the Puritan element as
it grew stronger could denounce it as that "noble science of heathen devilry",
it continued to be a popular pastime, even on Sunday—so much so in fact,
that James I sanctioned it, provided that it took place after divine service.

Much more direct contact with the people can be found in the broadsides
and ballads of the time. These were songs published on a sheet of paper, and
sold to the general public—usually the lyric only was given, but this was
illustrated with a crude woodcut. The first known printed sheet ballad is
Skelton's "A balade of the Scotyshe King", published in 1513, but it seems
likely that the form had already been long established.

In the earlier part of the sixteenth century many were published, though
few before the time of Elizabeth have survived. Their popularity and pointed-
ness seems to have been a constant source of worry to the authorities. In 1543,
some thirty-three London booksellers were prosecuted under the Act for the
Advancement of True Religion for issuing "printed ballads, rhymes and
songs" which were likely "to subvert the very true and perfect exposition
doctrine and declaration of the Scriptures". Again, in 1554, there was a

determined effort to suppress "ballads and other pernicious and hurtful devices", and in 1579, two men were hanged in Scotland for writing satiric ballads. Nevertheless, the genre increased rapidly in popularity. A hundred or so were licensed by Stationers Hall in 1569–70, and Chappell was able to trace the existence of at least some 250 publishers in the seventeenth century.

Many of the ballads were anonymously composed, but certain figures are known by name, particularly Thomas Deloney, whom Nashe called the "balleting silkweaver of Norwich", and William Elderton, who, Gabriel Harvey tells us, "armed himself with ale when he balleted, as old father Ennius did with wine". Deloney made a particularly great reputation for himself but, like most ballad writers, he was constantly running counter to official policy. Stow reports that

> Sir Stephen Stacy, Mayor, was brought to his hands a certain ballad, containing a Complaint of great want and scarcity of Corn within the realm. And forasmuch as it contained in it certain vain and presumptuous matters, bringing in the Queen, speaking with her people Dialogue wise in a very fond and indecent sort . . . he called before him both the Printer and the Party by whom it was put to print . . . The writer of this scurrilous ballad was one Delonie, an idle Fellow.

In his *Seven Centuries of Popular Song*, Reginald Nettel deals with the work of Deloney at some length, and it is therefore needless to do so here. But it is worth quoting some of his ballad "Of the strange and most cruel Whippes which the Spanyards had prepared to whippe and torment Englishmen and women", written at the time of the Armada in 1588:

> One sort of whips they had for men
> So smarting fierce and fell:
> As like could never be devised
> By any devil in hell.
> The strings wherof with wyre knots
> Like rowels they did frame,
> That every stroke might teare the flesh
> They layd on with the same.
>
> And pluck the spreading sinews from
> the hardened bloody bone
> To prick and pearce each tender veine,
> within the body known.

And not to leave one crooked ribbe
On any side unseene,
Nor yet to leave a lump of flesh
the head and foote between.

It would be easy to dismiss this as journalistic sensationalism or to be amazed at the gullibility of popular taste. To do so, however, is, I believe, an oversimplification of the phenomenon. For the Elizabethan was far more used to cruelty and barbarity than twentieth-century man, at least in times of peace; the heads of criminals, executed publicly, were exposed on London Bridge as a warning to all who could see. What is interesting is that though medieval man was no less barbaric in his daily life, he seemed uninclined to make literature out of such violence. Though, of course, violent acts are described, there does not appear to be the same love of lengthy and detailed description. Nor is this sensationalism confined to any one area of literature, in the way that one might now point to a significant difference between, say, the poetry of Auden and the *Sunday Pictorial*. For such elements appear, at times with little more subtlety, in the plays of the Jacobeans (compare the amputated hand scene in Webster's *Duchess of Malfi*). In this way, the ballad and the drama cast light upon each other. Even allowing for the discrepancy in dates, it might be argued that a popular attitude was forcing itself into the consciousness of the artist. It would seem that all areas of society were forced to extremes by the fact that the rigid framework of centuries was disintegrating, and had not then been replaced by a strong alternative pattern of thought, as took place after the Restoration. As happens so often in considerations of this period, parallels with the present age can be found (in the *avant-garde* drama for example) though the parallel is not entirely valid, because with a few notable exceptions, the popular world does not reflect this unease, at least not overtly.

The function of a ballad seller was that of a salesman who demonstrated his wares by singing them and talking about them. For this job, he needed personality but the prime interest of the public was in what he had to sell. This is in striking contrast to the current situation, in which it is the singer, or rather his image, and the emotions he triggers off, which are vital. It is possible to sit through a Beatles' concert without hearing a note, because of the shouting and screaming of the fans, for whom the appearance seems to be the moment of release. The epitome of the Elizabethan ballad seller is Shakespeare's Autolycus, in *The Winter's Tale*. Though, of course, he is larger than life, his general pattern of behaviour and mode of selling his songs seems to fit with the other available evidence.

Perhaps the most interesting songs to us are the amatory type, among the best and most popular being "Adewe Swete Harte" (1569) and the entry in the Stationers' Register for 3 September 1580—"a new northern dittye of the Lady Greensleves". Another very popular song was "Waly Waly" of which the first verse is given below.

Ex. 9

Waly Waly

If the tune was good, it was frequently used by other lyric writers, and in Scotland especially, there was a tendency to use the music of love songs for religious purposes: thus "Daintie come thow to me" became "Jesu come thow to me".

The sexual side of love, as we might expect from other art of the period, was more freely treated than is generally permissible today. Thus we can find "A mery new song how a bruer meant to make a cooper cuckold and how deere the Bruer paid for the bargayne", or, in the words of Nashe, we can listen to "such ribauldrie as Watkin's Ale".

One of the most important functions of the ballads was as vehicle for spreading news of topical events. The Armada brought forth a stream of ballads, though foreign events were also of interest. There was, for instance, "A warning to London by the Fall of Antwerp" (1577). Local news was equally well represented, as is shown by an entry in the Register such as that for 28 April 1598 of "The ballad of the burning of the town of Tiverton". Similar in type were the relations of unusual happenings, such as "The true description of a monsterous chylde born in the Isle of Wight" in 1564.

The freedom found in the topical songs was not so great as that found in the ribald ones, since a form of censorship appears to have been applied, as it was on stage productions. For instance, no ballads on the subject of the death of the Earl of Essex appeared until after the Queen's death.

There are other interesting differences between the popular tastes of the
sixteenth and twentieth centuries. For example, the hanging of verses on
trees, found in *As You Like It*, though admittedly a dramatic device, seems
more plausible when we realise that ballads were frequently hung on graves
as a token of grief or respect.

Another contrast is found in the attitudes to royalty. Though we today
have the occasional effusion, such as "In a Golden Coach There's a Heart of
Gold", at coronations and similar events, the interest of the average person
does not extend beyond a morbid curiosity. The rush to get out at the playing
of the National Anthem is strongly in contrast to the Elizabethan custom of
finishing a ballad with some form of prayer, such as the one which concludes
"The Belman's Good Morrow":

> Lord save our gracious soverayne
> Elizabeth by name
> That long unto our comfort
> She may both rule and raigne.

On the other hand, the ballads and broadsides appear to have been like
present-day popular music in that they offered better rewards than the more
sophisticated forms of art. More than one artist must have felt tempted to
agree with the writer of "The Return from Parnassus", who satirised this
fact.

The idea of following fashion was also known to the Elizabethans. Tastes
changed, though not at present-day speeds, as the following dialogue from
Love's Labour's Lost shows:

> Armado: Is there not a ballad, boy, of the King and the Beggar?
> Moth: The world was guilty of such a ballad some three ages since;
> but, I think, now 'tis not to be found; or if it were t'would
> neither serve for the writing or the tune.
>
> (I, ii)

The various ballads mentioned are not quoted, partly because they are
too lengthy, and partly because many of them are now easily accessible
(see Bibliography). Moreover, their interest is as whole works rather than
as creations whose separate constituents may give great pleasure and arouse
admiration in themselves. In this, we need an approach of the type suggested
with reference to Old English lyrics. A ballad, and indeed any popular lyric,

tends to be a direct and easily comprehensible expression of a single conception on the part of the author. Images and symbols with more than one level of meaning tend to be the province of the cultured poet. The lyric writer (at his best) is concerned with one moment of insight, one twist to a familiar pattern, which is quite sufficient material for a song; a complex of motives and perceptions is more the area of the novelist or dramatist. Indeed, the lyric which is to be set to music must be simple in its psychology and unambiguous in its message—an operatic plot that had the subtlety which we expect from non-musical drama would be constantly at odds with the music, partly in that two complex forms would be fighting for our attention, and partly in that music seeks primarily to engage our emotions directly, whereas literature in its higher forms also seeks to engage our intellect. The philosophical element is never far away in great writing.

It is for these reasons that a ballad has to be allowed to work through to its proper conclusion before it can be judged, and yet, paradoxically enough, will contain, like formulaic poetry, few lines which are not capable of alteration or omission without damage to the whole.

Before leaving the ballad for the moment, we should consider what is perhaps the most striking difference between sixteenth-century popular music and that of the present day—the sheer variety which then existed.

This may in part be explained by the material development of our society. The journalistic ballad has disappeared because of the development of the cheap newspaper. The satire that often went with such topics is perhaps now more easily and effectively put over by television. The patriotic element has fallen into disfavour since the advent of modern methods of warfare, universal conscription and the bombing of civilian populations.

But it would seem that, with the exception of certain types of "folk" musician, people feel that music is no longer suited to this type of function—or perhaps that music should be kept separate from it. The main interest of modern popular music is to reflect only aspects of love, and those over a narrower range than the Elizabethan ballad. In particular, it is surprising to find that when sexual freedom has become almost a cliché, our lyrics are far more inhibited. Can we, for instance, imagine any modern situation other than the stag party—and perhaps not there—where one might sing:

> What pleasure is there like to this,
> The Damsel then did cry,
> I've heard them talk of lovers bliss,
> O, what a foole was I
> So long to live a maid, ere I

did this same sport begin;
This death I now could freely die:
I prithee thrust it in.

I am inclined to believe that public freedom of this sort depends on the
stability of the underlying beliefs. Consequently, in a society where the
authority of religion, and the code of social behaviour is fundamentally unquestioned, it is possible to be extremely free in minor matters; the true way
is never in doubt. But in a society where values are changing, this type of
game suddenly becomes deadly serious; the insecure man dare not let his
position be questioned. In this, the "serious" artist and the folk may be out
of step; the popular faith takes longer to break down. For these reasons, the
above lines can brim over with earthy vitality, while Restoration sexuality, as
expressed in the comedy, can have a constant undertone of unease. Even now
this is so; while serious writers explore the extremes of sexuality, the popular
song remains almost without exception in an idealised world.

As in the medieval period, the drama is of interest to us, since it appears
to have been widely popular. Recent studies suggest the numbers involved
were quite large (one person in six) and that plays appealed to a very varied
cross-section of the community. It is this which is in part responsible for the
happy combination of the everyday and the elevated which Shakespeare and
others continually achieve.

However, a striking difference between the Elizabethan and the earlier
works is that drama became secular. This development was largely due to the
fact that in 1559, Queen Elizabeth forbade the stage to deal with religious
matters, because of the inflamed nature of people's feelings after the religious
troubles of the previous twenty-five years. This meant that whereas the
mystery cycles were full of hymns and Gregorian chant, Renaissance plays
contain love songs, functional music (such as dances and funeral marches),
entertainment pieces (catches and rounds, *e.g.* that song by Sir Andrew
Aguecheek, Sir Toby Belch, and the Clown in Act II of *Twelfth Night*) and
incidental music, to set a mood (the Statue scene in *The Winter's Tale*). The
depth of musical knowledge revealed in Shakespeare's works is well known,
and a similar knowledge is shown by the playwright Marston. Both writers
are always very accurate in their use of technicalities.

Of great interest are the songs which are found in plays throughout the
period. Music had always been thought apt for comedy since Classical times,
but in tragedy the position of music was less clear, since it was often thought
to be indecorous, despite Aristotle's statements to the contrary. Thomas Kyd
followed this prejudice against music in tragedy when in 1587 he wrote *The*

Spanish Tragedy which includes no songs and, a little later, Ben Jonson avoided the use of song in tragedy. In fact, with the exception of Shakespeare, whose dramatic use of song is outstanding (for example, the "Willow Song"), no playwright before Marston, in his *Sophonisba* of 1606, made use of song in tragedy.

It has already been stated that music was an important commercial attraction. One reason for this was that the medieval attitude to music as reflecting Divine harmony was still prevalent. It is, therefore, not surprising that it was considered in drama to be a touchstone of character—the man who did not like music was to be feared. So Caesar says of Cassius "He hears no music" (*Julius Caesar*, I, ii) and Shylock refers to "the vile squeaking of the wry-neck'd fife" (*Merchant of Venice*, II, v). Another reason was the increasingly emotional element in music. The power of music to move was, of course, known to medieval man, but to him, music only reflected emotion of a most general character. But in the later Tudor period it was expected to mirror the sense of the lyric more closely—tension had to be indicated by discord, and imagery by pictorial elements in the music (the word "ascent" by a rising phrase for example). This arose from the heightened interest in the lyrics and what they expressed. In the Middle Ages, the way in which words were fitted to the music was a minor consideration, and indeed violence was often done to the natural accents of a lyric. In the sixteenth century it was felt, however, that sound must follow sense. Sometimes the motivation was religious—Erasmus complains, in the early part of the century, that "Modern Church music is so constructed that the congregation cannot hear one distinct word." At other points, the motivation was a desire for more accurate self-expression: as Morley says,

> In this kind [the madrigal] you must possess yourself of an amorous humour, for in no composition shall you prove admirable except you put on and possess yourself wholly with that vein wherein you compose.

Such a conception of the lyric was new, and necessarily affected the music. In particular, it moved away from polyphony and abstraction towards monody and emotion. Though this clearly refers to "art" music, it was an important change because it meant that the cultivated artist was moving in the same direction as, and with similar ethos to that of the popular musician.

Since all classes of townsmen (at least in London) except the very poor could and did attend the theatre occasionally, they made demands upon the playwright both dramatically and musically. Consequently we find an amazing synthesis. In *Julius Caesar*, for instance, there is little doubt that Lucius' song (IV, iii) was a typical cultured song to lute accompaniment of the sort that might have been written by Dowland. On the other hand, the dumb-show and the closing jig persisted: for instance *Julius Caesar* closed with a jig, according to Thomas Platter, who saw a performance in 1660. It is worth noticing that the jigs were extremely coarse in their humour. So much so that, in 1612, they were banned by the Middlesex magistrates on those grounds.

Some of the songs were special compositions written by the leader of the theatre orchestra. These groups appeared to be an important part of musical life at the time. In 1621, for instance, the King's Men had twenty-one musicians on their books, which is a large number, but the cost of which must have been considered worthwhile. A few years later, in 1634, Sir Bulstrode Whitelocke mentioned "the Blackfryers Musicke, who were esteemed the best of the common musitians in London". Again, references to specific groups such as Sneak's Noise shows the emergence of a music profession (rather than court or Church musicians) which served the needs of the ordinary person. Sometimes songs for plays were written by well-known composers (for example, Thomas Morley's "It was a Lover and his Lass"), while others were anonymous. A famous one was "Calliro Custure Me", which is found in no less than fifteen plays of the period, including a snatch in *Henry V* (IV, i), as well as in the *Fitzwilliam Virginal Book*.

Ex. 10

Calliro custure me (William Byrd's version)

It is clear that the theatre was an important centre of popular culture for musical as well as for dramatic reasons during the Tudor and early Stuart periods. This state of affairs continued until 2 September 1642, when the Puritans closed the theatres, on the grounds that:

> Whereas publicke sports doe not well agree with publicke Calamities nor publicke stage-playes with Seasons of Humiliation, this being an Exercise of sad and pious solemnity and the other being Spectacles of pleasure, too commonly expressing lascivious Mirth and Levitye: It is therefore thought fit, and Ordeined by the Lords and Commons in this Parliament assembled, that while these Sad causes and set times of

Humiliation doe continue, publike stage-playes shall cease and bee forborne.

They were not opened again for plays until the Restoration in 1660.

This leads us to examine the effect which the Puritans had on the musical life, and to wonder whether England became as musically dead as is often believed. Dr Burney, the eighteenth-century musical historian, claimed that "Ten years of gloomy silence seem to have elapsed before a string was suffered to vibrate or a pipe breathe aloud in the kingdom."

One might have expected this because, since the Reformation, the Puritan element had been violently anti-musical. Their attitude may be summed up in the words of Charles Fox, the Quaker preacher, who spoke out against "all sorts of music and against the mounte-banks playing tricks on stages, for they burthened the pure life and stirred up people's minds to vanity".

Certainly two Acts of Parliament were passed by the Puritans, the first declaring that:

For the better observation of the Lord's Day . . . dancing . . . profane singing . . . and playing upon musical instruments was prohibited.

The second Act stated:

if any person or persons . . . commonly called Fidlers or Minstrels shall be taken playing, fidling, or making music, in any Inn, Alehouse, or Tavern . . . or shall be taken intreating any person . . . to hear them play . . . that every such person shall be adjudged rogues, vagabonds, and sturdy beggars . . . and be punished as such.

However, this seems to have been the full extent of their prohibitions, and it should be noted that these Acts were not passed until 1657, only three years before the Restoration. They seem to have been measures aimed at Sunday observance and vagrancy, and not at music as an activity.

As far as the Puritans' own personal lives were concerned, there seems to have been a wide variety of attitudes: so much so that while one, Solomon Eccles, burned his instruments on Tower Bridge as "vanities", the wife of Colonel Hutchinson, the noted Roundhead leader, could write of her husband: "He had a great love to music, and often diverted himself with a viol, which he played masterly." Indeed, Cromwell himself was very musical: he sang psalms after dinner, held musical gatherings, employed a keyboard tutor for his daughter, and a personal organist, John Hingston. Perhaps most revealing, to those of us who think of Cromwell as an austere character, is to find that at the wedding of his daughter Frances "they had forty eight violins, and much mirth with frolics, besides mixt dancing".

It is, therefore, not strange to find that the professional musician underwent a similar variety of fates. Those whose living was made through Church music suffered especially; so much so that, in 1656, John Hingston asked Cromwell to found a College because of the fact, "that by reason of the late dissolucion of the Quires in the Cathedralls, where the study and practise of of the Science of Musick was specially cherished, many of the skilfull Professors of the said Science have during late wars and troubles dyed in want".

The music of the Church was no longer intricately polyphonic in form. Though it is a subject which cannot be entered into deeply in this book, it should be said that popular needs had a profound influence on the development of Church music. The Anglicans, in attempting to clear away the ornate aspects of Roman Catholic worship, simplified their music considerably. They did not oppose music, as did some Puritans. In this, they followed Luther's dictum: "I desire that all arts, particularly music, be employed in the service of Him who has given and created them." But they felt a need to make the words intelligible and to involve the congregation in communal singing. The first great work in which this was done was John Merbecke's *The Boke of Common Prayer noted*, of 1550. The main principle behind this was to take old melodies, including plain chant, to regularise them metrically, so as to make unison singing possible and to tend to use one note only for each syllable. Hymns and psalms thus acquired a great strength by taking on some of the simplicity of popular music.

On the other hand, the new gravity with which the Reformed Churches regarded themselves made it impossible for their composers to use material which was popular in origin; religious and secular areas of life became compartmentalised. In the same way, the areas of experience which could be drawn on for religious lyrics became prescribed with a rigidity which has only begun to be relaxed in the present century.

The town waits, as servants of the Establishment, also suffered during the Commonwealth. In 1589, the ability of the Norwich waits had been such that Drake had requested (successfully) that they be allowed to accompany him on his next voyage. The London waits were so proficient that, in 1599, Thomas Morley dedicated his *Consort Lessons* to those "excellent and expert musicians". But they were dismissed from their posts—though this was hardly surprising when we consider that the traditional Puritan opposition to music made at least one Member of Parliament demand that "fiddlers and minstrels would be included [in an act prohibiting their activities] as they did corrupt the manners of the people and inflame their debauchery by lewd and obscene songs". It was only in 1660 that "the musical waits after many years sequestration were restored to their places and pensions".

Despite official disapproval, there was a sufficient interest in music to allow Jenkins, Locke and Lawes to make a living, while large numbers paid to see the virtuosity of the German violinist, Thomas Baltzar, when he toured this country. Also, we know that boys were still entered upon the eight-year apprenticeship, since the Clerkenwell Records, of 1657, show that an agreement was made between Henry Hazard, and Robert Strong, a musician of that parish.

Domestic music not only continued to be played, but thrived, at least among the middle classes, since some of the most important publications in this field date from the Commonwealth period. In 1652, John Hilton produced his famous album of catches and rounds *Catch that Catch Can* and, in the same year, appeared Playford's *Banquet of Music* as well as his *Music's Recreation on the Lyra Viol* (a popular chordal instrument). Playford's *Dancing Master* is, in fact, the source of much of our earlier popular music, since he records many dance tunes and, although some alterations have been made, we still have something like an accurate representation of popular dance music. A well-known example is "Portsmouth".

Ex. 11
Portsmouth

In this tune, we can see that the major key is used throughout, but in the following example, the older, modal approach is used, though the introduction of the F sharps, which bring the tune closer to the "normal" minor key, illustrates well the transitional stage which popular music was undergoing.

The conflict between a modal and a "standard" conception, demonstrated

Ex. 12
Pall Mall

in the above, is one of the factors which give the music of the period a great
charm to a modern listener. We must again be wary of assuming that the
same feelings were aroused in the original audience. In fact, it is only when
we can get beyond such feelings of "quaintness" that we can come to a real
understanding of the culture which produces a given folk music.

The appearance, in 1659, of the *Division Violist or an Introduction to the
playing on a ground* by Christopher Simpson is also of interest. This book
explained the art of composing variations on an ostinato bass. It thus emphasises the importance of improvisation, which we have always seen to be a
major factor in the performance and composition of popular music.

A striking testimony to the popularity of domestic music is Pepys' note in
1666, that during the Great Fire of London, one boat in every three which
was carrying furniture to safety contained a set of virginals. Even allowing
for exaggeration, and the fact that only the more well-to-do could afford to
hire boats to save large amounts of furniture, it still indicates the wide
popularity of this instrument among the middle and upper classes.

At the end of the period came a development which was highly important
in determining future tastes, namely the creation of an English opera. It grew
out of the masque, a lighter and more spectacular type of entertainment,
which had been popular since the 1590s, and had attracted such writers as
Ben Jonson and John Milton. From this form arose Davenant's *The Siege of
Rhodes* (1656), which was an attempt to find dramatic diversion through
music, since plays as such were forbidden. It was, in fact, not a masque, but
a three-act opera, since the music was predominant and the story was more
definite in outline than was customary in the masque. In addition, it had the
merit of being the first English dramatic production to use painted scenery
and women actors, as far as we can ascertain.

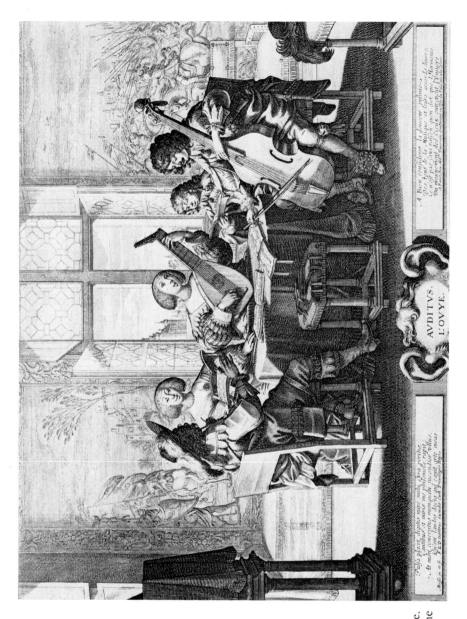

Auditus. Etching by Bosse.
Domestic music in the
18th Century

Farmer Giles and his
Wife showing off
their Daughter Betty.
Etching by Gillray

It contained some famous names. Captain Henry Cooke, "esteemed the best singer, after the Italian manner, of any in England", sang the lead in music composed by himself, Matthew Locke and Henry Lawes. The words were, of course, by Davenant, who was a very competent poet. The orchestra, led by John Banister the Elder, later of the King's Band, was accompanied by Christopher Gibbons, son of Orlando, playing the continuo part, and featured the violin playing of the virtuoso Thomas Baltzar. Davenant followed this opera with another, *The Cruelty of the Spaniards in Peru*, in 1658. Unlike the previous work, this was not privately performed, but was "represented daily at the Cockpit in Dury Lane at three afternoone".

It might seem that we have digressed in considering such an aristocratic form, but the relevance lies in the fact that in Italy, the home of opera, what had been an expensive aristocratic pursuit became in Naples, and more particularly in Venice, a popular form. In the latter city, in 1637, the first public opera house was opened, and though its boxes were sold to nobility from all over Europe on a subscription system, the general public were admitted free to the empty seats. As a consequence, the vociferous and frank comments of the gondoliers and others helped considerably to mould the shape of Venetian opera—in this way, a non-aristocratic taste was formed. The English opera similarly widened its scope and also gave rise to kindred forms aimed at a definitely non-aristocratic audience.

By 1660, the year at which this chapter ends, there was a thriving musical culture in England. Though the Reformation had hastened the divorce of Church music from popular song, and the Renaissance had encouraged the pursuit of the elevated style, the real effects of the Neo-Classical movement had yet to be felt. At the same time, interest in practical music-making was still strong—though professionals of high skill existed, they had not yet enforced a division between them and the amateur in the quality of composition which they performed. There was a resulting closeness of connection and depth of interaction between the consciously artistic and the popular on a scale which was never again to be equalled.

4 From the Restoration to the "Rocket" (1660–1825)

... I proposed to myself to proceed, the very
next morning, to an intelligence office, to
which I was furnish'd with written directions
on the back of a ballad Esther had given me.
JOHN CLELAND, *Fanny Hill*

Our next period begins at the Restoration, which is important from a musical viewpoint because of the new ideas which originated at the Court, and ends with the opening of the Stockton and Darlington Railway, in 1825. The selection of this date is quite arbitrary but it is nevertheless apt, because, as we shall see later, the railway facilitated and accelerated the process of industrialisation and the consequent decay of the rural economy. The process also brought about the rapid expansion of the towns, and the attendant movement among workers on an unprecedent scale. This was clearly to affect cultural attitudes. For the moment, however, we are more concerned with the effects of the emergence of a new form of British society, with new social relationships, after the Civil War.

Davenant's experiments with opera during the Commonwealth period foreshadowed the changes of musical style and attitude which were to take place after the accession of Charles II. He and his Court returned from France, where an attempt was being made to revive the ideas of classical Greece and Rome. As a consequence, Court taste was for plays like those of Racine and Corneille, and music like that of Lully. One of the king's first actions was to found a Court orchestra, in emulation of that at the French Court, called "The King's Own Band" and consisting of twenty-four violins. The very choice of instrument is significant of a new emphasis in music, in that the violin had largely been considered a coarse instrument, used until then, according to Thomas Mace, by "common fidlers". This popular dance instrument became the very centre of the instrumental resources of the most refined music. As a consequence of this change, by 1676, Mace was looking back at the glories of the former polyphonic period, explaining that "Our great care was to have all the parts equally heard", while the style had changed to the theme and accompaniment style of the French, because Charles II had "an utter aversion to fancies", and could "bear no music to which he could not beat time".

Closely linked with this change in attitude at Court was an even more far-reaching one: the decline of the idea that music was a necessary part of a man's accomplishments. Commentators no longer insisted on this—in some cases they positively discouraged it. Music might be an entertainment, but it was not an essential factor in moulding the spirit of those whose lives were to be spent in government.

Charles' attitudes also implied the creation of a *listening* class out of people who were originally participants. "Beating time" is the action of a member of an audience, whereas many of the musical creations of the previous age were meant to be enjoyed largely by taking part in the performance. That this was the beginning of the evolution of the modern concert-goer's attitude is made even more clear by the fact that at least one virtuoso, the Italian violinist Nicola Matteis, insisted, in 1674, on complete silence and attention for his performances at Court. All previous music had been to some degree incidental to the evening's entertainment and conversation. The chatter and comments of Theseus and his Court during the play in the last act of *A Midsummer Night's Dream* were not merely a dramatic device to permit the juxtaposition of visual and verbal comedy.

We have to add to this the fact that the king was thinking of music designed for, or at least based upon, the dance. This threw a new emphasis onto dance music, and tended to push music away from the intricacy which is inherent in polyphony, and apart from the loss of polyphonic interplay, there was a loss of freedom of rhythm which was not regained by serious musicians for over two hundred years. The emphasis on dancing as a social outlet (an increasingly important one in urban civilisation) is shown by the many editions into which Playford's *Dancing Master* ran. This was primarily aimed at the upper and middle classes in the towns, but the movement away from traditional dance (and music) had begun to take place in the country as well. The theme of the simple and old-fashioned tastes of the country dweller, is one with which we today are all too familiar, and which was widely held in the Restoration period. It had been sounded even before the Civil War in Shirley's *The Lady of Pleasure*:

> I would not
> Endure again the country conversation
> To be the lady of six shires—the men

So near the primitive making they retain
A sense of nothing but the earth, their brains
And barren heads standing as much in want
Of ploughing as their ground; to hear a fellow
Make himself merry, and his horse, with whistling
"Sellenger's Round"; to observe with what solemnity
They keep their wakes and throw for pewter candlesticks.
How they become the morris, with those bells
They ring all in to Whitsun ales, and sweat
Through twenty scarfs and napkins till the hobby-horse
Tire, and Maid Marian, dissolv'd to a jelly,
Be kept for spoon meat.

It is true to say that gibes of this type were in the first instance written to please a new, town-dwelling, fashion-conscious aristocracy. But the sentiments are found often enough elsewhere to support the attitudes of the rapidly increasing town population, which at this stage had not begun to question the advantages of urban life in the way that we are prone to do. We tend to think very highly of the Elizabethan era, to see it as full of life, and brimful of new discoveries. But the men of the Restoration era saw it as a time thankfully past; to them it was a barbarous, uncivil time, lacking in cultural delicacy, and lacking true emotion in its art. Thus, though the following complaint by Richard Baxter (1696) is primarily concerned with Sunday Observance, its tone is critical of old ways and old customs. He remembers his youth when

> One of my Father's own Tenants was the Town Piper, hired by the Year, (for many Years together) and the place of the Dancing Assembly was not an hundred yards from our door; and we could not on the Lord's Day either read a Chapter, or Pray, or sing a Psalm, or Chatechise or instruct a Servant but with the noise the Pipe and Taber and the Whootings in the Street, continually in our ears ... And sometimes the Morrice Dancers would come into the Church with all their Linnen and Scarfes and Antick Dresses, with morrice-bells jingling at their leggs.

Such changes brought certain aspects of cultured music much closer to the popular style, which had always been, of necessity, fundamentally monodic, and which was usually very rhythmic, so that it could be clapped and danced to. Even as sophisticated a composer as Purcell could cultivate an idiom very close to the folk style. His melody (Ex. 13) from *The Mock Marriage* (1695) was so folk-like that Gay used it some thirty-four years later in his ballad opera *Polly*:

Ex. 13

Melody by Purcell

This closeness of the two styles permitted an interaction between the two cultures, and meant that there was more opportunity for the ideas of sophisticated art to influence popular composition. A. L. Lloyd has noted the way in which the following ballad of about 1760, though keeping to a traditional framework and utilising traditional formulae, has a touch of the ornamentation and rather artificial imagery of the sophisticated poetry of the time, especially in stanza four:

> As I went out one May morning
> To hear the birds so sweet,
> I hid myself in a green shady dell
> And watched two lovers sweet.
>
> You courted me was what she said
> Till you got me to comply
> You courted me with merry mood
> All night with you I lie.
>
> And when your heart was mine, false love
> And your head lay on my breast
> You could make me believe by the fall of your arm
> That the sun rose in the west.
>
> I wish your breast was made of glass
> That all in it might behold
> I'd write our secret on your breast
> In letters made of gold.
>
> There's many a girl can go about
> And hear the birds so sweet
> While I, poor girl, must stay alone
> And rock my cradle and weep.

> There's many a star shall dwindle in the west
> There's many a leaf below
> There's many a curse shall light on a man
> For treating a poor girl so.
>
> Oh I can sing as lonely a song
> As any little bird in a cage,
> Who twelve long months have been gone
> And scarce fifteen year of age.

A lyric such as this, though superficially obvious in its content, shows the whole folk tradition at the start of its decline. A traditional theme is treated by giving a typically medieval opening (*cf.* "Now sprinkes the spray", in Chapter 2). The directness of the authentic folk style is still there,

> You courted me with a merry mood,
> All night with you I'd lie,

and the figurative use of

> You could make me believe by the fall of your arm
> That the sun rose in the west

is typically popular in origin. But the images come too thick and fast, and ideas such as:

> I wish your breast was made of glass,

like the underlying idea of the free and caged bird, are too contrived to have the true communal ring. And the latter half of the poem uses "sentiment" in a way which we associate with the Victorians. The singer is self-conscious; she uses tear-jerking phraseology (the last stanza), but we feel an element of self-dramatisation creeping in; the singer is moved, but not so much that she can't glance quickly at the audience to see that the appropriate response is forthcoming. The bird in a cage idea foreshadows that reversal of emotional values which took place in some areas of society in which excessive emotion over small things was accompanied by a steadfast refusal to face the bigger problems of the real world outside. The reader may feel with some justification that such an interpretation is going too far. The lyric is pleasant enough and would be more so with music, and it has a clarity and lightness which is most enjoyable. But I would suggest that the first tendencies towards a new approach are to be seen in it, and that these should be noted. It is a paradox of literature that it is, on occasion, capable of expressing ideas unequivocally and powerfully, but that, the nature of words being what it is, we are equally often obliged to chase what sometimes seems to be a will-o'-the-wisp in order to trace how we have moved from one clear position to another.

It is interesting to see how once a movement begins in a certain direction all factors seem to contribute to the process of change. The same is true of the above tendencies, which influenced and were influenced by the development of a professional musician class. Though this was created at first to entertain and not to dictate, these musicians had the leisure to develop a higher level of technique than the average amateur could hope to attain. Thus a gulf grew between the listener and the musician.

It is, of course, true that virtuosity had existed among professionals before, as in the Masses of the Netherlands School, or in certain compositions of the English virginalists (e.g. Bull's "Walsingham"). But these were display pieces, created by and for a small number of kept musicians, and the bulk of accepted music was within the range of the amateur. Its simplicity of technique did not automatically imply simplicity of conception, nor did it bear the stigma of not being advanced enough to be suitable for the professional. The gulf between listener and musician led naturally to the next unprecedented move: the organisation of public concerts.

Concerts had already been given, before the Restoration, by Cromwell at Whitehall, and probably the account of Oxford given by Antony Wood was true of other places; he mentions concerts in six colleges, and several private houses. These were probably like that recorded of a private house near St Paul's at which "some shopkeepers and foremen came, weekly, to sing a consort and to hear and enjoy ale and tobacco". The bulk of their repertoire came from Playford's Catch as Catch Can.

However, the person to take the final step was John Banister, in 1672. Formerly, he had been in the King's Own Band, but he now hired a room "over against the George Tavern in Whitefriars", and at four o'clock each afternoon put on concerts given "by excellent masters", at an admission fee of one shilling. Such a price must have excluded the poorer members of the community, but it still made music of the highest quality available to many who could never have kept an orchestra, or even have hired one for a special occasion. Performances in taverns were not unknown previously—Pepys records one on 18 February 1660—but Banister was the first to organise concerts regularly.

Banister's concerts continued until 1678, in which year Thomas Britton,

known as "the musical small-coal man" because he was a coal dealer of
Clerkenwell (the very trade is significant, since it clearly shows his social
origin and status), began to put on concerts once a week in the loft over his
storehouse at Jerusalem Passage. At first these were free, but later he had
to charge an annual subscription of ten shillings and a penny per meeting
for coffee. These concerts continued until 1714, and in the later years Handel
was a regular performer at them. Of course, only a very small percentage of
the population were as yet affected by organised concerts, but the beginnings
of a middle-class musical life had been created. It is also worth noting that
though the most cursory glance at economic history will show how few
people could have had time or money to follow musical pursuits, Pepys
tells us (25 January 1660) how he was invited by Lady Wright's butler into
the buttery, there to drink a glass of sack, and to hear the butler play a lute
piece. He also records that his wife's maid, Mary Mercer, was a competent
performer on the harpsichord and viol.

It was only a matter of time before the discussion which such performances
were bound to arouse became more formalised, and before Britton's concerts
came to an end, both the *Tatler* (1709–11) and the *Spectator* (1711–12) had
begun to include music criticism among their articles. From this time on,
there was a steady flow of music journalism.

The almost inevitable result of a gulf between audience and musician,
and of the unfamiliarity with musical aims caused by non-participation, is a
tendency to a lack of discrimination and a love of the unimportant or even
the unsatisfactory, because it contains superficially exciting or novel elements.
An example of this latter factor was the vogue of the harmonica, or to give it
its full title, the glass harmonica. So popular was this instrument that even
Mozart wrote a piece for it, and in 1746 Gluck gave a concert at the Hay-
market Theatre, which was advertised as "a Concert upon Twenty-Six
Drinking Glasses, tuned with Spring Water, accompanied with the whole
Band". About 1760, Benjamin Franklin improved the instrument by the
addition of a treadle, which saved the labour of running one's finger round
the edge of the glasses. The love of delicate and ethereal effects was also
made manifest in the popularity of the aeolian harp and the bell harp. The
former had gut strings and a soundbox and was put into gardens. The wind
set the strings in motion, so that they gave off harmonics. Thus the desires for
Nature ordered into harmony by the hand of man, in the form of a landscaped
garden, were reflected in sound; the ear could be delighted as the song of the
wind was made more beautiful. The bell harp was designed with the same
ideal in mind, but involved a human performer. Invented by John Simcock of

Bath in the early eighteenth century, it was a kind of psaltery, of which an account of 1767 says:

> Its form is like a bell and kept swinging whilst played on, whose strings are struck by each thumb, being armed with a split quill, whalebone or thin horn, which when artfully managed affords tolerable harmony.

Another account says it produced "the effect of a peal of bells borne on the wind".

Nevertheless, there was still a large amount of worthwhile musical activity in the home, as is shown by contemporary accounts, paintings, and by the large amount of music which is still known and played today (*e.g.* pieces by Mozart, Haydn, the Quantz flute works for Frederick the Great, and Telemann's *Tafelmusik*). Our interest is naturally centred upon those pieces which employ the better known modern instruments, in combinations easily arranged, but it is interesting to find, in view of present-day trends, that the lute, and English and Spanish guitars were very popular. The English guitar, not really a guitar at all, but a form of cittern, metal stringed and played with the thumb and first finger, arrived here from Italy in 1756, and, being a simple instrument to learn, enjoyed enormous popularity for a while. On the other hand, the Spanish guitar enjoyed a steadily increasing popularity until the 1830s. Handel, Haydn and Boccherini all played it. In fact, the violin virtuoso, Paganini, devoted himself to the study of it for three years, at one point in his career.

Another fretted instrument which became popular at this time was the mandolin. In 1713, we find the announcement of "a Concerto on the Mandoline, being an instrument admired in Rome, but never Publick here". It maintained a steady popularity which reached a peak in the late nineteenth century—a photograph of a Cambridge music shop of that period shows a window full of mandolins and banjos, comparable with the displays of guitars one sees today. Sonatas for mandolin with other instruments were in vogue, and Beethoven wrote a few pieces for it including a Sonata for mandolin and piano.

As pictures show, the harp was very popular among well-to-do families; the instrument took various forms. In the mid-eighteenth century there was a vogue for the Welsh triple harp, and in 1798, Edward Light, "Lyrist to the Princess of Wales", invented the dital harp, also called the harp guitar or harp lute. The latter name was very apt since the instrument had a lute body which continued upwards into a small harp. It was played with both hands, and finger keys were used to raise the pitch a semitone. By 1816, it had taken its final form, with twenty-two strings. The greatest popularity of the harp family was to come later however, in the Victorian era.

Music tended to form part of the very limited education of young ladies, and many gentlemen chose not only to make music at home, but to join a glee club. These were clubs at which the members drank, smoked and sang, and according to at least one engraving (of the Canterbury Glee Club in 1826) were attended by fairly large numbers (between fifty and a hundred members). In 1741, one John Immyns founded the first of these, the "Madrigal Society", a body originally attended by working men who loved the older style. However, such names as the "Noblemen's and Gentlemen's Catch Club" (founded 1761) show that the social range and musical aims of the clubs soon became more restricted. Thus, the "Glee Club" (founded 1787), and others of the sort, sang specially written music by such composers as Samuel Webbe (1740–1816) and Richard Stevens (1757–1857). However, the music was frequently of rather poor quality, both technically and emotionally, and the songs were not so much polyphonic, as what we should now call part-songs.

The ballad opera is perhaps the most important musical feature of the period, from our point of view. In Italy, and later in France, England and other countries influenced by the Italian style and ideas, opera was largely an aristocratic pursuit. It involved rich spectacle, large choruses and orchestras and it featured star singers. The themes were tragic and, as in the French classical drama, were treated on a grand scale, the writer aiming to express the noblest passions in the most refined manner. However, even more than in the drama, the form became stereotyped, the conventions became more rigid, and even the plots more fixed, so that the interest of the audience became more and more focused upon the star singers, especially the castrati.

This form was not suited to the rising middle class, who attended the commercial opera houses, and they demanded changes. From the insertion of comic interludes (intermezzi) between the acts a new form developed, the *opera buffa* or comic opera, in which the emphasis was on middle-class heroes, witty servants, dramatic situations and melody. Spoken dialogue was employed instead of recitative. The first in this genre was Pergolesi's *La Serva Padrona* of 1728.

Similarly, in France there developed the *opèra comique* and in England the ballad opera, which was in fact a play containing a great deal of music. It had no recitative, and attention was centred upon the large number of songs, taken from a variety of sources and including known traditional songs.

The first of these ballad operas appeared in 1725. It was by Allan Ramsay and was entitled *The Gentle Shepherd*. In verse, and utilising Scots dialect and tunes, it appealed to the growing fashion for art which reflected the simplicity of rustic life, and which contained rather exotic local colour. This apparent contradiction of my earlier remarks on country life serves to illustrate the way in which at any period, our artistic generalisations are only half-truths. Very often, opposites may be found in the same period, and even in the work of the same persons. In this age, practical men regarded country life as backward and undesirable. At the same time they took a greater interest in natural surroundings than perhaps in any earlier age; nature had, however, to be regularized. Similarly, though the life of the town was all-important, in their idealised world of the imagination, eighteenth-century men turned to a pastoral conception, in which emotions were simple; man was a "noble savage" unspoiled by the corruption of civilisation. The pastoral combined with music clearly provided an even better opportunity for indulging these Romantic ideals.

The Gentle Shepherd came to London in 1727 and was followed in 1728 by the still popular *Beggar's Opera* of John Gay, which was set among rogues and vagabonds, and was full of simple yet beautiful traditional tunes. It is the complete antithesis of the serious opera of the aristocratic classes, and is an expression of the need for sentiment, in a more realistic and lower social setting, which was found among the middle and working classes.

The popularity of this form was immediate and enormous. No less than fifteen ballad operas were produced in the following year, and in the peak year, 1733, some twenty-two ballad operas were staged. They created great difficulties for the serious opera writers—Handel's statement that "ballad opera pelted Italian opera off the stage with Lumps of Pudding" (the name of the last tune in Gay's work) is well known. It is hard for us to imagine the kind of excitement which these productions engendered, especially as today the conditions of opera-going are far more formal than they were then, even for the *opera seria*. The Restoration audience was far less respectful than its modern counterpart. All the records show that Etherege's complaint that the audience went

> From one Playhouse to the other Playhouse
> And if they like neither the play nor the Women,
> They seldom stay any longer than the combing
> Of their Perriwigs or a whisper or two with a Friend

was, if anything, an understatement. A contemporary letter regrets, diplomatically, that "Ann Barwick, who was lately my servant, had committed rudeness last night at the playhouse by throwing oranges and hissing when Mrs. L'Epine, the Italian gentlewoman, sung."

A sympathetic audience was equally demonstrative. In a *Spectator* of 1711, Addison describes the audience at the *opera seria*:

> The chorus in which that opera abounds gives the parterre frequent opportunities of joining in consort with the stage. This inclination of the audience to sing along with the actors so prevails with them, that I have sometimes known a performer on the stage do no more in a celebrated song than the clerk of a parish church, who serves only to raise the Psalm and is afterwards drown'd in the music of the congregation.

Addison was here speaking of French audiences, but the custom passed to England, and as one might have expected was, if anything, even more popular at the ballad opera with its simple tunes. This custom led Colley Cibber in *Love in a Riddle* (Drury Lane, 1729) to sing:

> Since songs to play are nowadays
> Like to your meals a salad;
> Permit us then, kind gentlemen,
> To try our skill by ballad;
> While you, to grace our native lays,
> As France has done before us,
> Belle, beau and cit, from box and pit
> All join the jolly chorus.

Chorus:

> Then, freeborn boys, all make a noise,
> As France has done before us:
> With English hearts all bear your parts,
> And join the jolly chorus.

Despite the fact that ballad opera, as a form, died out within about twenty years, it was symptomatic of a new popular need, for it was followed by similar forms of musical drama. It was also not alone in aiming at this particular form of entertainment, since it had been preceded, in 1711, by the production of the first pantomime (in the modern sense) at Drury Lane. This form of music-play has never died out, though it has had various changes of manner. The most significant developments were probably made by Joseph Grimaldi, son of the ballet master at Drury Lane, and originally a child star— he danced at Sadler's Wells at the age of two years and four months. His first great adult success came, however, in 1800–1 at Drury Lane, but the pantomime which made his name was *Mother Goose* produced at Covent

Garden, Christmas 1806. In this, he sang the song most closely associated with him, and popular for some thirty years after his death in 1837, "Hot Codlins" (roasted apples). The lyrics suggest that the song was aimed at an adult rather than a child audience, since there is a streak of "naughtiness" running through the song, carefully avoiding the unmentionable while leaving the audience in no doubt of the forbidden subject. The first stanza will illustrate this:

> A little old woman her living she got
> By selling hot codlins, hot, hot, hot,
> And this little old woman who codlins sold
> Though her codlins were hot she felt herself cold:
> So to keep herself warm she thought it no sin
> To fetch for herself a quartern of —

Looked at from one point of view, this is typical Victorian horseplay, illustrative of a rather immature and unsubtle outlook, which contains a certain malicious element in that it always takes on weaker opponents. Perhaps this is merely my prejudice; but is it not really the humour of the people who consider someone to be a bad sport, if he does not feel able to laugh with quite such vigour as they do, when he sits rather painfully on the tintack they have placed on his chair? The typically English humour, found in the twentieth century in the Old Mother Reilly films, is perhaps better illustrated by the third stanza.

> This little old woman, while muzzy she got,
> Some boys stole her codlins, hot, hot, hot,
> Powder under pan put, and in it round stones;
> Says the little old woman, "These apples have bones"
> The powder the pan in her face did send
> Which sent the old woman on her latter —

My comments may be the result of a biased reading, but what is less contentious about the song is that in it the middle- and working-class attitudes are still indistinguishable. It is clearly robust and earthy, its sentiments spring out of everyday existence, and are far from *Love in a Village*, with its artificial rusticity. As in the Restoration drama, comedy comes far nearer to reality than tragedy.

This area of nineteenth-century experience is one that is still under-stressed; we are far more familiar with their prudery and their sentimentality. I therefore offer a couple more examples of Grimaldi's humour, so that the reader may be better able to draw his own conclusions. His reliance on basic humour is found in the song "Tipitywitchet", which depends for its effects on hiccups, sneezing, yawning, laughing, and crying:

> This very morning handy
> My malady was such
> I in my tea took brandy
> And took a drop too much
>   (Hiccups) Tol de rol, etc.

Of the same type, was the kind of situation which rocked the house—Grimaldi would make a hussar's uniform out of coal-scuttles, a pelisse and a muff. (We might compare the Western Brothers.) It is fair to conclude by mentioning that Grimaldi was very talented, and could sing, dance, act, tell jokes and do acrobatics. In fact, his name "Joey" has been applied ever since to clowns.

It is reasonable to say that between them, the ballad opera and the pantomime opened up the way for an entirely new stream of taste, which was in fact a parallel culture, developing its own tastes and standards which were by no means always the same as those of the serious artistic world. It did for music what Richardson's novel *Pamela* did for literature: it gave expression to a new and highly lucrative sphere of middle-class sentiment. It called into being a class of musicians whose outlook was shaped and limited by the demands of its new public. This was no different in one sense from the position of a composer like Haydn, who depended on a patron. A divergence did, however, take place. The first reason for this was that the serious artist found and continued to expect, as he still does, a high degree of independence from his audience. He felt a consequent duty to warn or instruct, but not necessarily to please. The composer writing for the middle class had to be constantly aware of the commercial effects of his actions, and was consequently limited, since his audience wished, first and foremost, for entertainment. The commercial composer might arouse melancholy, provided he knew well that his audience would accept it; but there was no room for tragedy. The situation of the Tudor Court, in which Cornysshe was required to write for the Chapel and the dance, and used a common language (though with different degrees of subtlety) for both, had gone, and still has not returned. Until the nineteenth century, the composer was a man who was required to have, and had, such versatility—Mozart could produce work as varied as the piece for glass harmonica and the *Requiem*.

Perhaps the last important English composer of relevance to this phase of our topic was Thomas Arne (1710–78). His musical life was amazingly varied. In 1740, he produced a masque for the Prince of Wales (in which the song "Rule, Britannia" first appeared). But he also wrote the music for the musical drama *Love in a Village*, which was typically bourgeois in taste. He wrote domestic music, conducted a concert of catches and glees (1768), led the Drury Lane orchestra, wrote an oratorio, *Judith*, and was the chief composer at the Vauxhall Gardens—a pleasure gardens where one could walk, eat, drink, listen to light music, watch fireworks, or make amorous assignations in the bowers. And these examples are not isolated instances of his activities. His range and his output were amazing by modern standards. As we come nearer to our own time, we find a steady widening of the gap between the popular and serious artist. A composer like Robert Farnon may set out to capture a popular audience or a composer such as Stravinsky a cultured one and win acclaim, and even respect for it. But the man who, like George Gershwin, tries to live in both worlds, may easily find himself not really accepted by either.

We can see how this widening gap between the aristocratic-cultured taste and the bourgeois-sentimental taste was beginning to appear by making a few simple comparisons. Here is a lyric by Gray, typical of the refined style. It was composed in 1761 to a tune by Geminiani, but was not published until 1780; making it more representative of the latter part of our period.

> Thyrsis when we parted swore
> Ere the spring he would return
> Ah! what means yon violet flower!
> And the buds that deck the thorn!
> 'Twas the lark that upwards sprung
> 'Twas the nightingale that sung!
>
> Idle notes! Untimely green
> Why this unavailing haste?
> Western gales and skies serene
> Speak not always winter past
> Cease, my doubts, my fears to move,
> Spare the honour of my love.

In this, the thought is one which is satisfactory as the basis for a lyric—that, as the lover promised to return before the spring, the signs of spring which the singer sees must be deceptive. The idea is expressed in language which, according to the tastes of that time, was suited to the topic. The images, though conventional, have the dignity of formality and a certain decorousness. The setting is also conventional—a pastoral scene, in which the lover is a shepherd, with a Greek name. Granted the conventions, it is a simple, but adequate lyric.

In contrast to this carefully cultivated elegance, we find that the middle-class mode had an everyday setting, as is seen in the mid-century "Sally in our Alley" of Henry Carey. Two verses will serve to illustrate the difference in tone.

> Her father he makes cabbage nets
> And thro' the streets does cry 'em,
> Her mother she sells laces long
> To such as please to buy 'em:
> But sure such folks could not beget
> So sweet a girl as Sally:
> She is the darling of my heart,
> And she lives in our alley.
>
> When she is by, I leave my work,
> I love her so sincerely;
> My master comes like any Turk,
> And bangs me most severely;
> But let him bang his bellyful
> I'll bear it all for Sally
> She is the darling of my heart,
> And she lives in our alley.

Lyrics such as the above should not be credited with some kind of "sincerity", lacking in Gray's. These songs were written, for a definite financial reward, by middle-class musicians for a middle-class audience. Indeed, if the concept of sincerity has any real value at all in the evaluation of such songs as this, it may well be suggested that the conscious striving after low language ("But let him bang his bellyful") and the suggestion that she was too good to be begotten by "such folks" is, if anything, degrading in its treatment of the working man. However, such ideas are only valid if we apply twentieth-century attitudes to an age which just did not see things in the same light as we do.

Nevertheless, the attempt to portray "low life" is worthy of further examination. The following extract comes from a song by John Percy and William Shield called "Wapping Old Stairs":

> Your Molly has never been false, she declares,
> Since last time we parted at Wapping Old Stairs,
> When I vow'd that I still would continue the same,

And gave you the 'bacco box mark'd with my name.
When I passed a whole fortnight between decks with you,
Did I e'er give a kiss, Tom, to one of your crew?
To be useful and kind with my Thomas I stay'd,
For his trousers I wash'd, and his grog, too, I made.

To us there is clearly a strong element of humour in this lyric, but before we decide that this was the intention of the authors, rather than heart-string tugging, we should remember the excesses to which a love of dewy-eyed sentiment took the middle classes. This was the age of the aeolian harp and weeping on the death of a canary, of the "black dog" Melancholy and of Mrs Radcliffe.

What is interesting, because it is new, is the association of sentiment with working-class characters, and the inclusion of details of working-class life. The aristocratic culture of earlier centuries was only really interested in the expression of the noble passions of noble people. Such feelings were not possible in the lower-class person, who was of grosser mould, and fit only to be represented as a bumpkin. It should be remembered that Perdita in *The Winter's Tale* drew attention because

nothing she does or seems
But smacks of something greater than herself
Too noble for this place.

On the other hand, the details of "low life" are not the products of working men writing about themselves, and their inclusion should be distinguished from genuine sympathy for the lower orders. It is noteworthy that when such people sang, they were, in fact, only interested in the *un*common (the passion, and the knight in armour) and not in what was commonplace to them. The interest in "authentic detail" may be taken to illustrate not a mixing of the classes, but a greater demarcation of them. Thus the following lines from Charles Dibdin's *The Waterman*, of 1773, were of interest to a middle-class audience precisely because of their detachment from ordinary life, and because they were therefore in a sense exotic:

Then farewell my trim built wherry,
Oars and coat and badge farewell,
Nevermore at Chelsea ferry,
Shall your Thomas take a spell.

The details of the above lyrics are, of course, accurate, unlike those of pastoral writing, and not a little of this must spring from the fact that many composers came from the lower classes of society. For instance, William Shield (1748–1829) had been a boat builder's apprentice, Allan Ramsay (1686–1758) was a bookseller and rugmaker, and Charles Dibdin (1754–1814) was the son of a parish clerk. It may be argued that in romanticising the lower classes they were, in fact, expressing the ideals which they held about themselves, in the way that many people today would feel *Coronation Street* and similar television programmes express what they are like in all their important aspects. But the degree to which the commercial pressures of a harsh age must have influenced their work must always be borne in mind.

The search for novelty and the demand for portrayals of a life different from that of the average member of the middle class was also made manifest in the vogue of "Celtic" songs and poems. We have already mentioned Allan Ramsay's opera in this connection, and it is to this same period that we owe the writing down of much beautiful Scots folk song. This was often done by putting new words to an old tune, as Robert Burns did in his "My love is like a red, red rose".

The Welsh, too, were not neglected. John Parry, who became famous enough as a harpist to be portrayed by Hogarth and Joshua Reynolds, published a book of *Traditional Welsh Tunes*, in 1742, for harp and harpsichord. Some of these were genuine, others were just typical of the music of London, and were written by Parry himself.

Most popular of all, though, were the Irish tunes, in connection with which the most important work was done by Tom Moore, who produced his *Irish Melodies* between 1807 and 1834. Unlike Parry's, these were largely genuine, and introduced and made popular such songs as "The Harp that once in Tara's Halls" and "The Minstrel Boy".

An age attracted by the Celtic peoples, China, Peru, and Turkey, not unnaturally also found an interest in the Negroes of the Colonial plantations. This interest, which from the start leaned towards the "coon" and "nigger minstrel" type of image, was to continue to the present day. As early as 1788 Charles Dibdin wrote:

> One negro, wi my banjer
> Me from Jenny come
> Wod conning yieie
> Me savez spy
> De buckra world one hum
> As troo a street a stranger
> Me my banjer strum.

It is interesting to see that the basic minstrel pattern is already there, but that the lyrics have still the sound of a foreign song: they are not yet white songs with a few Negro clichés added.

This love of the exotic, in the sense of things which are not a part of one's normal existence, together with a love of sensation that probably sprang from a day-to-day life which was becoming ever more ordered and peaceful, manifested itself most strongly in the "Gothick Cult". The richer people had "grottoes" and "ruined abbeys" built in their grounds, and both they and the poorer part of the population threw themselves happily into the novels of Mrs Radcliffe. It was in this vein that the following song was written by Shield and O'Keefe. Entitled "The Wolf", it opened:

> While the wolf on nightly prowl
> Bays the moon with hideous howl,
> Gates are barred in vain resistance,
> Females shriek, but no assistance,
>
> Silence, or you meet your fate,
> Your keys, your jewels, cash and plate.
> Locks, bolts and bars soon fly asunder
> Then to rifle, rob and plunder.

Spine chilling galore, with the comforting knowledge that no wolf had howled in Britain since 1728.

Another growing element in middle-class song was patriotism, but, cynical though it may sound, it is hard to deny that the majority of the songs which urged the valorous pursuit of duty, came from those who slept peacefully at home, allowing professionals to sail the seas or fight the foe, expanding the empire and trade.

Sometimes, a note of self-awareness is heard, as in Henry Fielding's *Grub Street Opera*, of 1731:

> When the mighty roast beef was the Englishman's food,
> It ennobled our hearts and enriched our blood;
> Our soldiers were brave and our courtiers were good,
> Oh the roast beef of England,
> And Old England's roast beef.
>
> But since we have learned from all-conquering France
> To eat their ragouts as well as to dance,
> Oh what a fine figure we make in romance,
> Oh the roast beef of England,
> And Old England's roast beef.

But in contrast to this, we find that many of our best blood-stirring patriotic songs date from this period: "Hearts of Oak" (David Garrick, 1760), "Tom Bowling" (Charles Dibdin), "The Arethusa" (William Shield), and "The Snug Little Island" (Thomas Dibdin, from *The British Raft*, an anti-Napoleonic opera of 1797).

We must beware of jumping to the conclusion that these were the spontaneous expression of intensely patriotic souls. It cannot be stressed enough that the professional songwriter had arrived, and he wrote to order. It is only just to admit, however, that Dibdin's brother was a sea captain and that he inspired "Tom Bowling"; in fact, a quotation from this was carved upon Dibdin's tombstone. The very number of patriotic songs of this era shows that they must have reflected genuinely held sentiments. Our own age, embittered by the results of excessive patriotism, makes too much of the willingness of eighteenth-century writers to produce sentiments congenial to their noble and merchant patrons. There was, after all, by the standards of the time, a great deal of democracy and liberty, which had been hard won in the civil unrest of the previous century. Whilst we should not forget sentences of a thousand lashes, and other disgraceful aspects of our naval history, we should bear in mind that so extreme a radical as Voltaire found the English system very admirable, and a model of democracy. The exhortations to "freeborn boys" were not therefore without some basis in genuine pride.

On the other hand, the response of the rural population to these was shown by Cecil Sharp's work to be negligible. For the inland population, the sailor was an exotic element in their ballads; he came and went again quickly, and from a structural point of view held the same position as soldiers, outlandish knights and characters with a magical element. In coastal areas, of course, sea shanties were found, in which the sailor was a real character with the problems of the time. The shanties and sea songs reflect the terrible conditions of the naval and merchant ships:

> The winds were foul, the ship was slow,
> *Leave her, Johnny, leave her,*
> The grub was bad, the wages low,
> *It's time for us to leave her.*

Similarly, the popular "Blow the Man Down" is a song of the men of the Black Ball Line. This was notorious for hiring desperate characters and the song reflects the violence which can still be found in dock areas:

> They gave me three months in Liverpool Town,
> *To me way-ay, blow the man down*
> For kicking this policeman and blowing him down
> *Give us some time to blow the man down.*

This type of song really flourished in the first half of the nineteenth century, until the advent of steam, but they contrast strongly with songs of the Dibdin type, which continued to be popular in drawing-rooms and music halls until the end of the century. The appearance of a whole range of stirring shanties in the nineteenth century can easily obscure the fact that the shanty was a kind of Indian summer of the folk song proper. Industrial changes accelerated a process which had, if one interprets the comments about earlier fashions correctly, begun about the time of the Civil War. To some extent, these changes worked by invalidating the content of songs which sprang from a rural society. But strictly musical forces were also at work. Early in the Middle Ages, popular music had become predominantly Ionian in mode (that is, it used the major scale form). Increasingly the modes were standardised and modal songs became regarded as archaic survivals. At the same time, the adoption of the major/minor system permitted the influence of literate musicians to permeate through to a new degree. A common musical language made it easy to accept their compositions, at first alongside the genuine folk material, and later in place of it.

The process of change can be seen in various tunes which were recorded at different stages of their existence. A tune known as "Quodlings Delight", used by Farnaby in the *Fitzwilliam Virginal Book* (No. 144), is next found in *The English Dancing Master* of 1650, under the name "Goddesses". It later became (in the eighteenth century) the well-known "The Oak and the Ash", in which form only the final cadence remains modal.

Ex. 14

(a)

Quodling's Delight (Fitzwilliam Virginal Book Version)

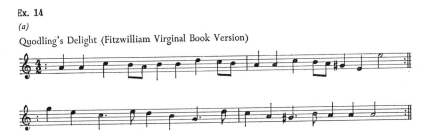

(b)
Goddesses

(c)
The Oak and the Ash

Similarly, the eighteenth-century "British Grenadiers" seems to derive from the tune "Nancie", used in the sixteenth century by Morley (*Fitzwilliam Virginal Book*, No. 12).

Ex. 15
Nancie

Sometimes the change is not only harmonic; for instance, the slow tune "A Virgin Unspotted" became the lively "Admiral Benbow".

The type of change that was taking place in the lyrics has already been discussed, especially with reference to "Bird in a Cage", but a few words are needed about the ballads, which at this point still kept most of their forthrightness, as is shown by this extract from an eulogy of ploughboys by a country lass:

> Oh, I'll take off my greenest gown
> And I'll take off my smock of brown
> On a bed of straw we will lie down
> And there I'll hug my ploughing boy.

Chorus:

> Then it's oh, oh, oh, and it's lovely oh,
> To hear him hup hi and whoa
> And make his furrow straight to go
> What's better than a ploughboy?

It may be that it was this kind of ballad which drove the writer of *Rural Economy in the Midlands* (1796) to complain that

> The fears of prudent employers is directed to the troops of balladsingers who disseminate sentiments of dissipation in minds which should have been bred in principles of industry and sobriety.

It is more likely, however, that it was the agricultural workers who were causing uneasiness by their complaints of this kind:

> On cabbage cold and taters
> They'll feed you like the pigs
> While they sit at their tea and roast
> And ride about in gigs.
> The mistress must get "Ma'am" and you
> Must lift your cap to her
> And before you find an entrance
> The master must get "Sir".

As another contemporary ballad pointed out, eight shillings a week was not much of a wage for a man with a family.

Nevertheless, the decline in the traditional folk song had begun, and such musically talented people of the working class as could find any outlet at all, must have been drawn to the towns, where it was possible to have a life which was easier than that of a labourer and, as in the present day, offered richer rewards. This process naturally tended to impoverish the countryside musically, not only draining it of talent, but also encouraging the idea of music as entertainment rather than communal expression.

Countrymen who became musicians did draw freely, for a while, upon traditional material. William Shield's famous tune, the "Arethusa", was not, in fact, originally by him, but was a country dance-tune known as the "Princess Royal", to which he put the harmonies. Similarly, Carey's original tune for "Sally in our Alley" was replaced, after his death, by the traditional tune, "What though I am a Country Lass".

But the pressures were constantly upon musicians to imitate the fashionable (French and Italian) styles, and to avoid the "uncouthness" of modal tunes. It was the mood of the time to reject these, as it was to regularise Shakespeare. We can see this fashion reflected in the comments of Sir John Hawkins in his *History of Music* (1776), about

> fidlers and others, hired by the master of the house; such as in the night season were wont to parade the city and suburbs under the title of waits. . . . Half a dozen fidlers would scrape "Sellengers Round" or "John Come Kiss Me" or "Old Simon the King" with divisions till themselves and their audience were tired, after which as many players on the hautboy would in the most harsh and discordant tones grate forth "Greensleeves", "Yellow Stockings", "Gillian of Croydon", or some other such common dance tunes and the people thought it fine music.

One can see that the waits were falling into disfavour as archaic survivals of a past and unmourned age, a conclusion which can be confirmed by the satire of the *Tatler* of 9 September 1710:

> By letters from Nottingham, we have advice that the young ladies of that place complain for want of sleep, by reason of certain riotous lovers, who for this last summer have very much infested the streets of that eminent city with Violins and Bass-Viols between the hours of twelve and four in the morning . . . as the custom prevails at present there is scarce a young man of any fashion . . . who does not make love with the town music.

The theme of provincial "rudeness" gives way to another theme of the period, that of lack of moderation in the drier satire of John Cleland (1766).

> But at the ancient yule, of Christmas time, especially, the dreariness of the weather, the length of the night, would naturally require something extraordinary to wake and rouse men from their natural inclination to rest, and from a warm bed at that hour.

William Gardiner noted with mixed surprise and delight that the Leicester waits had a more modern approach:

In the dead of night . . . on one occasion I heard the waits parade the market place, playing the minuet from Haydn's *Quartet in D minor*, and was much thrilled.

These examples come, as does much of my information on this subject, from Professor Bridge's article on town waits (see Bibliography). He also quotes a passage from Burney's *History*, which is very relevant to our purpose:

John Ravenscroft was one of the waits of the Tower Hamlets and, in the band of Goodman's Fields playhouse, was a Ripieno violin, notwithstanding which, he was a performer good enough to lead in any such concerts as those above described and to say the truth was able to do justice to a Concerto of Corelli or an Overture of Handel. He was much sought after to play at balls and dancing parties and was singularly excellent in the playing of Hornpipes in which he had a manner that none could imitate. It seems that this was a kind of music which of all he most affected; so that by dint of a fancy accommodated to these little essays, he was enabled to compose airs of this kind equal to those of the ablest masters; and yet so little was he acquainted with the rules of composition that for suiting them with basses he was indebted to others.

A tune of Ravenscroft's follows:

Ex. 16

Tower Hamlets   John Ravenscroft

The attitudes implicit in this passage are most enlightening. We note that, like Arne, Ravenscroft could be associated with "balls and dancing parties", but that Burney is pleasantly surprised that he was "able to do justice to a Concerto of Corelli". There is a suggestion of surprise also in the statement that "this was a kind of music which of all he most affected". He had a natural facility for composing hornpipes, but he was not "acquainted with the rules of composition". Reference to Ravenscroft's piece will show why Burney should express admiration: it is perfectly "regular", and contains none of the archaic features of some of the ballads of the time; though an instinctive musician, Ravenscroft had assimilated completely the modern style. Burney expresses admiration for this kind of ability elsewhere:

> I remember very well in my musical life and have heard one of the four waits of Shrewsbury vamp a bass on all occasions, being unable to read the one that was written.

We find that another of the distinctions between art music and popular music, one that still exists, was beginning to appear. The increasing emphasis on development away from the suite form used by earlier composers was now excluding the similar virtues of dance music as being too limited. This was, in turn, encouraging a different kind of approach to musicianship. An intellectual element was appearing in composition; one had to obey rules, or even had to learn them in order to compose. In popular music, however, the forms remained simple enough for them to be improvised, and it was quite common for a dance musician to be musically illiterate, but capable of excellent improvisation. The distinction still holds. A glance at any harmony book will show how many pages must be mastered before even a simple hymn tune can be composed, whereas must modern pop groups and their composers have a minimal musical literacy.

Apart from the obvious financial moral this seems to offer, we may (more seriously) wonder whether a music which depends as little on intuitive talent as modern serious music is not in a very dangerous position, particularly when we recall the well-known abilities of Bach, Mozart and Beethoven to improvise. It would appear that, at least, to ignore this aspect leads to a very cerebral music, which is felt by many listeners to have lost the power to communicate. Whether or not such a suggestion is valid, there is little doubt that part of the strength of jazz and popular music is that the music springs spontaneously from the depths of the personality, and as a consequence has only a limited element of conscious organisation.[1] We have seen in this chapter how the change in social organisation, with the emergence of a strong middle class, encouraged what had been, hitherto, a two-stream tradition

[1] This theory has been developed more fully, since the time of writing, by the critic Henry Pleasants in his book *Serious Music—and all that Jazz*.

(aristocratic and peasant) to split again and to produce a distinctive bourgeois tradition, with its own standards. Some of these standards are, in fact,
still to be found (for instance, the love of novelty and of exotic, escapist
material). The next stage was the destruction of the authentic "folk" tradition
by the Industrial Revolution, and its supplanting by a new and still-extant
musical culture.

5 The Age of Victoria (1825–1911)

The modern popular song reminds one of the outer circumference of our terribly overgrown towns. . . . It is for the people who live in those unhealthy regions, people who have the most false ideals, who are always scrambling for subsistence, who think that the commonest rowdyism is the highest expression of human emotion; for them this popular music is made, and it is made, with a commercial object, of snippets of slang.
SIR HUBERT PARRY, 1899

The age of Victoria was paradoxical in that at the same time as the decline of "folk" music, mentioned in the last chapter, was brought to its completion, there burst forth an unparalleled interest in music among all levels of society.

On the one hand, the old music was dead in the towns, and virtually so in the villages; nothing was being composed in the idiom, and its performance was restricted to a diminishing number of old people whose interests were considered unfashionable. Flora Thompson, writing about village life in the '80s in her book *Lark Rise*, tells of Old David, a man of eighty-three, who sang an old ballad of which she says: "It was out of date, even then, and only tolerated on account of his age." Similarly, the traditions of participation of all kinds had declined quite rapidly. Her grandfather had played the violin in the village choir; the only instrument remaining in the whole village of thirty households was a melodeon, on which a boy played by ear. In contrast, Emily Brontë had described the Gimmerton band in the following words, written in 1847:

> Our pleasure was increased by the arrival of the Gimmerton band, mustering fifteen strong: a trumpet, a trombone, clarionets, bassoons, French horns and a bass viol, besides singers. They go the rounds of all the respectable houses and receive contributions every Christmas and we esteemed it a first rate treat to hear them. After the usual carols had been sung, we set them to songs and glees. Mrs Earnshaw loved the music and so they gave us plenty.

Both this and the descriptions of music found in Thomas Hardy's *Far From the Madding Crowd* are, of course, fictional and set in an earlier period, which suggests that we need to make allowances for the idealisation of rural communities; but the basic facts and their illustration of a thriving musical culture in the countryside seem to be reasonably clearly established. The descriptions show that there had been a fairly dramatic change in the situation in the middle of the century.

It is not surprising that there was a similar or even worse position in the towns. All traditional forms seem to have decayed, so that music was increasingly concentrated in the areas outlined in the previous chapter. The waits, for instance, had become a rather moribund ancillary to civic ceremonies, where they continued to exist at all; the London authorities decided to fill no more places after 1854.

Among the working class, activity was, for a time, very limited indeed. The Town Clerk of Burslem recorded:

> In the forties the number of men who could read music here without the help of an instrument was comparatively few, and of women not more than three or four in the district.

This comment was made, as one can see, to illustrate the lack of formal *singing* in the area, but it is nevertheless true to say that town-dwelling owners of instruments among the working class in the first half of the century were few and far between.

One area seems to have been an exception to national trends—the North-East. There the old music and customs were kept alive a little longer. H. M. Neville in his *A Corner in the North* (1909) wrote:

> There are still many who remember the visits to our villages of the travelling dancing master. These were men of the working class, and often of an idle jovial disposition, fond of dancing and good fiddlers. The travelling dancing master would stay in the village for two or three months in the winter, and give his lessons in a hired room, or a loft lent for the purpose. The members of the class and a few friends paid him a small sum. From time to time he gave a more public dance, which he called a "small occasion", and at the close of the season "a grand ball" for his own benefit. This practice was long in vogue, and no doubt it did much to preserve the knowledge of the old Border and Scotch dances. It ceased in the English Border about thirty years ago, but is still maintained in some parts of Scotland.

The miners in the area continued to compose songs of contemporary relevance in the old modal style. The first datable song of this type was "The

Collier's Rant", collected by Joseph Ritson in his *Northumbrian Garland* (1793):

> Oh marra, oh marra, this is wor pay week.
> We'll get penny leaves and drink to our beek.
> And we'll fill up our bumper and roond it shall go.
> Follow the horses Johnny lad oh.
>
> *Chorus:*
> Follow the horses, Johnny me laddie,
> Follow them through, me canny lad, oh,
> Follow the horses, Johnny me laddie,
> Hey lad, lie away, canny lad, oh.

The lightheartedness of this type of song soon gave way to much more intense expressions of the rigours of life in mines that were sunk ever deeper, without adequate safety measures. The "Blantyre Explosion", though collected in the present century, is of this type. It tells of a disaster in 1877 in which 310 men were killed. The traditional phrases and setting of the lover's complaint are sensitively used by the author:

> By Clyde's bonny banks where I sadly did wander
> Among the pit heaps as evening drew nigh,
> I spied a fair maiden all dressed in deep mourning
> A-weeping and wailing with many a sigh.

We guess that the maiden's lover, Johnny Murphy, has left her, but the writer shows instinctive artistry in choosing a situation in which our normal expectations will be confounded; their hopes bring out the senseless tragedy of the disaster:

> The wedding was fixed, all the guests were invited
> That calm summer evening when Johnny was slain.

Confronted with these songs, I always find literary analysis to be something of an impertinence, and such terms as "artistic" to imply artifice in its worst sense. The songs are not complex in form or diction, and yet they convey a spontaneity which is often lacking in songs made for entertainment, because they are the expressions of people needing to express real and often tragic situations. In particular, their approach to the violence with which the miner's everyday existence was and is surrounded, whilst being deeply emotional, always has a deep dignity which, as we shall see later, is lacking in much urban song on the same topics. Our response to "That is Love", for instance (see p. 99), is one of repulsion at a sordid interest in the gruesome. We can only respect the grief of the "Blantyre Explosion"; our only way of examining these songs should be to listen to them.

Not all aspects of the miner's life were mournful, as the following lyric shows. This lyric is also of interest in being a rather startling survival of an old form. It is a discussion of the relative merits of the old-style pit cage and the new safety cage, but its manner is that of a Dunbar "flyting" of the fifteenth century. Compare the miners,

> Wor aud cage to the patent says "Aa'll warrant thoo, thinks thoo's clever,
> Because they've polished thoo wi paint—but thoo'll not last for ever

with Dunbar's:

> Renunce, rebald, thy rymyng, thow bot royis,
> Thy trechour tung hes tane an heland strynd;
> Ane lawland ers wald mak a bettir noyis.

(Renounce, rebel, your rhyming, you merely rave; your treacherous tongue has taken on a highland manner: a lowland arse would make a better noise.)

The cages fight, and the poem ends:

> the patent won the battle
> It took the brakeman half a shift to clag them up wi' plasters
> Wor aud cage sent his notice in, just to vex the masters.

This song is a little exceptional, in that the miner's humour was more in evidence when dealing with his personal life. The collections of C. E. Catchside-Warrington include this good-humoured dig at a familiar situation:

> Of all the plagues a poor man meets
> Along life's weary way
> Thor's nyen among them all that beats
> A rainy washin' day.
> An' let that day come when it may
> It always is ma care
> Before Aa break ma fast to pray
> It may be fine and fair.

Chorus:

> For it's thump thump souse souse
> Scrub scrub away
> Thor's nowt but glumpin' i' the hoose
> Upon a washin' day.

It is perhaps significant that the creators of such a vital tradition moved with the times, and created their own music halls. These seem to have been lively places with a boisterous humour, springing from, rather than produced for the popular taste. The most famous music-hall character in this area, for instance, was George Ridley, who turned to entertainment after a pit accident. One of his great hits was "Cushie Butterfield" (tune: "Pretty Polly Perkins"), a full-blooded character of the Clementine type:

> Aa's a broken-hairted keelman, and aa's ower heid in love
> Wiv a young lass in Gyetside an' aa caal her me dove.
> Hor nyem's Cushie Butterfield, an' she sells yaller clay,
> An' hor cousin is a muckman, an' they caal him Tom Grey.
> *Chorus:*
> She's a big lass an' a bonny lass,
> An' she likes hor beor,
> An' they caal hor Cushie Butterfield,
> An' aa wish she wes heor.

The singer is far from the traditional lover who "sees Helen's beauty in a brow of Egypt":

> Ye'll oft see hor doon at Sangit when the fresh harrin comes in.
> She's like a bagful o' sawdust, tied roond wiv a string.
> She wears big galoshes tee, an' hor stockins once was white,
> An' hor bedgoit's laelock, an' hor hat's niver strite.

Ridley was also the author of that "national anthem" of the Geordie, "Blaydon Races" (1864).

The people who enjoyed the village dances and the music hall were sceptical, as they still are, of "art". This may be illustrated by the following, written on the occasion of a tour of the North-East by the virtuoso violinist Paganini:

> The curtain flew up and a lady did squall,
> To fine music played by a Cockney bit manny.
> Then frae the front seats aw seun heard my friends bawl:
> "Hats off, smash your brains, here comes greet Baggy Nanny."
> An ootlandish chap seun appeared on the stage,
> And cut as odd capers as wor maister's flunkey.
> He skipped and he fiddled as if in a rage—
> If he had but a tail he'd a passed for a monkey.
> Deil smash a gud teun could this bowdykite play—

The Enraged Musician. Engraving by Hogarth
"The almost inevitable result of a gulf between audience and musician . . .
is a tendency to a lack of discrimination"

THE BEGGARS OPERA

*Brittons attend — view this harmonious Stage
And listen to those notes which charm the age
Thus shall your tastes in Sounds & Sense be shôn'n
And Beggars Opras ever be your own*

Sold at ý Print Shop in ý Strand nett Catherine St.

The Beggars Opera. Engraving by Hogar

His fiddle wad hardly e'en please my auld granny—
So aw seun joined my marrows and toddled away,
And wished a good neet to the greet Baggy Nanny.

The other industrial areas seem to have had a much less vital popular
culture: new songs were largely restricted to social topics. A. L. Lloyd
quotes one which demonstrates the immense hostility which the introduction
of new machinery aroused:

Come all ye croppers stout and bold
Let your faith grow stronger still,
For the cropper lads in the County of York
Have broke the shears at Foster's mill.

The wind it blew, the sparks they flew,
Which alarmed the town full soon,
And out of bed poor people did creep
And run by the light of the moon.

Around and around we all will stand,
And sternly swear we will,
We'll break the shears and the windows too,
And set fire to the tazzling mill.

Such violence was not surprising in view of the conditions reflected in the
"Four Loom Weavers":

We held on for six weeks, thought each day were the last,
We've tarried and shifted till now we're quite fast,
We lived upo' nettles, while nettles were good,
And Waterloo porridge were 't best of us food.

Agricultural workers had their complaints too; "The Honest Ploughman"
remembers better days:

The farmers' wives in every way themselves the cows did milk
They did not wear the dandy veils and gowns made out of silk.
They didn't ride blood horses, like the farmers' wives do now,
Their daughters went a milking and the sons went to the plough.

If the figures we have are accurate, it was the urban ballad, however,
which was the most popular: sales could easily be in the thousands, and the
ballad of Rush's murder in 1849 sold two and a half million copies. But despite such sales it declined as rapidly as the rest of the traditional culture,

though for different reasons. By 1861, it was possible for a writer in the *National Review* to comment:

> For several years the fact that the street ballad singer is disappearing from amongst us has been forcing itself more and more on the unwilling minds of ourselves and the few others who, from some strange and perverse idiosyncrasy, take an interest in this ancient if no longer honourable profession.

His sentiments are echoed by John Ashton in *Modern Street Ballads*, of 1888:

> A new generation has arisen who will not stop in the streets to listen to these ballads being sung, but prefer to have their music served up to them "piping hot", with the accompaniment, of warmth, light, and beer and tobacco (for which they duly have to pay) at the Music Hall; but whether the change be for the better or not may be a moot question.

One of the fascinations of history is the way in which it illustrates how many attitudes thought to be modern are in fact recurrent. One of these is nostalgia for a past age because of dissatisfaction with the present. The added irony, that the "decadence" of one era becomes falsely remembered as "the good old days" in the next, is seen clearly in Christopher Pulling's words:

> The Victorian music-hall catered for the ordinary man in the street, and he liked his art to be like his life, full-blooded and rich. He had not had his ideas corrupted by Hollywood.

More interesting still is the statement which Pulling makes about the pierrot shows, produced by one of the original pierrots, Charles Heslop: "The saddest thing, in my mind, is the deterioration of audiences. We got really rather highbrow in lots of our stuff before 1914." As the poet puts it, "The times are eternally changing and we with the times." Clearly, when dealing with the twentieth century, we shall need to tread carefully, since there is perhaps no sphere of activity which is more prone to this kind of excess, founded on affectionate admiration, than the one which we are considering: it is an area of art with immense (one might say disproportionate) power, but, for the most part, of so ephemeral a nature, that our judgements can become wildly ludicrous in a lesser space of time than it takes for many a great work to become understood.

The urban ballad was, in the first half of the nineteenth century, a very lucrative business, and nowhere more so than in the hands of the most famous of ballad publishers, James Catnach. He came to London in 1813 and set up his press at Seven Dials, which finally had some 14,000 ballads at its disposal. Five of the writers he employed are known, but most were anonymous. They were paid one shilling for a ballad, often written at great speed, and headed with a crude woodcut, which was frequently of little or no relevance to the subject, and was nearly always of great antiquity.

The form seems to have disappeared for several reasons: an advance in education accompanied by the arrival of cheap newspapers (thus making the topical ballad largely redundant); the music hall, which took over comic and amatory topics; the introduction of penny song-books, which clearly gave one more for one's money; and the opposition of the recently formed police.

The latter days of the ballad saw a change in tone, in the form of greater sensationalism. One very popular form this took was "verses written by the wretched culprit on the night previous to his execution" of which the one given below is typical, though of a more polished and acceptable form than many:

JAMES MACDONALD

You young and old that are so bold, I hope you will draw near,
For it's one of the cruellest murders that ever you did hear.
It's all of a fair servant girl, her age was scarce sixteen,
And the humbling of her pride was my delight, when something
    came between.

This girl she was a servant girl and I was a farmer's man,
All in the county of Oxford we went walking on the green.
And when she told what ailed her, I gave her this reply:
O Annie we will go no further, for here you have to die.

O James think of your baby dear, and do not give me fright,
Don't think of double murder on this dark and grisly night.
I pray to God all on my bended knee, that if you'll spare my Life
I'll promise never more to trouble you or ask to be your wife.

But what she said was all in vain, I swore I'd hear no more,
And I cut her throat with my clasp knife and left her in her gore.
And when that I seen her body a-lying on the ground,
I turned and quickly ran from there, where I should not be found.

'Twas on a Monday morning all by the break of day,
By chance there was a farm girl come passing by this way,

She seen this girl a-lying all hidden in the fern,
And when she seen the shape she was, her heart with grief was torn.

She cried aloud for help to come and soon the news was round,
And they searched the country high and low the murderer to find.
Then quickly they at once surrounded me, I told to them my name,
And they spit on me and took me prisoner, and locked me up in gaol.

And here I lie with troubled mind until my final day,
And when that they have found me guilty, the judge to me did say,
It's all for your cruel murder, your death you know must pay,
So James Macdonald I will hang you all from the gallows tree.

The somewhat oblique way in which the girl's pregnancy is mentioned is typical of this period. The sexual forthrightness found in earlier centuries had become unacceptable outside the barrack room and similar places (a position which is still largely so). The compiler of *Curiosities of Street Literature* (1871) noted that:

> the moral tone of the ballads if not lofty, is certainly not bad, and the number of single stanzas that could not be quoted in these pages on account of their gross or indecent language is very small.

The decline in "folk" creation was paralleled by a rising demand, particularly among the middle classes, for ready-made music of all kinds; the theatrical, the concert performance, the religious, and especially the domestic.

In the drawing-room the instruments mentioned in the last chapter continued to enjoy great popularity. A catalogue issued by Charles Sheard, in 1895, lists favourites such as "After the Ball" and "Ta-ra-ra-boom-de-ay", set for violin, mandolin, flute, clarinet, cornet, and violoncello. The flute was considered to be an especially suitable intrument for gentlemen in the middle of the century.

It will be noticed that the harp, despite its earlier popularity, particularly in the early years of the Queen's reign, was omitted from the list. This was because it fell out of favour very rapidly in the latter half of the century, a fact deplored by Stainer and Barrett in their *Dictionary of Musical Terms* (1876). They added the rather unkind explanation that "as the fair performers grew old, the charms of the harp decayed, and although the instrument is still played and taught, it is not cultivated to the extent that its merits might seem to warrant".

A more likely explanation is that, since its main function was as an accompanying instrument, it gave way to the piano, which is both more versatile, and, I believe, more easily learned. The increasing chromaticism of Victorian music made it technically more difficult to manage on the harp, which can only produce the chromatic notes by altering the original (diatonic) ones with pedals. To the pianist, however, accidentals present minimal technical problems. Moreover, the harp is notoriously difficult to tune, whilst it could be put out of tune very easily by the sort of heat one gets in a drawing-room. The fact that it was also a satisfactory piece of furniture must also have been a reason why the piano, and especially the square piano, which had been a luxury instrument at the beginning of the century, rapidly gained favour. Such a firm as D'Almaine of London produced a *Catalogue of Reduced Prices*, and offered instruments from the price of thirty guineas upwards. This indicates the possible market when we consider the general level of wages—a half-sovereign for an agricultural worker, and a little more for the man in the factory. We can see how the piano became a status symbol; when one could afford one, one had risen in the world.

The market for public performances also grew, thus permitting the production of more massive works, particularly choral ones. The symphony orchestra grew in size and resonance, and choirs also increased in size to perform a repertoire in which the firmest favourites were Mendelssohn's *Elijah* and most popular of all, Handel's *Messiah*.

Not all were concerned only with their own cultural life, however. Many of the better-off members of society felt a great sympathy for the less fortunate, and a desire to take positive action to help them. For this reason, in 1849, the vicar of Cheadle, Cheshire, tried to improve the standard of Church music in his area by combining various choirs and giving them rehearsals and instruction. Sometimes a benevolent employer, such as J. & G. Meakin of Hanley, would try to encourage music by purchasing instruments to form a military band among their employees.

Others sought to help by making music, rather than by helping others to do so, and thus in 1878 the People's Concert Society was formed to give musical performances to the inhabitants of the poorer quarters of London, while in the provinces Mr Meakin gave £200 to Hanley Corporation to provide high-class concerts for working men. The desire of people for this experience can be shown by the fact that the average attendance at these concerts was 3,000 people.

Perhaps the most important move to help the nation's musical life was in 1841, when a conference of Nonconformist teachers appointed John Curwen to look into these problems and especially into the lack of musical knowledge and education among working men.

Curwen saw that the difficulty, as far as the performance of the works of the great composers was concerned, lay to a great extent in the fact that the average workman could not read music, and did not have the time to obtain the skill. He therefore sought an easy way of reading music, and found it in a method being used by a Miss Sarah Ann Glover of Norwich to teach singing to children.

In Curwen's hands this became the system known as Tonic Solfa, a method by which one learns to sing a scale and to give the notes the familiar names of doh, ray, me, etc. One then learns to sing from music written in this form and not from the ordinary musical staff. This is more complex to explain on paper than to learn, and the method caught on. In 1853 the Tonic Solfa Association was formed, and Curwen himself founded a publishing house, which ran a magazine *The Musical Herald* and helped to support a Solfa College in London to train teachers; this was very popular, from 1870 onwards, among teachers from the new Elementary Schools.

The work done by these bodies was spread all over the country, but typical was the Potteries, where a local manufacturer George Howson, and the Town Clerk of Burslem, mentioned above, spread the new teaching. Powell made a transcription of *Elijah* among other works, and both men organised classes, choirs, and competitions; a new element in popular musical culture.

Typical of the type of man they taught was James Whewall, of Red Street, Staffordshire, a man who organised and ran a choir so successful that it not only won local competitions, but even the Welsh National Eisteddfod, and that three times running.

It was no exaggeration when Powell remarked, thirty years after the introduction of the Solfa method to his area, that, in contrast to the earlier state of affairs, "the power to sing at sight had become so common as to excite no remark". It is also for this reason that, though literature is often prone to glamourise, that Arnold Bennett was describing a true state of affairs, when he described a male voice quartet in *Clayhanger*:

> They sang at dances, free-and-easies, concerts and Martinmas tea-meetings. They sang for the glory, and when there was no demand for their services, they sang to themselves for the sake of singing.

Bennett goes on to observe "the free, natural mien of the singers, proudly aware that they were producing something beautiful, that could not be produced more beautifully".

The love of craftsmanship found among working men enabled them to improve their skill to a point where leading composers could be commissioned to write special show pieces, to allow a choir to display its ability: this was especially true of the Huddersfield and Leeds choirs. It helped men who were in danger of a total degeneration under frightful industrial conditions to regain their self-respect.

Literally thousands of people were attracted to these choirs, as is shown by the one-thousand-man entry from the Potteries for the Tonic Solfa Jubilee Festival of 1891, the fifteen-thousand attendance at the funeral, in 1905, of James Garner, probably the Potteries' most noted and popular choir leader, and, most important for future generations, the three-thousand attendances at concerts, which meant that in 1888 Hanley Town Council built a concert hall to hold them. Thus, two centuries after the first efforts of Bannister and Britton, performances of good music came within the reach of all, and good music was performed by all sections of society. On the other hand, though the people could draw aesthetically on the concert hall, this did not immediately result in a kind of musical Utopia, as the separate streams of music continued to exist, though perhaps more closely linked than ever before, or after.

It is now necessary to look more closely at the nature of the music which was being so widely disseminated.

Perhaps highest in the artistic scale of values, and certainly the most popular, was the choral music of the latter half of the century. This took either the form of grand-scale *Messiah*-type pieces, or, more often, short lyrical pieces. Fairly representative is the following programme of 1889:

Madrigal	"Matona, Lovely Maiden"	Orlando di Lasso
Anthem	"Judge me, O God"	Mendelssohn
Anthem	"Come Unto Him"	Gounod
Glee	"Hushed in Death"	Hiles
Partsong	"A Slumber Song"	Lohr
Soprano Song and Chorus	"Now Tramp o'er Moss and Fell"	Bishop
	"God Save the Queen"	arr. Henry Leslie

The general characteristics of the taste of the time are quite clearly indicated in this; the comparative lack of solo singers and preference for combined work, the prevailing slightly sombre mood, despite a livelier beginning and end, and a strong leaven of religious music. More striking are the facts that only one of the composers was not of the nineteenth century, and that composers now long forgotten were highly esteemed. It is hard to imagine the performance of so much contemporary music in the present day, especially by amateurs.

On the other hand, despite these healthy tendencies, it should be noted that though the performers were all quite distinctly of the working class, the music was entirely in the "Classical" tradition. According to one's taste, one can see this as a lamentable loss of their own traditions, or as a point at which, paradoxically, in view of the prevailing social conditions, the more artistic side of the music had become so freely and genuinely available to all classes, that it was indeed a universal language, and that (more or less) good music was truly and widely respected.

In contrast to this, the division between the serious opera and the lighter forms of musical drama continued to grow wider, perhaps partly because of the tastes of the Queen, who was a frequent visitor to such productions. For Victorian tastes, the plot had to be cut down, so as to make more possible the "plugging" of attractive songs, whose real destination was the drawing-room. This attitude and its effect on the serious opera can well be seen in the following extract from a review of Meyerbeer's *The Huguenots* in *The World of Fashion* for November 1836: "As an opera it may possess some merit on the stage, but in the drawing room it is dull and profitless and has by no means our recommendation."

A major figure in this sphere was Alfred Bunn, manager of the Drury Lane Theatre. He had many successes, but perhaps the most noted was *The Bohemian Girl*, which he produced in 1843. In it, appeared a song which remained a great favourite of drawing-room amateurs throughout the century:

> I dreamt that I dwelt in marble halls,
> With vassals and serfs at my side;
> And of all who assembled within those walls,
> That I was the hope and pride.
> I had riches too great to count, could boast
> Of a high ancestral name;
> But I also dreamt, which pleased me most,
> That you loved me still the same.

To the modern reader, the final line comes as a rather absurd anticlimax; the sentiments are too unreal, and the aspirations set out earlier are felt to be rather naïve, if not actually undesirable. But we should bear in mind the historical situation, in which such sentiments were acceptable over the whole artistic spectrum; there is only a difference of degree between this kind of song and those of Schumann; and Balfe, the composer, also wrote the music for "Come into the Garden, Maud", which was by no less a poet than Tennyson. This illustrates yet again what has become a commonplace of this book, the notion that in our age serious and popular artists live in separate worlds, because their ideals, and the means by which they express these, have become almost totally divorced—imagine W. H. Auden writing the lyrics to *Oklahoma*.

In the '50s and '60s the operettas of Offenbach thrived and in the following decades Gilbert and Sullivan swept the stage. The real period of success came after the building of the Savoy Theatre in 1881, the reasons being that the music was light and singable and also that it parodied other forms, especially the Italian opera.

The widening division between the serious music lover and those who sought only the lighter forms, with a clear-cut, memorable melody, but perhaps little else, can also be shown by Flora Thompson's description of a travelling German band:

> Most of the music they played was above the heads of the hamlet folk, who said they liked something with a bit more "chune" in it; but when, at the end of the performance, they gave "God Save the Queen", the standers-by joined with gusto in singing it.

It is noticeable that such bands as this, along with the man with the barrel organ, and the street singer were by now the only survivors of the old wandering minstrel tradition. This was so because the lower classes had turned their interest to the music hall, in which we see the real beginnings of the modern popular pattern.

Music had been performed in taverns and similar places since time immemorial, but had usually been informal and spontaneous, in the way that it still is. At the turn of the nineteenth century, however, a move towards a more formalised entertainment began to take place.

Public music of not too exacting a variety, which could be accompanied by eating and drinking, had been available for a long time in the public gardens. Marylebone was the first of these, having been established in the seventeenth century; it was mentioned by Pepys in 1688. Vauxhall Gardens had opened in 1732, and was perhaps the most famous; Ranelagh followed in 1742. As was mentioned earlier, the activities of these places included music, refreshments, and balloon ascents; most important they were excellent meeting places for lovers—we could do with such places today. The last garden of any size to be opened was the Cremorne Gardens in Chelsea (1831), which was some twelve acreas in area. Admission was one shilling before 10 p.m. and two shillings thereafter. But the popularity of these places began to wane, partly because of the obvious problems of weather, but also because they began to attract a rowdy element. Consequently, they began to close down in mid-century, and were all gone by the 1880s. When the Cremorne closed in 1877, the *Standard* commented that "The open air dissipation of Cremorne Gardens has been replaced by the indoor dissipation of the music hall."

One way in which the irresistibly rising demand for entertainment was satisfied was by Song and Supper Rooms, which first appeared in the 1820s. Most famous of these were the Cyder Cellars, the Coal Hole, and Evans' (opened in the '40s) which was frequented by Thackeray,

> Going to the play then and to the pit was the fashion in those merry days, with some young fellows of my own age. Having listened delighted to the most cheerful and brilliant of operas, and laughed enthusiastically at the farce, we became naturally hungry at 12 o'clock at night, and a desire for welsh-rabbits and good old glee singing led us to the Cave of Harmony, then kept by the celebrated Hoskins, among whose friends we were proud to count.
>
> We enjoyed such intimacy with Mr. Hoskins that he never failed to greet us with a kind nod; and John the waiter made room for us near the President of the convivial meeting. We knew the three admirable glee-singers, and many a time they partook of brandy-and-water at our expense. One of us gave his call dinner at Hoskins's and a very fine time we had of it. Where are you, O Hoskins, bird of the night? Do you warble your songs by Acheron or troll your choruses by the banks of black Avernus?

Though the material of the entertainments was popular, the clientele were definitely of an upper-class "bohemian" set. The clubs were very much all male; ladies were not admitted to Evans' until the '70s, though the other places had opened their doors to them a few years previously. The moral tone thus had that ambivalence which we customarily associate with the Victorians. Consequently, when a friend of Thackeray's noted the arrival of an elderly colonel, in the company of a sixteen-year-old boy, "writing on his card to Hoskins, [he] hinted to him that a boy was in the rooms, and a gentleman who was quite a greenhorn; hence that the songs had better be carefully selected". Obviously the nightingale of Avernus, despite his many virtues, needed guidance on how to behave in the most polite company.

The authorities were unhappy about the existence of these clubs, and in 1872 fixed 12.30 a.m. as the closing time for all public entertainments. This rapidly brought about the closure of the Song and Supper Rooms.

The music hall proper grew out of the drinking habits of a lower level of society. Many taverns found musical entertainment so popular, among both sexes, that they found it worthwhile to put on special performances in back rooms, with an entrance fee of sixpence or a shilling. The popularity of these was such that in some cases they became the main attraction of the house. The rooms were often enlarged, and new ones were constructed with entertainment in mind. The first of these was the Regency in Fitzroy Square (1815) which in 1865 became the Prince of Wales Theatre. The numbers of such halls rose rapidly in the '30s and '40s, but the real heyday of the music hall was heralded by the Theatre Act of 1843, which deprived Drury Lane and Covent Garden of their monopolistic right to put on stage plays; public houses and saloon theatres had only escaped the law by an emphasis on music. The new act also removed trivial restrictions, and decreed that such houses could be recognised either as theatres or as "palaces of varieties", with the right to present shows after 5 p.m. and to sell refreshments. After 1866, they were also allowed to put on matinées.

Thus it was that in 1848 Charles Morton, owner of the Canterbury Arms tavern in Lambeth Marshes, built a hall at the back of his property. After alterations, it was reopened in 1851 to seat 1,500 people; the audiences were mixed. Accompaniments were played on the piano or the harmonium, and the artistes were paid out of the bar profits. Though by this time only one of about twenty London theatres, the Canterbury is generally felt to have been the first of the great music halls.

This type of entertainment was popular because it was sufficiently different from ordinary life to attract those who had a little money to spend, yet was without the frills and inhibitions of the "refined" theatre; one could buy beer, smoke, eye pretty girls and sing with gusto. It was also the first social centre, other than the tavern, for the new city culture, which had lost the rural means of social intercourse, but had not yet developed the football match, the dance hall and Brighton beach. These came into being later in the century in response to a pressing social need.

Most important, from our point of view, is that the music hall drew upon the talent of the common people, partly because it was the only *working-class* means of creative expression, but mostly for financial reasons. The aristocratic-bourgeois culture was, as we saw above, available to all, but not all working men felt able to express themselves through this medium. Some

felt a kind of independence which manifested itself as an uneasiness with the
"serious" works; they were like a set of ill-fitting clothes. Furthermore, they
found, as the Negro did in the USA half a century later, that one of the few
ways for a man to win some sort of respect, to break out of a state of permanent
poverty and to rise above his "station" was to entertain, since here one relied
on gifts of personality which few other people had. Light entertainment had
always been able to make a man popular and to feed him, but at this period
it became what it has since remained: a business offering rewards normally
only obtainable by inheritance, with capital, or after years of work. These
were now to be gained almost overnight by those who had the right kind of
talent.

George Leybourne, a mechanic from the Midlands, was typical of the new
pattern of entertainer, only possible in an industrial society, with its mass
audiences, which made possible very high fees, while each individual paid
very little. Leybourne's greatest fame came at the Canterbury Arms, Lambeth Marshes; his "act" was built around the song "Champagne Charlie is
my Name". Romantic conceptions about the vitality of a self-confident pro-
letariat need to be tempered just a little with the realisation that this song
was written as part of a publicity campaign by the champagne shippers, who
subsidised the bar to the sum of £20 per week in order to popularise the
drink. Nevertheless, Leybourne's salary rose from one guinea a week to
twenty-five, and at the height of his career he was earning £120 a week, a
sum which, allowing for the changes in the value of money since that time,
still compares well with the rewards which most present-day "pop" stars get.

Much has been written about the music-hall artist, usually complimentary,
and sometimes verging on idolisation. In particular, attention has been
drawn to their boisterousness, their forthrightness, their theatrical capabilities, and the spirit of their audiences.

Certainly, the life of a star involved then, as it does now, a great deal of
gruelling hard work for the few moments of glory. In 1878, the Great
MacDermott had a timetable as follows, at one point:

4.15	8.15	Royal Aquarium
	9.10	Metropolitan
	10.00	London Pavilion
	10.50	Collins

Charles Heslop, though talking about pierrot shows, gives an insight into the
requirements which must have applied by and large to any variety artist:

"You had to learn to hold an audience on your own for at least eight minutes, to extemporise and to work on a small stage."

Such facts oblige us to pay the music-hall artists the respect which one gives to any professional for mastery of his craft. But at the risk of being the next in the chain of over-adulatory critics whose judgement will appear particularly wild to the following generation, I would like to offer a few counter-arguments to the claims of music-hall devotees.

On crowds, for instance, we have the words of Thomas Burke: "In the past people were individuals who liked, now and then, to gather at a music hall and be one of a great mass." He remembers "the spectacle of a crowd when it came out", humming choruses and with bright eyes, whereas people at the cinema, "come out as if there were nothing in life worth living for". We are all cinema-goers, and so may put such ideas to the test for ourselves.

Equally unconvincing to me is the comment of Christopher Pulling that "In the strict Victorian age it delighted the lads by its licentious innuendo or effrontery", and the similar comment of Reginald Nettel on the following lyric:

> A smart and stylish girl you see,
> Belle of good society;
> Not too strict but rather free,
> Yet as right as right can be.
> Never forward, never bold—
> Not too hot and not too cold,
> And the very thing I'm told,
> That in your arms you'd like to hold.

> Ta-ra-ra Boom-de-ay-

"This is the spirit of the music halls—the uplifting of man as he is and not into something he ought to be."

But I suggest that Mr Pulling's comment on Marie Lloyd, that she "knew the great English public will open its arms to vice, provided it is presented as a frolic", is a double-edged remark, and perhaps pinpoints that which I find difficult to accept about this type of song. And since we seem to be among a spate of categorical statements, let me call for three cheers for the good old ballads, and hurrah for:

> The Fair Maid of the West
> Who sold her maidenhead for a Highcrown'd Hat.

We certainly cannot leave the music hall without mentioning briefly the other types of entertainment which it engendered among the classes which found it not suitable for respectable entertainment. The success of the Savoy Operas is well known, but that of Mr and Mrs German Reed is less so. Between 1855 and 1895 they held Illustrative Gatherings which were entertainments in the tradition of the one-man shows of Charles Dibdin and John Orlando Parry, though of a more innocuous type, "to provide dramatic amusement for that class of society which was reluctant to visit theatres". Typical of their repertoire was *A Casket of Comic Songs* which set out to be "a source of instructive and innocent recreation" to the family. The most licentious piece in this work was Grimaldi's "Hot Codlins". The German Reeds were imitated by others, whose glory has faded, unmourned by art.

The increasing vogue for family holidays by the sea also produced a more innocent offshoot of the palace of varieties—the pierrot show. The first of these was Clifford Essex's Pierrot Banjo Team which appeared in July 1891 at Henley Regatta. Seaside engagements were forthcoming, and shows were produced three times a day, under the title of *The Follies*, weather and tide permitting. Versatility was vital as companies were small. But this was an excellent training for the young professional, and the challenge of the conditions is said to have brought out "a freshness of style, a natural spirit of humour and an ingenuous enjoyment of their own entertainment which suggests the amateur rather than the professional". To some extent, sheer financial necessity forced the artists to give of their best, as wages came from a collection, and the sale of penny song-books.

In the countryside, too, the beginnings of the twentieth-century pattern were to be seen. In Flora Thompson's *Waggon and Horses* "men and boys still sang the old country ballads and songs, as well as the latest music-hall successes", but this was only because of a lack of contact with the towns, since, with the exception of the railway and the telegraph (neither of which was available in *Lark Rise*) communication was as it had always been, by horse and on foot. For this reason, the spread of music was achieved more by chance than by intent. Quite typical was Alf, the only owner of an instrument in *Lark Rise*, of whom we hear that "if the baker or any other caller hummed the tune of a new popular song in his hearing, Alf would be playing it that night on his melodeon". The inadequacy of this, and the consequent postponement of the final decay of the rural tradition until communications improved, is shown by the way that the young men interpreted the new songs: "The most popular of these would have arrived complete with tune from the outer world; others, culled from the penny song-book they most of them carried, would have to have a tune fitted to them by the singer."

Nevertheless, the old country songs were doomed, and it is fortunate indeed that such men as Cecil Sharp and Ralph Vaughan Williams set to work as soon as they did, or we should have little or no record of the popular music of earlier times. The disappearance of the country songs was so quick that a matter of fifty years was sufficient to bring it about, in all except a few very remote areas. Even in so removed a place as the Isle of Man this was happening, according to Dr Clague, who managed to save much of the traditional Manx music. As elsewhere, the decline was due to a fall of population, owing to movement to the cities of the mainland. The emigrants then brought a new cultural force to bear on those left at home. Again, the whole process, though perhaps deplorable to the historian and to the artist, can only really be regarded as inevitable.

Music would here seem to be analogous to language in that those elements which are no longer relevant to life as it is actually being lived, become meaningless and archaic to the majority of people, and fall out of use. At the same time new elements are brought in, and are widely accepted, despite the efforts of purists to prevent this and to "maintain standards", provided that such new elements meet a need to express a concept for which there has been no suitable word, structure or pattern up to that point. This in turn suggests that assertions of artistic deficiencies, such as will be made in the second part of this book, have a very limited validity, and may perhaps be no more than a condemnation of the points at which two aesthetic approaches, one's own and the one under consideration, diverge. It may further be possible that any art of a popular rather than "cultural" type can only mirror the society from which it springs, and that any criticisms should therefore be levelled not at the artist but at the society in which he lives.

Having looked at the background in which nineteenth-century popular music was created, we must now turn to an examination of the music itself.

Perhaps the predominant impression of the age is a sentimental one. The desire to have the heartstrings sounded strongly and often, which emerged in the eighteenth century, developed even further. Lyrics became, by and large, more elevated, more remote from everyday life, and melody writers found the chromatically-based tensions of serious music ideal, in diluted form, for whipping up emotions cheaply. In all forms of popular music there was a continued move away from the "purer" more abstract type of sound towards the production of emotion by the use of music of a more fixed connotation. There was to be no doubt about what the music was about or what one was to feel. The desire to dramatise the external and to represent it by "realistic" and onomatopoeic effects, which developed in the eighteenth century, and became the programme music of Beethoven's *Pastoral Symphony* and similar works was exaggerated in later years into an attempt to portray even more exactly in music, essentially visual or verbal ideas, a tendency which was very much suited to popular taste.

The difference between the popular and the serious in this vein was only in the degree of the exaggeration, and the technical subtlety of the means of portrayal. Whereas Liszt or Schumann still wrote works of fairly general implication, and therefore left scope for individual interpretation of the composer's vision (an essential in so abstract an art as music), the popular composer became quite specific in the stimulus he used and in the emotion he was trying to arouse. Typical was a *Piano Fantasia on the Relief of Lucknow*, which incorporated a "Hindu Chant" and "The Campbells are Coming". Similarly, a concert at the Agricultural Hall, Islington, in 1868, to celebrate the Abyssinian Expedition, featured the Band of the St George's Rifles and the pipes and drums of the Guards, and portrayed "the formation of the Avenging Army", a "hurrah for the Dangers of Africa", "the revels of savages in wild fastnesses", "the war hymn of the Belochees" (for bassoons, ophicleide and euphonium), "elephants dragging cannon", a "march through glooming defiles", a "cornet solo of 'Home, Sweet Home', by the expectant prisoners", their "dreams of deliverance", "the grand assault", and "See the Conquering Hero Comes". So much do tastes change in a century.

The Victorian love of sentiment is most clearly seen in lyrics, however, and in these we see that the love of tears, found in eighteenth-century audiences, had become even more pronounced:

> In the gloaming, oh my darling,
> When the lights are dim and low,
> And the quiet shadows falling
> Softly come and softly go;
> When the winds are sobbing faintly
> With a gentle unknown woe,
> Will you think of me and love me
> As you did once long ago?

For us, the excesses of such mournful ditties frequently result in an unintentional humour:

> I left my love in England,
> In poverty and pain,
> The tears hung heavy in my eyes,
> But hers came down like rain.

Sometimes we find a song, such as the one below, that appears to show a concern for others rather than an indulgent self-pity, but it may be argued that here the writer is guilty of tastelessness in that he is shedding painless tears for his own entertainment over a position in which he has no likelihood of finding himself:

> Underneath the gaslight's glitter,
> Stands a little fragile girl,
> Heedless of the night winds bitter,
> As they round about her whirl,
> While the hundreds pass unheeding,
> In the evening's waning hours,
> Still she cries with tearful pleading,
> "Won't you buy my pretty flowers?"

The tendency to revel in melodramatic situations was also applied to domestic life, the apparent realism of which masks at first glance the excessive sentiment on which the song is based:

> See a father, standing at his cottage door,
> Watching a baby in the gutter rolling o'er
> Laughing at his merry pranks—but, hark, a roar.
> Help, oh help him, gracious heav'n above.
> Dashing down the road there comes a madden'd horse;
> Out the father rushes with resistless force:
> Saves the child—but there he lies a mangled corse.
> That is love, that is love.

An unsatisfactory love relationship was clearly suitable for such an approach:

> Why did he forsake me
> Him I loved so well.
> Hark the bell is tolling
> Bidding earth farewell.
> Frantically, her hands high
> In the air she throws:
> A sigh, a leap, a scream, 'tis done,
> As o'er the bridge she goes.

In such lyrics there is an element of the grotesque, in unadulterated form, reached in the last verse of Henry Russell's song "The Maniac":

> For lo you, while I speak, mark how yon demon's eyeballs glare!
> He sees me now; with dreadful shriek he whirls, he whirls me in
> the air!

Horror, the reptile, strikes his tooth deep in my heart, so crush'd
  and sad.
Aye! laugh, ye fiends, laugh, laugh, ye fiends,
Yes, by Heav'n, yes, by Heav'n, they've driven me mad!
I see her dancing in the Hall—I—ha, ha, ha, ha, ha, ha, ha, ha,
I see her dancing in the Hall
Oh! release me! oh! release me!
She heeds me not
Yes, by Heav'n, yes, by Heav'n, they've driven me mad!

The last lyric might be explained as the survival of the Gothick craze,
with its continual appeal to horror and melancholy, but I prefer to see it as the
reductio ad absurdum of a tendency found throughout the songs of the age.
It is not merely the artificial diction which is at fault, despite the fact that
it draws upon the clichés of the eighteenth century long after the classical
desire to dignify and ornament had declined and been left behind by the
more serious poets. Nor is it a matter of faulty poetic technique, even though
this can make it difficult to sense the sincerity of a less able poet. The crux
of the matter lies more in the whole stance which the writers take towards
their subject-matter, and their tone towards their audience. Their approach
is unpleasing to the serious modern lover of the arts in that it is morally
unhealthy; moral sentiments are used to provide an excuse for a gloating
upon violence—and a violence from which, despite the many difficulties of
the social situation in Victorian England, such as factory conditions or infant
mortality, the writers were largely cushioned. This point has already been
made in connection with the Northumbrian songs.

The tone of the lyrics is also a constant source of irritation, in that the
writers are incapable of understatement. They rely on a constant frontal
attack upon the emotions which grates tremendously upon a modern ear.
The following illustrates this well:

Father, dear Father, come home with me now,
The clock in the steeple strikes three,
The house is so lonely, the night is so long,
For poor weeping Mother and me.
Yes, we are alone, for Benny is dead,
And gone to the angels of light,
And these were the very last words that he said,
"I want to kiss Papa good night."
Come home, come home, oh Father, dear Father, come home.

A lyric such as this brings in a whole range of highly emotive situations, any one of which would be sufficient material for a better artist. A type of appeal which is singularly hard for us to accept, in view of the amount of senseless mass violence in our century, is the very popular Victorian exhortation to trust in Providence:

> On such a night the sea engulph'd
> My father's lifeless form.
> My only brother's boat went down,
> In just so wild a storm.
> And such perhaps may be my fate,
> But this I say to thee:
> Fear not but trust in Providence,
> Wherever thou mayst be.

We are, perhaps, least sympathetic to songs of a patriotic or nationalist nature, a fact which is not surprising in view of the twentieth century's experience of total war. Typical, is the song which gave a new word to the language at the time of the Russian crisis of 1877. G. H. Farrell, a bricklayer, who had become the Great MacDermott, sang it at the London Pavilion:

> We don't want to fight, but by Jingo if we do,
> We've got the ships, we've got the men and got the money too.
> We've fought the Bear before, and while we're Britons true,
> The Russians shall not have Constantinople.

Another song appeared as a sequel to this, which said:

> If it's Jingo to love honour, then Jingoes sure are we.

As a result, feeling was aroused, Gladstone's windows were smashed by demonstrators, and Parliament, which had been in doubt about the course of action to take, voted £6,000,000 for military use. This type of attitude, and the songs which reflected it, was only to disappear when a majority of people had suffered the bitter disillusionment of the Great War.

However, we should not think of all Victorian song as being melancholy and mournful or even sober and serious. There was for instance:

> I thought the last of all my cares
> Would end with my last minute:
> But though I went to my long home,
> I didn't stay long in it.
> The body snatchers they have come,
> And made a snatch at me;
> It's very hard them kind of men
> Won't let a body be.

The love of puns found in this lyric illustrates another aspect of the rather childlike nature of Victorian humour, and is linked with the coining of catch-phrases, such as "Wotcher, me old brown son" and nonsense words, such as that invented to satirise the first lady doctor, about the patient who had "got the ooperzootic and I don't know where it is".

The horseplay found in Grimaldi's humour continued to be popular throughout the period. An example from the middle of the century is the story of a fried fish shop heroine who, after various slapstick, including pouring a bowl of batter on her rejected swain, says:

> I got together a mob of boys to pelt him in the street.

This tendency to what might now be called "sick" humour is shown more clearly in the song "The Lost Child", which asks:

> Why should he leave the court, where he was better off
> Than all the other boys,
> With two bricks, an odd shoe, nine oyster shells,
> And a dead kitten by way of toys?

It is interesting to note the way in which a song shows us how limited is the "freedom" which is so often proclaimed these days: it is difficult to imagine a present-day popular audience finding anything satisfactory in this type of song. It is only with an understanding of historical background that such songs can bring anything like a sympathetic reaction from us.

The Victorian fondness for mocking the "toff", might also be seen in the same light, despite the almost unanimous admiration which this aspect of Victorian song has aroused. The humour of "Burlington Bertie" is undoubtedly subtle, and the more effective because of its delicacy:

> I'm Burlington Bertie, I rise at ten thirty,
> And saunter along like a toff.
> I walk down the Strand with my gloves on my hand,
> And then walk back again with them off.

But such lines as the following are rather puerile in their humour, and even a little malicious:

> But nothing weally wuffles me—I don't see why it should
> Whatever comes along I never cwy;
> No the only thing that wowwies me at all is simply this,
> I cannot keep my eyeglass in my eye.

In the Northumbrian "Baggy Nanny", mentioned earlier, philistinism was mollified by its good humour. But the following lines, spoken by the Great Vance, in a song about Martha Gunn, the bathing-hut attendant (1868), merely illustrate the disturbing tendency of certain types of English audience to view everything outside of their own pattern of existence in a destructively humorous light. One is not sure whether to be more concerned about the points where they laughed at Martha, or about those where they laughed with her.

> Bathing strengthens the interlect, braces the body, cleans the system, puts new life in the blood, old heads onto young shoulders, fills the pocket, drives away care, cures corns, warts, bunions, Pilgrim's progresses, water on the brain, new-ralgia, old-ralgia, velocipedes, bicycles, telephones, tella-crams, and all the Primrose 'ills the flesh is heir to.

Possibly it was the first realisation of the difficulty of having anything like what Wesker's Beattie Bryant calls "majesty" in a slum city, rather than an intellectual mockery of the excesses of the form, which turned writers to satirise the ballad. We find, for instance, the lament of a milkman—"Pretty Polly Perkins of Paddington Green"—and the tale of "The Ratcatcher's Daughter of Islington".

The method of a satire was to take a standard ballad situation and to treat it in a more lifelike manner, as in Henry Clifton's "The Weeping Willer", a tale of a forlorn maiden which ended:

> She looked at the Willer above,
> And said, "I'll hang in my garter,
> But what a mistake, if the garter break,
> I shall be drowned in the water."
> She looked at the water below,
> And her nerves began to totter,
> "I'm not very bold, and I may take cold,
> I'll wait till the water is hotter—milder."

The last word is typical of one form of humour found throughout the song; that obtained by the substitution of more "genteel" words for common ones.

Exceptional situations were not always needed. Humorous effects could also be obtained by the contrast of a serious emotion with a particularly lowly setting:

> I am the right man
> Be then my bride;
> A regular nightman,

> And dustman beside.
> While cats'-meat calling,
> You look so smart,
> I, in love falling,
> Then lost my heart,
> Rouse, Blowsa bella,
> Get up my dear;
> Come from your cellar,
> Bob Dusty is here.

As in all ages it was the love song, in its various forms, which constituted the bulk of popular music. At its best, the Victorian ideal of love was a most delicate conception, with an idyllic view of the loved one and of the love situation. The following lyric comes from the end of the Victorian period (1907), but it epitomises the attitudes of at least half a century:

> Under the weeping willow tree
> Woo'd by the summer weather,
> Lull'd by the voice of bird and bee,
> Just you and I together,
> Watching the swallows dip and fly,
> My heart on your breast I pillow,
> Letting the cares of life slip by,
> Under the weeping willow.

This is not far from the nostalgic memories evoked by Matthew Arnold:

> Where is the girl, who, by the boatman's door,
> Above the locks, above the boating throng,
> Unmoor'd our skiff, when, through the Wytham flats,
> Red loosestrife and blond meadowsweet among,
> And darting swallows, and light water-gnats,
> We track'd the shy Thames shore?

But the vision of beauty is more detached from real life than in earlier ages. Chaucer's Troilus could admire his Criseyde with all the spirituality of the code of Courtly Love, but it was also entirely natural to him to become her lover. In this period the patronising protection of the innocent by the worldly wise, which we saw in the Thackeray extract, is never far away.

Perhaps this was only symptomatic of a disintegration which was bound to take place in a society which maintained in its marital attitudes a (literally) medieval viewpoint long after the theological basis which medieval Catholicism had provided had ceased to be of importance. Moreover the disturbance caused by the French and American revolutions had begun the gradual change in position which was to result in the emancipation of women. The first signs of a rising discontent are to be seen in the following lines of Harriet Grote, written in 1855:

> Full many a sorrowful and tragic tale
> Enfolded lies beneath the semblance frail
> Of wedded harmony and calm content.
> How oft the heart in aching bosom pent,
> And careworn thoughts are borne abroad unseen,
> Veiled in the aspect of a cheerful mien,
> By the sad mourner of a home unblest,
> A faith dishonoured, and a life opprest.

Such ideas had not even reached the point of enjoying public attention let alone of public support, and consequently the songs largely fall into two categories—lachrymose seriousness, or the traditional "wife" jokes. Some of the versions of this are, however, a little surprising in their topics. We tend to suppose that the "faith dishonoured" was a commonplace, but not spoken of. On the other hand, the Great Vance sang in 1868, of "The Husband's Boat", which took the husbands down at the end of the week to join their wives and families, who were already at Margate. On the boat, the husband's thoughts turn to matters far from the domestic:

> Imagine my surprise, then, I chanced to turn my eyes, when
> I saw a lovely damsel who was looking straight at me,

then

> We got into conversation, I stood a cold collation;
> We soon got near to Margate pier; the time went quickly by.
> Around her taper waist, then, my arm I just had placed when
> I heard a voice that brought me to my senses instantly.

> Spoken: "Oh, look Ma. There's Father. Isn't it kind of him to bring your dressmaker with him on board?"

And the cover illustrates this lascivious proceeding.

The Victorian audience was also capable of accepting a realistic and earthy humour on occasion. Here, from 1866, is part of a song called "Children Objected To" by J. A. Hardwick: it deals with a problem which still has relevance:

> You may seek in the East, you may seek in the West,
> Where "Lodgings To Let" your eyes may arrest,

> Each family man will find, how high he bids,
> Though with gloves on his hands, they object to his kids.
> If rooms in this town you wish to obtain,
> Young fellows, directly a girl's heart you gain,
> Make this bargain tho' she may not like it when wed,
> Have no children—each sleep in a separate bed.

More frank, and with a subject in the spirit of an earlier age, is this extract from a Cockney lyric:

> Should one of the females get in a queer way,
> John his exit must make without any delay,
> Though my lord be the father—'tis common 'mongst the town
> They're sure to be father'd on unlucky John.
> Three females are kept,
> So blithe and so bonny,
> And to keep 'em in order
> They now want a Johnny.

Nevertheless, the most successful songs financially were ones which were less frank, but were "naughty" in implication. It is from these as much as anything that the popular ideas of the "Naughty Nineties" and the "Gay Edwardian Era" have sprung. The great success of Marie Lloyd was due largely to the exploitation of this mixture of "naughtiness" and coyness in such songs as "Oh Mr Porter", "Can't Find My Way Home", "The Naughty Continong", "Then You Wink the Other Eye", and "How Can A Girl Refuse?"

The town had now produced a culture (I use this word here in the widely known sense in which it was used by T. S. Eliot) whose attitudes contrasted sharply with those of the countryman. This situation was rapidly changing, as is shown by the account of the Rev. Sabine Baring-Gould, one of the first folk song collectors, of village attitudes to traditional songs:

> When I came to enquire what the younger men knew—men of forty and fifty—I could find nothing old, only Christy minstrel songs, music-hall pieces, and, of course, Salvation Army hymns. They laughed and curled their lips contemptuously when asked for the songs sung by their fathers and grandfathers.

Nevertheless Flora Thompson's book shows how the countryman had a definite idea of propriety which meant that "men's tales", which she suggests were "coarse, rather than filthy . . . were kept strictly to the fields . . .

and songs and snatches on the same lines were bawled at the plough tail and under hedges and were never heard elsewhere". Thus of a man who was wont to improvise "dragging in the names of honest lovers, and making a mock of fathers of first children" she says that "nine out of ten of his listeners disapproved and felt thoroughly uncomfortable".

Clearly, the type of song in question would have been inacceptable in most parts of a town as well, but the picture of a fair-dealing and clean-living countryman is still there and was in reality remarkably close to the idealised pictures which writers have at times created. Perhaps the root of the matter is that the pattern of life which was being lived in the villages prohibited the growth on any scale of vices that could flourish and be profitable in a town. There also seems to have been a more homogeneous moral climate, which was enforced upon the few who might have ignored it; it appears to have been almost impossible to continue to live in the villages whilst flouting their standards and conventions. The poorer wages of the agricultural labourer must also have helped to restrain him, and in sexual matters the continual contact with animals probably helped to form a healthy attitude, whereas it was quite possible to live in complete ignorance of such things in the town. Symptomatic of these things is the fact that in the country women never went into the public house, and that there was rarely any drunkenness.

It is not surprising to find that many of the songs sung publicly were of the "ballad" type, and concerned ideal situations and a world of fantasy. The frequently sung ballad of Lord Lovell, a piece of great antiquity, opens:

> Lord Lovell stood at his castle gate,
> Calming his milk white steed,
> When up came Lady Nancy Bell,
> To wish her love God speed.

While he was away, she died, and when he returned and found this, he died in great sorrow. The song ends:

> And they buried her in the chancel high,
> And they buried him in the choir;
> And out of her grave sprung a red, red rose,
> And out of his sprung a briar.

> And they grew till they grew to the church roof,
> And then they couldn't grow any higher,
> So they twined themselves in a true lovers knot
> For all lovers true to admire.

Humour was much lighter and lacked the unpleasant undertone of some of the city songs. An example of this is the half-nonsensical "King Arthur":

> When King Arthur first did reign
> He ruled like a king,
> He bought three sacks of barley meal
> To make a plum pudding.

The tale of this gigantic pudding continues through several verses, and ends

> And what they couldn't eat that night
> The Queen next morning fried.

Among the most popular songs were those of a convivial and communal nature, such as "The Barleymow":

> Oh, when we drink out of our noggins, my boys,
> We'll drink to the barleymow.
> We'll drink to the barleymow, my boys,
> We'll drink to the barleymow,
> So knock your pint on the settle's back;
> Fill again, in again, Hannah Brown,
> We'll drink to the barleymow, my boys,
> We'll drink now the barley's mown.

Rural songs were full of references to former times. Sometimes these were of a very general nature, such as in the following children's song, which clearly referred to a problem of more lawless days:

> "Who's that going round my sheepfold?"
> "Oh, it's only your neighbour Dick."
> "Do not steal my sheep while I am fast asleep."

Sometimes the date of origin is fairly clear, as in this next children's song, which probably dates from the coronation of George IV:

> Queen, Queen Caroline,
> Dipped her head in turpentine,
> Why did she look so fine?
> Because she wore a crinoline.

In contrast to this continuous delving into the past, we find that town songs are full of modernity:

> On the new velocipede so gaily,
> You'll see people riding daily,
> Everyone should try one, everyone should buy one,
> See the new velocipede.

The lightheartedness of this fashionable song of 1868, and of the more famous "On a Bicycle Made For Two", was more often found than the sombreness of the following song, but this too was very much of its time, and reflected the appalling poverty in which many people lived, in a way which one feels conveys a definite sincerity:

> Bags of hay laid on the floor,
> For hunted wretches on to snore,
> For one, but holding three or four,
> All night in a London workhouse.
> In, one by one, the casuals crawled,
> In filthy tatters, raiment called,
> Like raging fiends they yelled and bawled,
> While by the Daddy overhauled,
> Who doled to each a slice of "toke"
> Which eager, dirty fingers broke,
> No word of thanks for that was spoke,
> At night in a London workhouse.

The constant reflection of the new and vital, even though depressing, urban surroundings is still of interest to us, in that though it often renders the songs out of date, it nevertheless enables us to get much closer to understanding how these people thought and lived. This is the appeal of the domestic details of the following song:

> He's bought a bed and a table too,
> A big tin dish for making stew,
> A large flat iron to iron his shirt,
> And a flannel and a scrubbing brush to brush away the dirt,
> And he's bought a pail and basins three,
> A coffee pot, a kettle, and a tea-pot for the tea,
> And a soap bowl and a ladle,
> And a gridiron and a cradle,
> And he's going to marry Mary Ann—that's me
> And he's going to marry Mary Ann.

In conclusion, we must now look at a fashion which lasted throughout the period, but which was to have even greater significance in that it began some very great changes. I refer to the minstrel show.

The sporadic interest of the eighteenth century has already been mentioned, but it is now necessary to add that this interest became a craze after 1828, when an American showman called T. D. Rice wrote a song called "Jump Jim Crow":

> Wheel about, turn about
> And do just so,
> Ebry time I wheel about
> I jump Jim Crow.

Based on the idiosyncrasy of an old Negro observed by Rice in Louisville, USA, this song became the centrepiece of an act which became enormously popular. The humour was of a very simple kind, as a later stanza shows:

> Dis head, you know, am pretty tick,
> Cause dere it make a hole,
> On de dam macadam road
> Much bigger dan a bowl.

As John Ashton put it: "We may wonder what merit our grandfathers and fathers found in it, but it created an absolute furore."

The next stage was the formation of Minstrel Companies, which sang, told jokes and danced. One of these, Bryants Minstrels, ran for sixteen years in New York, and was popular in England, where the fashion became so strong that the Prince of Wales took banjo lessons from James Bohee, a noted performer of the time.

The first minstrels to visit England were Whitlock's Virginia Minstrels, a white company, in 1843, but a more famous American company was Edwin P. Christy's Minstrels, who visited London in 1857. It was in that year that the most famous English troupe was formed, the Moore and Burgess Minstrels; this was a large company, being some seventy men strong. The minstrel show remained extremely popular until the end of the period, the last famous minstrel being Eugene Stratton, whose greatest song was "Lily of Laguna". The form has had waves of popularity since then; the television success of the Black and White Minstrels is a recent example.

The minstrel companies appeared in large public halls, but they were imitated in less imposing surroundings all over the country. Flora Thompson's tiny hamlet was entertained once a year by a minstrel troupe. The Squire took certain of the village lads and taught them the songs, and on the night they dressed up in red and blue, blacked their faces, rattled bones, joked and sang. Not surprisingly, the street musicians also followed the

fashion. Henry Mayhew interviewed such a one, whose comments are revealing:

> When we started the songs we knew was Old Mr. Coon, Buffalo Gals,
> Going ober de Mountain, Dandy Jim of Caroline, Rowly Bowly O and
> Old Johnny Booker. We stuck to them a twelve month. . . .
> There are all sorts of character in the different schools, but I don't
> know of any runaway gentleman or gentleman of any kind among us,
> not one; we're more of a poorer sort, if not a ragged sort, for some of us
> are without shoes or stockings.

Originally the songs were Negro or Negro-inspired, and the closing dance
of the first half—"The Cakewalk"—was a take-off of white ways. Also, in
the final "hoedown", the whole company formed in a circle, clapping, round
one dancer, in a manner taken directly from the Southern-Negro "ring
shout". At least one Negro, James Bland, achieved considerable fame with
his "Oh, Dem Golden Slippers" and "Carry Me Back to Old Virginny".

But this was nothing to the fame of the white minstrels, most notably
Stephen Foster, who wrote songs which typify the minstrel style and are still
popular, such as "Beautiful Dreamer", "Old Folks at Home", "Old Ken-
tucky Home" and "The Camptown Races".

For a period, during the American Civil War, a more serious element was
introduced, but this soon passed, and the style returned to the straightforward love ballad and to the typical "coon" humour, such as:

> John lay on the railroad track,
> De engine came slap on his back;
> John didn't cry, nor wince, nor whine,
> But cried "Do dat again, you'll hurt my spine."
> Walk along John, all through the town.

As one might expect, the "coon" shows could not have continued so long
and so successfully had they not been prepared to widen their repertoire.
Thus Flora Thompson's Squire and his "Negro Minstrel Troupe" sang:

> A friend of Darwin's said to me
> "A million years ago" said he,
> "You had a tail and no great toe"
> I answered him "That may be so,
> But I've one now, I'll let you know
> G-r-r-r-r-r-r out."

This latter word was "emphasised by a kick on Tom Binns' backside by
Squire's boot".

Such a song was halfway between the genuine "coon" song and the typical
English music-hall song, but the minstrels went further. Nothing could have
been more typical of the Victorian drawing-room than this song of the
Ethiopian Troupe:

> When the snow was falling, falling,
> On a bitter winter night,
> I and little Mary watch'd it,
> Wrapping all the world in white.
> Came a little robin redbreast,
> Hungry, shivering and in pain,
> And we heard him faintly tapping,
> Tapping on the window pane.
> Robin's gone to sing with Mary,
> In my dreams I hear the strain,
> And I wake and hear the echo,
> Tapping on the window pane.

For some people this love of the mock-Negro life was accompanied by,
and perhaps stimulated further, an appreciation for music that was genuinely
Negro in origin. As early as 1848, an English critic, reviewing a performance
by Juba, a famous Negro dancer, could see a significant difference in style and
quality between him and his white imitators, but this type of appreciation
grew much more widespread over the next twenty-five years. It was a time of
religious revival and Moody and Sankey were stirring the souls of many, when
a group of Negroes, the Jubilee Singers, came to England, singing religious
songs in order to raise money for the recently founded Negro university,
Fisk, at Nashville, Tennessee. They were highly popular in the United
States; indeed a letter to the *New York Tribune* praised them as being
representative of "the only true native school of American music. We have
long enough had its coarse caricatures in corked faces." But it is unlikely that
it was solely the perception of the superiority of the Negro originals which
in England produced a response which makes us think twice if we are accustomed to imagine our forefathers as undemonstrative. They drew crowds of
7,000 at Mr Spurgeon's Tabernacle in London, at the Corn Exchange,
Edinburgh; and at a concert for the Freedmen's Missions Aid Society, in
1873, "the dense audience rose to their feet, hats and handkerchiefs waved
in the air, and the deafening applause was kept up until the singers answered
with 'God Save The Queen' ".

They performed before Queen Victoria, breakfasted with the Prime
Minister, Mr Gladstone, and gave an extempore service by the King

William Monument in Hull "to a crowd that filled the street farther than the voice of either speaker or singer could be heard". Their effect (at least temporarily) appears to have been quite remarkable, since "tears trickled down the cheeks of many to whom the sound of prayer or religious song was apparently almost unknown".

It will be seen from the above that the cause of the intense excitement which the Jubilee Singers generated was primarily religious. This area of nineteenth-century popular life needs a little examination, since it is relevant to the concept of an increasingly demonstrative popular audience, demanding increasingly powerful musical stimulus.

In the United States a great following had grown up for vigorously expressed fundamentalist Christianity. Known as "The Great Awakening", the movement had as one of its most distinctive features the "camp meeting". In form, it was very close to already existent Negro religious practices, since these meetings were held in the open air, and a considerable atmosphere of hysteria seems to have been aroused. The general pattern of the meetings was an alternative between "hellfire" sermons and lusty hymn singing, usually in a call and response form; the hymn tunes utilised folk tunes, but the lyrics were rewritten. An example of this style is:

Ex. 17
Camp meeting hymn

He comes, he comes the Judge se - vere, Roll Jor-dan roll. The sev-enth trum-pet speaks him near, Roll Jor-dan roll. I want to go to heav'n, I do Hal-le - lu -jah Lord. We'll praise the Lord in Heav'n a - bove, Roll Jor-dan roll.

This was originally a song celebrating the return of Admiral Vernon in 1739; the chorus was added in camp meetings. Some 800 tunes of this type are still extant.

In 1805 "Crazy" Alonzo Dow came to England to save the country from heathendom, and in 1807 he held the first English camp meeting in Mow Cop, on the Staffs-Cheshire border; out of this sprang the Primitive Methodist Church. A second wave of strongly expressed evangelism came later in the century, with the movement led by Moody and Sankey.

Dwight L. R. Moody was converted in 1855 and devoted himself to evangelism some years after. In 1870, he was joined, in Chicago, by Ira D. Sankey and they collaborated to produce *Sacred Songs and Solos*, music of a simple nature, based on the three primary triads, and a lively rhythm. Most of the music was compiled, rather than composed, by them. The popularity of their methods was quite startling; they claimed, not without reasonable evidence, to have "reduced the population of Hell by a million souls" in America and England.

It is not therefore surprising that in such a religious climate William Booth, who, since 1864, had been holding services in tents and the open air in London, was inspired, in 1878, to create the Whitechapel Church Mission, and with it the Salvation Army. At first, the military dress and organisation of the new church caused considerable hostility, based on a misunderstanding of its aims; early meetings were often broken up by fights. But the devoted service of the Army in poor areas soon earned them the popular esteem which they still enjoy.

As is well known, Booth is said to have been the originator of the famous query, "Why should the devil have all the good tunes?" Whether or not the story is apocryphal, the statement sums up his attitude, which was to use any means which were not sinful to save souls. He realised that the attention of many people could be captured if the services were simple, and the tunes catchy, and so took to using existing tunes, as the camp meetings had done, with new lyrics. The repertoire included music-hall songs; and the extremely popular "Champagne Charlie" was soon pressed into the service of the Lord. In so doing, he was taking up a tradition which dated from the days of Anglo-Saxon Bishop Aldhelm. The implementation of stricter copyright laws put a stop to this practice, though not to the lively military-band style for which the Army is still known. The attitude that popular idioms may and should be used in a Christian cause is still accepted by the organisation, as has been seen in the recent success of the group called the Joystrings.

We can see how the popularity of religion and of minstrel shows had prepared the way for an influx of Negro music. The minstrel show attuned people to the idea of accepting inspiration from Negro sources, though a highly Westernised variety, but the emphasis of the religious movements on a strong physical response, leading to the ecstatic release of "salvation", made it possible for Europeans to accept music which was much more authentic. The most striking musical feature of the songs of the Jubilee Singers was thus noted by the editor of them, Theodore F. Seward: "the first peculiarity that strikes the attention is the rhythm. This is often complicated, and some-

The Padstow Hobby, old and modern photographs

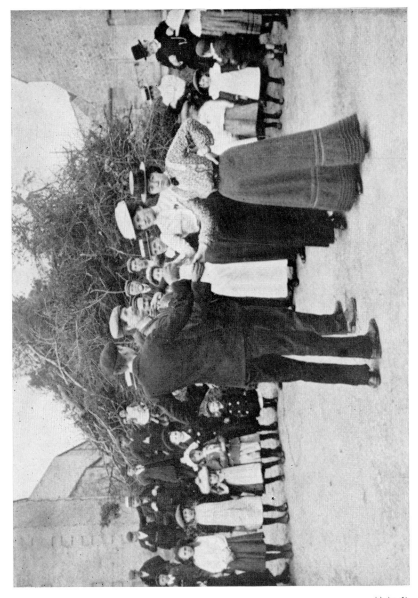

Traditional dancing as it survived into the 19th Century at the Northumbrian Baal Fire

times strikingly original." He speaks also of the effect of this rhythm, "the beating of the foot and the swaying of the body, which are such frequent accompaniments of the singing. These motions are in even measure and in perfect time; and so it will be found that, however broken and seemingly irregular the movement of the music, it is always capable of the most exact measurement." This description, which might well be applied unaltered to much modern popular music, shows perfectly how the first elements of the style of the present day were already emerging, some thirty-five years before the end of this period. But the first big impact of the new style did not come until 1911, in the form of Irving Berlin's "Alexander's Ragtime Band".

6 The Work of Cecil Sharp and the Folk Song Collectors

Folk melodies are a real model of the highest
artistic perfection. To my mind, on a small
scale, they are masterpieces, just as much as, in
the world of larger forms, a fugue by Bach or
a Mozart sonata.
BÉLA BARTÓK

Until the turn of the present century little of our traditional rural music had
been written down. It was only at the turn of the century that various lovers
of this music, of whom the most important was Cecil Sharp, felt this fact
strongly, and saw that if something were not done quickly, it would be lost
forever. Among the most hardworking of these collectors was Ralph Vaughan
Williams, whose own music, as is well known, takes much of its spirit and
inspiration from English folk song.

The result of these valuable efforts was to produce a collection of some
thousands of songs of very varied quality, type and age. We therefore now
have a very good idea of the nature of English folk song, but comparatively
little indication of the stages of its historical development. Sometimes, there
is internal evidence which will give a rough date, such as a date before or
after which, for some reason or other, the song cannot have been written,
at least in its present form. Thus the song "All Things Are Quite Silent",
which is about pressganging, is likely to have been written before about 1835,
when this means of obtaining men fell out of use. Similarly, "The Death Of
Queen Jane" must presumably have been written after 1573, when Jane
Seymour, a wife of Henry VIII, died. For some songs, we have external
evidence, such as for the words of "Ye Mariners All", of which a version is
found in a penny song-book, *Little Warblers*, of 1838.

On the other hand, for most songs we have little background information,
and even when we have some facts, we have to allow for the probability of
change and reworking, such as we saw in Chapter 4. For instance, the origin
of the tradition in which "Death and The Lady" was written is known to
have been medieval, but it is not known at what date the song was actually

composed. There is, therefore, a persistent difficulty of dating songs and of making inferences from these datings.

After years of careful work, Cecil Sharp set down his conclusions about the English folk song tradition in a book that is still so satisfactory in its analysis that I shall not hesitate to refer to it several times in the next few paragraphs.

In it, he stressed the sense of urgency which dominated his work, since the tradition started to die out very rapidly after the Industrial Revolution (from about 1840 on); thus he found it was "as a rule, only a waste of time to call upon singers under the age of sixty: their songs are nearly all modern". Moreover, he drew attention to the fact that this process of decline had already been under way long before: the Society of Antiquaries of Newcastle-on-Tyne attempted, in 1855, to collect the old Northumbrian ballads, but recorded sadly that they were "Half a century too late".

Nevertheless, sufficient songs were collected to give fascinating illustrations of the way in which the attitudes of a period found musical expression. The tune "The Miller of Dee" is a good example. Version (a) below, the most well known, comes from the eighteenth-century ballad opera *Love in a Village*; it is interesting to compare (b) the original aeolian melody, noted by Vaughan Williams. We can see clearly illustrated the way in which music had to conform with eighteenth-century ideas of order and reason. Version (c) was sung in the nineteenth century by a Kilburn street-singer—it is thus an urban version of the rural tune.

The differences between (b) and (c) are perhaps surprising to us as we would expect similarities between the "unpolished" versions, but they become less so in the light of Cecil Sharp's interpretation of the nature and origin of folk song, which he sees as a "spontaneous utterance" of a type "prevalent among the unlettered classes". The original invention is therefore altered by every new singer until an accepted version or versions remain. Every new singer will therefore subconsciously contribute his idea of what is better, or more desirable, to the song. The result of many such alterations is

Ex. 18

(a)

Miller of Dee (from 'Love in a Village')

(b)
Miller of Dee (coll. Vaughan-Williams)

(c)
Miller of Dee (Kilburn singer's version)

to reflect the character of the people whose song it is, or as Sharp put it, "The racial character of a ballad or song is due therefore, not to communal invention, but to communal choice." He thus feels that "the real antithesis is not between that of the town and that of the country, but between that which is the product of the spontaneous and intuitive use of untrained faculties, and that which is due to the conscious and intentional use of faculties which have been especially cultivated and developed for the purpose".

These ideas of the communal creation of a song and of the consequent reflection of communal or racial characteristics in a song, are by no means accepted without reservation by present-day scholars, but the finer points of the argument need not concern us here, since the topic of this book, as defined at the outset, does not clash with such ideas. Since my aim is to examine "the music of the people" in the sense of such music, irrespective of type and origin, as was listened to and performed by a majority of the population, it can include both the "spontaneous utterance" and that produced by the "conscious and intentional use of trained faculties".

The aim of the first part of this book has thus not been to divide music into "folk" and "popular" but to consider the musical life of the country as first two, and later three streams of taste, each with a different set of aesthetic and moral values and with a consequently differing musical manifestation of these. It is, of course, true to say that, on the one hand, the "conscious use of trained faculties" has been an important distinguishing feature between the peasant tradition, on one side, and the middle-class and aristocratic traditions on the other. Furthermore, the use of such training has always been linked with so different a set of aims and emphases that we have called the result "cultured" or "sophisticated" or "art" music to draw attention to its conscious interest in comparatively intellectual qualities, such as formal construction.

On the other hand, I do not see this as being sufficient in itself as a means of analysis and categorisation of all the types of music which we have had to deal with. These can and must, as I see it, be classified also according to the aesthetic and moral attitudes which they assert. Furthermore, in so doing they reflect the values of the social groups, or "classes", from which they sprang, or for whom they were written. Some readers may feel that the use of the term "class" so far has been over-frequent and undesirable, and perhaps even too loosely applied, especially in the last couple of chapters. To such readers, I must point out again, as I did in the Preface, that I am only making such distinctions as were accepted as normal by the people of previous eras. If I am wrong in my assertions, it is not because such class distinctions did not exist, but because I have made a false correlation between these and the forms of music which are the material of this study. It will be noticed that in discussing the present century, with its changed musical and social conditions, I divide society into two groups—the lovers of "cultured" music and those who listen mostly to the "popular".

Returning to Cecil Sharp's work, we find that he confirms our earlier impressions of the dominance of the major/minor system. Only one-third of his songs are in the modes, and it is to be noted that though as we live in a century when serious and popular musicians tend to seek liberation from the major/minor system, we see the modal songs as "quaint" or "beautiful", to most listeners of one and two centuries ago they were archaic and old-fashioned. We should remember that, in Flora Thompson's book, the singer of "The Outlandish Knight" was "tolerated only because of his age".

This tendency was one which contributed to the decline of the folk tradition: another factor was the irregularity both of metre and of number of bars:

Ex. 19
The Lowlands of Holland

The increasing insistence on the "squareness" and regular metre of dance music, mentioned earlier, contributed greatly to the decline of interest in songs in "free rhythm".

A further factor was the difference in the style of singing between town and country singers. This is of special interest in view of what has already been said about the urban culture. This is how Cecil Sharp describes "the conventional method of singing adopted by folk singers. During the performance the eyes are closed, the head upraised, and a rigid expression of countenance maintained until the song is finished. A short pause follows the conclusion, and then the singer relaxes his attitude and repeats in his ordinary voice the last line of the song or its title. This is the invariable ritual on formal occasions." The singer enunciated the syllables clearly, and maintained an unbroken stream of melody, with a pure intonation and even tone. Thus, he says:

> When, for instance, an old singing man sings a modern or popular song, he will sing it in quite another way. The tone of his voice will change and he will slur his intervals, after the approved manner of the street singer.

Cecil Sharp had said, "Folksingers like to sing in as high a pitch as possible, and will often apologise for not being able, on account of age, to sing their songs high enough." The tone of the street-singer appears to have been much broader, with a heaviness of technique well suited to the sentimentality which we have already noticed in much of the nineteenth-century urban song. They also used a range of vocal techniques which produced an effect very far from the pure "stream of melody" of the traditional rural style. A. L. Lloyd describes it as follows:

> The street singers commonly pitched their songs about a fifth higher than their voice would really take, and they used voice breaks, slides, and high rasping wails, and in that way lines which look on paper merely sad and tearful become as thrilling as an Indian war whoop.

The differences between the old and new traditions are manifested not only in the techniques of their music, but in their content. Thus, songs of hunting and drinking (the pastimes of a richer section of society) were no more popular than were songs containing domestic detail (such as "Mary Ann") among folk singers. Similarly, patriotic songs were written by the trained composers (for example, Dibdin)—such themes are not found much in the old folk music.

The songs divide into three main types; the work song (and sea shanty), the ballad, and the love lyric. As the origins of all of these have been noted in previous chapters, it is only necessary here to add a few notes on their nature. I strongly advise the reader to open up a new world for himself, if he has not already done so, by studying these at great length, and most of all by singing them (see Bibliography).

The ballads are too long to quote here, but fairly typical is "Lord Thomas and Fair Eleanor", a sad story of a lord who loved a maiden, who was stabbed by a rival. In revenge, Lord Thomas strikes off the rival's head, and then commits suicide. From the bodies of the lovers grow two rose bushes which intertwine (cf. the ballad of Lord Lovell in the previous chapter). Many ballads are set in such a knightly background: they are usually songs of love, often linked with some mysterious happening, and frequently sad. Probably the most important other single subject is the sailor, who, witty, charming, and free-and-easy, tends to return to sea, leaving the girl lovelorn and with child. Such ballads are often very beautiful though they are not always to the taste of our time. Perhaps this is because these songs rarely reflect much of the day-to-day background from which they came. On the other hand, one might expect a greater popularity for those with a knightly story in view of the Englishman's persistent love for his aristocracy, which only seems to have begun to diminish at all when the knight lost his armour.

The ballad is the most common English folk form, perhaps because it had not only the attraction of tune and mood, but of story and fantasy. Indeed, the latter is perhaps the most distinctive feature of the rural ballad. Urban lyrics may be sensational, sentimental or over-ornate, but their situations are fundamentally those of life. They lose the traces of magical and ritual influence which had lingered for centuries in peasant communities.

By lyric, I mean songs concerned with one mood and situation only, rather than with narrative. The following is a good example:

Ex. 20
Nelly the Milkmaid

NELLY THE MILKMAID

Nelly was a milkmaid, bonny, brisk, and gay,
Always took delight with young Roger for to play,
One day she decided some pleasure for to take,
And asked her missus' leave for to go to the Wake.

"Oh Nelly," said her missus, "I'd have you to take care,
And of that young rogue, Roger, I'd have you to beware;
So, Nelly, you may go, but this promise you must make,
Do not frolic with young Roger coming home from the Wake."

So dressed in all her best, young Nelly did repair,
And, as she expected, young Roger he was there,
They danced and they sang, they had beer, ale and cake,
And many were the pleasures that they had at the Wake.

The Wake being over, they homeward went their way,
Until they came to the new cocks of hay,
Then Roger kissed young Nelly and her promise she did break,
And she frolicked with young Roger coming home from the Wake.

When eight months were over and nine coming on,
Young Nelly was the mother of a fine, lovely son,
"I will call it," said she, "I will call it for his sake,
I will call it 'Young-Roger-coming-home-from-the-Wake'."

This is typical of the folk style and its subject, which, dealing as it does
with the inevitable result of indulgence in the pre-contraceptive age, is a
frequent one (though by no means the only one). To me, the greatest attraction lies in the tone of such songs, which face reality but are not morbid.
In this, the older songs differ from the urban lyrics of the last century or so,
which so often wallow in a sea of self-pitying tears, or brood on one or two
aspects of a very limited concept of the relationship between man and woman.
In particular, the physical relationship is either ignored, referred to in veiled
terms, or half-represented, so that one might imagine that there was nothing
more to do in love than to kiss goodnight on the doorstep. Compare the rather
unhealthy flirtatious tone of the following:

If a maiden means to marry,
On a houseboat she should tarry,
And a man she's sure to catch;
For the picnics and the dances
Will afford her endless chances
To bring him to the scratch.
For when the moon is mellow
Up on deck she takes a fellow
Whom she thinks she wants to wed.
And she flirts with him reclining
In a blouse that lacks a lining
And he's bound to lose his head.

This surely has an unpleasant undertone nearly as pronounced as that of
"The Husbands' Boat".

In the older folk songs, there is an immense vitality arising from an awareness and frank expression of the physical realities. Cecil Sharp mentioned
that he had collected "a large number of folk songs, which transgress the
accepted conventions of the present age". A half-century later, this is still
largely true, which I see as a pity, since I strongly maintain that we have lost
something important, when the term "popular" cannot be applied to a song
like that of the young apprentice, who, meeting a boastful doxy by the way-
side, told her to

"Cease this idle prattle."
He laid her on the ground,
And made her buttocks for to rattle.

Despite the pleasure which such songs can give, though, it is lines such as the following of which the lover of folk music is thinking, when he criticises modern popular music:

> A blacksmith courted me, nine months and better,
> He fairly won my heart, wrote me a letter
> With his hammer in his hand, he looked so clever.
> And if I was with my love, I'd live for ever.

These lines have the artistic simplicity and emotional balance which are for me the great attraction of the older English folk songs. There is no attempt at conscious art, and yet the soundness of the culture from which they spring means that their directness is artistically convincing. They contain the two elements needed for the best art to be produced—an acceptance of the existence of the commonplace and everyday side of life (which by itself can be boringly trivial or ridiculously overdramatised) linked with a vision of the greater forces in life, which by themselves can be self-consciously artistic, out of touch with reality, or insufferably pompous and devoid of genuine human sympathy. They are the expression of people who have lived among and with others, instead of in a world of fantasy, intensified by the isolation which is at present fundamental to modern city life.

It remains, before finishing this section, to mention the folk song in the present century, which means effectively the industrial folk song. To go beyond 1900 is in this case reasonable, since not only would the singers themselves wish to be identified with the tradition, but also it is impossible to detect any obvious changes of direction in the way in which this is possible when considering the "entertainment song".

Comment has already been made upon the use of traditional idioms in industrial contexts; these have inspired a whole body of collectors, most notably Ewan McColl and A. L. Lloyd. In his book *Come All Ye Bold Miners*, Lloyd mentions that in 1951 a competition was organised by the National Coal Board, in connection with the Festival of Britain celebrations. This produced some hundred songs, but many of these were not traditional, being merely parodies or stage songs; moreover the number is small when we consider the thousands which were collected by Cecil Sharp. We are therefore obliged to admit a great falling off in the creation of this type of song since the last century. A fine exception to this was "The Gresford Disaster", of the thirties:

> You've heard of the Gresford disaster
> The terrible price that was paid

> Two hundred and forty-two colliers were lost
> And three men of a rescue brigade.

The bitterness of the song is very great:

> The Lord Mayor of London's collecting
> To help both our children and wives
> The owners have sent some white lilies
> To pay for the poor colliers' lives.

As recently as 1957, Ewan McColl collected a song from locomotive fire-man Charlie Mayo, of the King's Cross Loco Depot, called "The Colour Bar Strike". The sentiment was laudable enough but, like the eighteenth-century ballads, it lacks some of the strength of earlier songs of the type, because it has become too aware of a climate which approves "the poetic":

> But though the Union won that fight
> The pressures there are rising higher,
> Smoke rises in the engine sheds,
> And where there's smoke there's always fire.

It ends:

> Man, don't let smoke get in your eyes,
> Know that flame and keep it bright.

The search for truly working-class modern material is thus likely to be in vain; it would seem that it has become unfashionable for working men to give vent to such grievances through song. The songs which are being written come, as far as I can discern, from a small number of people who are excited by "folk music". One may quote the song "Twenty One Years", written by Ewan McColl in 1949, for a programme about road transport:

> 'O I am a wagon driver, boys,
> Bill Healey is my name.
> Year in, year out, I roll my load in the heavy transport game.
> I keep my wagon rolling boys, however tired I feel.
> I've been serving up my twenty-one years behind the steering wheel.
>
> I know all the runs, and all the bends from Hell to Breakfast time.
> I know every kip and caff, my boys, I know all the Highway.
> I've eaten all my cake at Dirty Dick's, at the Jungle signs they
>   know me,
> I've been serving up my twenty-one years on chips and mugs of tea.

> When I turn my wagon in, my boys, and I've had my chips at last,
> Plant me by the road where I can hear the wagons pass;
> Bury me by Scotch Corner of the road outside Carlisle,
> And I'll lie and hear the heavy stuff go tearing up the miles.

Mr McColl's choice of medium, the Aeolian mode, seems to me to reflect a problem of creation of this type, in that it is not the living language of popular expression, nor has it been for some centuries, as the past few chapters have shown. To utilise the medium, therefore, is to bring in an alien idiom, requiring superior knowledge. Such a position is manifestly contrary to the situation described by Cecil Sharp, in which the musical culture is held in common, and is therefore freely handled or reshaped by all who care to do so. A tradition of this type was described by T. S. Eliot:

> What I mean by tradition involves all those habitual actions, habits, and customs . . . which represent the blood kinship of the same people in the same place.

That is to say, culture, if sound, is unconscious of most of its nature. Language, music, and subject-matter will have no sense of unfamiliarity to the audience. There will of course be a need for merit, but the poets will be concerned with technical difficulties, and will "find it expedient to occupy their conscious mind with the craftsman's problems, leaving the deeper meaning to emerge from a lower level". Such a situation no longer obtains among the common people, at least with regard to traditional song: sadly enough, the latter is largely equated with "art" (classical music, etc.), which is an alien and middle-class pursuit. As a consequence, a man of working-class origin only becomes aware of what is fine about our old traditions, and only uses them, when he has already assimilated much of the ethos by which the artist works—to use a simplification, when he has become one of the bourgeoisie. This need not entail the taking up of the obvious material positions (employment, possessions) which a caricature of the term "middle class' implies. But the artist is of the middle class, is tolerated, and even supported by it.

The problem for men like Ewan McColl is that they have become self-conscious; they can never again be completely and utterly involved, in the way indicated by Cecil Sharp and Eliot, with what they are creating. There must always be an element within them which belongs elsewhere. Put crudely, a song of social criticism may arise out of the deepest and most sincerely felt sympathy for a given injustice, but it does not arise from a constantly felt necessity; the "Durham Lockout" was written by a man who was locked out.

In conclusion, one may ask whether there is any truth whatever in the feeling among the central figures of modern folk music that something is lacking in our contemporary popular music, and that this may be replaced by reviving this tradition, for this is the serious aim of the true folk singer. The editorial of the quarterly magazine of the English Folk Dance and Song Society showed full awareness of these dangers, in October 1965:

> Folk is still considered by too many, who should know better, as the poor relation of this country's national culture, and yet it is an essential part of that culture. Many think that interest in "folk music" is merely an attempt to put the clock back to "Merrie England", to live in the past. They see us donning our smocks every evening and playing fiddles in the inglenook.
>
> The Formal Arts, by contrast, are by their very nature still not wholeheartedly acceptable or even available to many members of the community. . . .
>
> Traditional music is our national heritage, and it is also an expression of the pattern of human continuity.

Let me first say that if, due to faulty self-expression, I have given the impression that I imagine Ewan McColl or A. L. Lloyd affectedly donning smocks or wielding pickaxes, I wish to correct this at once. No one who knows the work of these men can have anything but the greatest respect for it, or a conviction that it is immensely valuable.

My belief, however, is that their efforts are not, and cannot be sufficient to alter the course of events; they are swimming against too powerful a tide. Songs of industrial protest (the industrial must clearly dominate our attention in our society) arose out of pressing need; if similar needs arise, and let us hope they will not, a new body of songs will undoubtedly be created. When men are moved sufficiently, they will protest, and one of the ways in which they will do this will be singing. But I doubt that we shall have many songs of the "Twenty One Years" type. There seems to be little evidence that man has ever wanted to sing of his job, except in criticism; his attention has always been focused on the perennial human problems, especially upon religion and love.

The potential range is further limited, however, by the fact that the climate of opinion is largely against organised religion, and thus against the religious song; it is clearly outside the scope of this work to discuss whether this will in future generations be judged as a fault. Certainly many critics would feel that the greatest works of art have been, and can only be created by an artist with an intense desire to express deep religious feeling. This would seem to indicate that the main concern of the modern popular song must be love.

Though the criticism, that the popular song lacks range, may therefore be answered in this way, I believe it is undeniable that our age has lost a certain type of verbal spriteliness or wit; and as the sentiments of all works of literature are bound to be reasonably similar, it is in this that literary virtue will consist. The following would be a fairly crude example of the older lyrics:

> Sometimes I am a Butcher,
> And then I feel fat Ware, Sir;
> And if the flank be fleshed well,
> I take no farther care, Sir;
> But in I thrust my Slaughtering-Knife,
> Up to the haft with speed, Sir;
> For all that ever I can do,
> I cannot make it bleed, Sir.

Regrettably, the best we can offer is like the following:

> My husband's a pork-butcher, a pork-butcher, a pork-butcher,
> A bloody fine pork-butcher is he.
> All day he stuffs sausages, stuffs sausages, stuffs sausages.
> At night he comes home and stuffs me.

At its worst, the modern folk ballad seems to revel in sheer coarseness, and to consist merely in a very loud declamation of the maximum number of obscenities:

> There was an old monk of great renown
> Who f—d all the women of London town.
> The old s—d, the dirty old s—d
> The b—r deserves to die.

Foreigners have often noted not our tendency to swear, which is common to all men, but our total lack of imagination in so doing.

In contrast to the above, the author of "The Merry Bagpipes"—an account of a meeting between a "country damsel" and a "jolly shepherd" who played the pipes—shows a sharp and attractive wit:

> Altho' I am but a silly Maid
> Who ne'er was brought up at Dancing-School
> But yet to the Jig that thou hast paid,
> You find that I can keep time and rule;

Now see that you keep your stops aright,
For Shepherd I am resolv'd to view thee,
And play me "The Damsel's Chief Delight"
Then never doubt but I'll dance to thee.

It should be noted that the immediately preceding remarks have concerned themselves with lyrics; they should not be taken as necessarily apply-
ing to music. The assumption that modern popular music is equally weak,
needs much closer analysis; it is to this and related problems, many of which
have only arisen in the twentieth century, that we must turn in Part Two of
this book.

Part Two

English Popular Music in the Twentieth Century

Music hath two ends, first to please the sence, and that is done by the pure Dulcor of Harmony . . . and secondly to move ye affections or excite passion. And that is done by measures of time joyned with the former. And it must be granted that pure Impuls artificially acted and continued, hath great power to excite men to act but not to think. . . . The melody is only to add to the diversion.

ROGER NORTH, *Musicall Grammarian*, 1728

7 The Development of Popular Music in the Twentieth Century

It gives a sensual delight more intense
than the Viennese waltz or the refined
sentiment and respectful emotion of
the eighteenth-century minuet.
(from an article on Jazz)
New Orleans Times Picayune,
20 June 1918

At the turn of the century, there were few signs of the immense changes that were to come over British popular music. The "folk" tradition was already dying and it had been left to Cecil Sharp and the folk song collectors, the most commonly known of whom was Ralph Vaughan Williams, to save the rapidly disappearing remnants of the tradition, in some cases for the school room, but more often for the library. Perhaps the most significant event for us was not a musical one: the population of London rose until, by 1940, it had doubled since 1880. At the same time, the standard of living rose, though slowly, in the towns. All this meant bigger markets.

However, in the United States the beginnings of new trends were already to be seen. A pianist called Scott Joplin enjoyed a certain popularity because he played a new type of piano music called "ragtime". His music became more widely known, mostly through the dissemination of piano rolls, until ragtime became a craze among the younger generation. The regular two-in-a-bar rhythm of the left hand created a basic pulse at a fairly lively tempo, and the music played by the right hand acquired a distinctive flavour from the incorporation of certain elements of Negro music, and a definite jauntiness through its use of forms of cross-rhythm not usually met with in other dance music and variously ascribed in origin to Negro music and to the banjo style of the singers of the Appalachian mountains. It should be stressed that Joplin was not the "inventor" of the music, in the way that Schoenberg might loosely be described as the "inventor" of the "twelve-note system" of composition; he was merely the best-known exponent of a music which was still taking shape.

This music definitely appealed to something which was nascent in the young of the period, and though mild in effect to the more satiated modern ear, was certainly considered somewhat extreme and radical. *Avant-garde* composers, such as Debussy and Stravinsky, turned their attention briefly towards this new dance music, though their compositions remained almost unknown to the average person, who soon discovered a dance, familiar to us from the minstrel shows, to fit the new style. It was called the "Cakewalk". It reached Britain in 1906, and enjoyed a quite startling popularity, despite the opinions of the older generation that it was both "wild" and "Trans-atlantic".

This was probably the first time that a fashion or "craze" had played an important part in shaping the course of popular music. The ballad opera may be granted as an exception to this, and some might wish to claim the Savoy Operas as well. There are significant differences between the three, though. The Gilbert and Sullivan works were successful but unique; they created no new tradition, and used a traditional musical language. The ballad opera, by contrast, was a good example, of the kind of art which gives expression to tendencies already to be found in society, and by uniting them successfully acts as a generating point, from which a whole stream of taste can arise. The same is true of ragtime; the difference was that as well as creating an outlet for existing tastes, it introduced a new language, and one that has been shown by subsequent developments to be capable of utilisation and even expansion by composers of popular music, without a sense of plagiarism.

The Cakewalk was followed, in the years before the Great War, by several new and revolutionary dances, in particular the Turkey Trot, the Bunny Hug and the Foxtrot. At the same time, dancing gained rapidly in popularity as a form of social recreation. Though public dances had existed for long enough, it was only now that the gayer young things, at least, could start to go to public dance halls. There were still many taboos, and the "decent" tended to avoid such places, but the pattern of life which in towns had destroyed certain forms of social intercourse had, sooner or later, to provide an alternative, and this was it. By 1910, the first dance marathon is recorded, and the cheap popular dance was an established institution.

It should be noted, however, that at this time the public was still equally fond of the older dances, such as the Viennese waltz, and thus the love of the ragtime dances may well be regarded as much as a temporary taste for the exotic, as for a whole new style of music. It has to be borne in mind that this was the heyday of what is now known as "Old Time Dancing", and an examination of the dates of composition of these dances will in fact show that a majority of them were invented during the first decade of this century. It is not, therefore, surprising to find that the Broadway sensation of 1914 was the Tango (though this did not become popular in Britain until 1925), a dance which we now consider to be most sedate. Nevertheless, the fact that it was in 1912 that W. C. Handy published the first of his highly successful series of Negro "blues" is indicative of the beginnings of a revolution in public taste.

In the latter half of the second decade of the century Great Britain was, of course, engaged in the "war to end all wars", but in the United States life went on unaffected until our next date of importance, 1917, the year in which they entered the war. On 26 January of that year, a group of white men, playing a music which was copied from bands at that time playing only with all-coloured musicians in Negro halls, appeared for the first time at Reisenweber's Club, New York. Their style was by no means an exact copy of the peculiar "roughness" of Negro music; indeed, because of this and because it contained many "barnyard" effects, it may well be thought of as being little more than orchestrated ragtime. Nevertheless, the sound was sufficiently different to be quite startling and to achieve immediate popularity on an unprecedented scale.

It was in 1919 that this new sound, henceforth to be known as "jazz", was brought by its originators, the Original Dixieland Jazz Band, to England, at the Hammersmith Palais, so that the new style, though as we have seen, clearly of nineteenth-century origin, may well be said to have been a post-war phenomenon. I shall not discuss the sociological significance of this, at present, but shall leave it for later discussion (especially in Chapter 12).

I had not originally intended to mention Tom Brown's Jazz Band, since it is of no significance to our theme, and of no importance except to the afficionado of traditional jazz history. But the fact that Reginald Nettel (see Bibliography) discusses it in his chapter on modern popular song compels me to state the relevant facts, so that the reader who is not too familiar with this area of music may avoid obtaining misleading ideas.

It may well be that the Brown band first brought the previously obscene word "jazz" into acceptable usage; the point has little more relevance than a discussion of who first invented the word "television". But there are several important facts that need to be understood about the Original Dixieland Jazz Band. These are that they were white, and thus acceptable to the mass of Americans, they were very popular over a wide social range, they appeared at a critical moment (the year of the American entry into the War), and they were the first band of this type to record. The latter fact is probably the most significant of all; but it gave rise to the mistaken belief, accentuated by the claims of their leader Nick La Rocca, that they "invented" jazz. The immense amount of research done by American musicologists on this topic makes it possible to state quite categorically that jazz was of Negro origin, and that it was invented by no one man—it evolved over several decades after the American Civil War. Perhaps this misconception about the invention of jazz—like the Shakespeare–Bacon controversy, with which it can be equated both in type and degree of error—may now be laid to rest.

The twenties is a period about which much has been written by those who saw it as a golden age, and it would obviously be easy to destroy this myth by referring to such events as the bombardment of Corfu by Mussolini in 1922, the General Strike of 1926, and the Wall Street Crash of 1929. Nevertheless, from our point of view, the impression is fairly valid, since the "Jazz Age" was a time of unparalleled boom for popular music; so much so that by the thirties, Constant Lambert was driven to speak of "the appalling popularity of music".

The reasons for this are not hard to find. In the first place, the value of money increased in real terms for the only time in this century, while those who were fortunate enough to be in work also tended to be enjoying shorter working hours than ever before (the average working week fell from 55 to 48 hours). More important was the enormous expansion of mass media. Newspapers increased in popularity until the *Daily Express* had the largest daily circulation in the world, and the cinema, ever growing in popularity, took a great leap forward in 1926 with the first "talkie". It is of note that this was called *The Jazz Singer*, featuring Al Jolson: this very fact is indicative of the commercial potentialities which the producers felt the combination of popular music and film to have. In ten years, public taste had changed beyond all recognition.

The forms of mass entertainment were of even more relevance to popular music. The first was the gramophone which, though no novelty at the end of the War, took on a new dimension with the introduction of electrical recording techniques in 1925. A new quality was given to the result, which made it immensely more attractive as a commodity.

At the same time, the music was even more widely disseminated, both in recorded and live forms, by the radio. On 14 September 1920, the first radio broadcast took place, and, in 1922, the British Broadcasting Company was formed. By 1926, it had become so powerful a force that it was decided to make it into a public corporation, and within five years was an entertainment enjoyed by the large majority of the population.

It is not, therefore, surprising to find that an enormous amount of popular music was composed and performed, and that fortunes were made which, even allowing for inflation, were on a scale hitherto inconceivable. The famous bandleader Paul Whiteman, for example, had a gross income of $1,000,000 a year.

What is surprising, despite all that has so far been said, was the sweeping popularity, after so many centuries of a European tradition, of the American-inspired music, of so different an emotional foundation, which may loosely be termed "jazz". I should explain, for the benefit of the more purist followers of this music, that I use the term to signify all music, regardless of quality or alleged style, which is inspired by a clearly recognisable, though less easily definable, American approach to music known to us all. I propose to clarify this definition in Chapter 8.

After the first success of the Original Dixieland Jazz Band, in 1917, a host of similar bands were formed, perhaps the most well known being those of Paul Whiteman and Ted Lewis. At the risk of censure I will suggest that the most popular English band at the time was the Savoy Orpheans.

A regular way of proceeding from this point on, would be to list large numbers of names. I feel, however, that apart from the dangers of monotony which are inherent in such a process, it is unnecessary, and even confusing. In the world of the modern arts we all know something, by reason of our position in time. What is needed is a drawing of attention to significant figures or movements; details can be added at will by the reader.

In 1921 a new dance, the Shimmy, appeared, and in 1922 a new cornetist became known from his performances at the Lincoln Gardens, Chicago, with the King Oliver Band. His name, soon to become a household word, was Louis Armstrong. The following year, 1923, saw the emergence of another new dance, the Blues, and a new style of popular singing, the "whispering baritone", at the time considered the most emotive of vocal sounds, and nowadays considered the most dated and ludicrous. This desire for novelty, and the changes to extremes at high speed are typical of fashions in this century, and, I suggest, only of this century.

In the same year, in London, appeared a show which was perhaps the epitome of the highly fluid state of public taste. The show *You'd Be Surprised*, was described as a "jazzaganza"—the very word is symptomatic—and as well as containing the latest "jazz" numbers, also featured minstrels, such was the varied nature of public taste. Most amazing, to us, there was interpolated a ballet by Milhaud, danced by Ninette de Valois. I think it is true to say that though similar things are sometimes done today on TV "spectaculars", they are never given long runs in the theatre, nor are the composers of such high quality. In particular, the teenager, though very up-to-the-moment in tastes, has a much more limited field from which he actually makes his choice. Perhaps we may ascribe this to the fact that theatre audiences were very much still middle-class in the twenties.

This show reflects the various attempts that were being made to establish contact between "jazz" and "the Classics" (dealt with in more detail in Chapter 9), which were taking place at the time. The next year saw perhaps the most famous attempt, from the jazz side, to appeal to "respectable" audiences. On 12 February, at the Aeolian Hall, New York, before an audience including several of the great names of serious music, Paul Whiteman produced a concert of "symphonic jazz", in which the high spot was George Gershwin playing his own *Rhapsody in Blue*. Such attempts resulted in a great deal of heated discussion on the status and value of the new style so that, as often happens, more significant moves went unnoticed.

In the same year, the Charleston became the rage to such an extent that it is often now considered to be the most typical dance of the period. Its importance as an influence is that its most outstanding feature is a syncopated rhythm which is an absolutely essential part of the dance. As far as I know, this was the first occasion on which such a factor became widely accepted and unconsciously understood. The rhythm is a common enough one in both Eastern Europe and the Caribbean, but it was completely alien to the Western European tradition. Thus we have a point at which the new popular tradition can be shown to be diverging widely from the old. The full significance of this will be analysed in Chapter 8.

Reginald Nettel suggests that there was an imaginative assimilation of the new style during the General Strike. He mentions that some of the miners formed bands, "the songs they played were the popular songs of the day" and that "they called these bands jazz bands for want of a better name", he continues: "The instruments they used were called in the musical trade 'kazoos', and by the miners themselves 'bazoukas'." He then goes on to offer the idea that, "A new line of folk-culture was making a beginning." In view of this claim, it is necessary to draw attention to the craze of 1924 for the music of the Mound City Blue Blowers (banjo, comb and paper and kazoo). During its enormous popularity, this group recorded and toured Europe.

At the same time the catholicity of taste of the average listener of the twenties must be emphasised. The older styles were still accepted, and the old instruments still played. The violin and cello were still found in dance bands, and music which would now be called "Palm Court" was still widely popular. One of the most famous popular English singers from the end of the decade onwards was Gracie Fields, "the singing millgirl". The voice of the "lass from Rochdale" could hardly be described as "jazzy". Even within the ultra-fashionable world, there was a great love of "sweet and sentimental" songs; for example, the song "Tea for Two" which appeared in 1925 in the musical *No, No, Nanette*.

The year 1926 saw a musical by Jerome Kern, *Sunny*, alongside various "Ruritanian" comedies, and this vogue for things American continued into 1927, with a musical by Gershwin, *Oh Kay*. In the United States, a new figure, Duke Ellington, began to make a name for himself at the Cotton Club. In 1928 Jerome Kern's *Showboat* came to London, but by 1929 public taste had begun to get over the first intoxication with the new sound, and the first of the Latin-American dances, the Rhumba, became popular in this year. At the same time, Noël Coward's *Bitter Sweet* came to the London stage, with a comment by the author that he (and the public) wanted romance after the "endless succession of slick American Vo-do-deo-do musical farces in which the speed was fast, the invention complicated, and the sentimental value negligible". Perhaps there is a moral here, since it was only in this year that anyone dared to put on a war play (*Journey's End*). These trends were accentuated by the Wall Street Crash on 24 October of that year, with the ensuing Depression.

The effect of these events on music, a luxury industry, was quite catastrophic. By 1934, record sales were down by ninety-four per cent in the United States and many companies went bankrupt. The "economic blizzard" put an end to the boom for most musicians. Only the best, or rather the most popular, could survive, and the fate of the pianist Jimmy Yancey, who became a baseball groundsman, was typical. On the other hand, the singer Bing Crosby was still able to become a rich man, largely because the *musical* effect of the economic situation was to force people even more quickly into a state of affairs which had been crystallising during the previous decade. The public now had to choose very carefully what they wished to buy, and in so doing to clarify their tastes. Such clarification rapidly became categorisation—purchase by name or style—rather than the indiscriminate buying of the previous ten years.

In the twenties the differences (often quite vast in both style and musical quality) between the various idioms within the "jazz" world were largely a matter of dispute between musicians. The situation described by Eddie Condon in his book *We Called It Music*, or by Milton "Mezz" Mezzrow in his *Really The Blues* in which a sharp line was drawn between jazz and non-jazz, sweet and hot, and New Orleans and Chicago styles was really one only

meaningful to a small number of American musicians (mostly white) who
regarded the new style as a way to express a musically revolutionary attitude.
On the other hand, many musicians had few such concerns. The Negro was,
generally speaking, still willing to accept a role of dance musician and entertainer, and the more commercially minded among the white musicians
(usually classically trained) accepted the whole business as an unfortunate
concession to a fallen public taste, which had to be made if one was to live
and make profits. Furthermore, many musicians of some standing accepted
the whole style as jazz, and allowed themselves to wander freely within the
idiom, as did Duke Ellington, or to move from quite abstract music to
straightforward clowning, as did "Fats" Waller. Most important, the public
took the same line and accepted pretty well anything in the name of
jazz.

But there was, nevertheless, some awareness of the differences, technical
and aesthetic, which were to be found in the jazz world, and the Depression
helped to form and accentuate the rigid divisions which have since remained
a dominant musical and economic factor in the world of jazz or popular
music.

The most important division then, as now, was between pure jazz and
commercial music, or "hot" and "sweet", as they were then known. The more
abstract or ferocious type of music, accompanied as it was by great advances
in technical difficulty in many cases, was too much for the average ear,
especially as such music frequently strayed far from the hitherto accepted
standards of melody and beauty. The comparison of, say, "Whispering" with
"Royal Garden Blues" will show the type of difference and its extent. The
result was that the majority of the public began to reject such sounds and to
demand "memorable" tunes, played without much alteration and with a
sweet tone, a saxophonic equivalent of the most maudlin violin tone. In this
redirecting of taste they were assisted in making their choice by the ever
solicitous musical salesmen of Tin Pan Alley. It was for this reason that Bing
Crosby chose to leave behind the more "jazzy" style which he had admired
in the Bix Beiderbecke Wolverines and to adopt the more familiar style of
crooning found, say, in "White Christmas". In this country, such a style
enjoyed an enormous popularity throughout the thirties, largely because of
the inaccessibility of the hot records, the best of which were made by
Negroes, and were therefore often only issued in Negro areas under the
heading "Race Recordings". Also, we must not discount the weight of the
old tradition and the widespread antipathy to things American.

Symptomatic of this split between styles was the appearance of papers favouring the hot style, such as *Downbeat* magazine, in the United States, in 1934. For once, England had taken the lead, the *Melody Maker* having appeared some time earlier. This paper still tends to concentrate on jazz proper, whereas the rival *New Musical Express* deals almost exclusively with the more commercial type of music. Much more specialised, was the short-lived magazine for collectors, *Jazz Information*, which appeared in 1939 and which had a steady stream of successors, most of whom have been forced, sooner or later, to discontinue publication because of a lack of funds. It is paradoxical that the most hot, extrovert, and *physically* appealing music, should have become an interest so much confined to an intellectual minority.

The watchwords of the music of the thirties might well have been "melody" and "simplicity". While some quite complicated but beautiful melodies were being written by such composers as George Gershwin, Cole Porter, Jerome Kern and Hoagy Carmichael, the simplification went on apace of the more lively styles, for which there had always been a certain demand. It is noticeable that the Conga, which appeared in 1937, was a far less subtle dance than its Latin-American predecessor, the rhumba, of 1929.

The main product of the situation was a form of music which was much less popular here than in the United States, but which needs to be mentioned because of its later effects on British music, and was generally known as Swing music.

In the early thirties, there had evolved in Kansas City a style for "big band" (usually three trumpets, two trombones, five saxophones, piano, bass, drums and guitar), which aimed at generating a great deal of excitement by the use of loud, hard-hitting effects, a steady pushing four-in-a-bar rhythm, and by the constant repetition of simple melodic phrases (the jazz name for this is "riffing"). The most competent band of this type was the Count Basie Orchestra.

Originally designed to please migrants from the South, this music attracted the attention of various white leaders, especially Benny Goodman. The almost hypnotic effect of the music on the unsophisticated did not escape the eagle eyes of promoters looking for a style to please a new generation of teenagers, who took a fair measure of freedom as much more of a right than did their predecessors of ten years before, and who were now, in a country expanding after the Depression, beginning to have more money to spend than ever before. Goodman's agents launched a publicity campaign, which was by no means the first in this type of music, but was perhaps the first to attempt consciously to create an image of the musicians which differed from their actual life and character. The subtle and morally questionable use of information by these people has been well examined by Francis Newton in his book *The Jazz Scene*, and is interesting in the way in which it shows how a new dimension was added to the techniques of publicity. Instead of slogans which were little more than bombast (*i.e.* of the "world's greatest" type), a more subtle approach was made towards people's minds, in order to find out what they wanted, or even needed, to hear and to formulate the publicity in this manner (*i.e.* the "her best friend wouldn't tell her" approach).

Benny Goodman made his first success in 1935, and by 1938 had captivated his audiences to such an extent that he was able to hire and fill a New York cinema for his performances, at which there was screaming and jiving in the aisles by the "bobbysoxers", as they were then called. These near-riotous scenes were to become more and more a part of the American and later the British popular music scene.

The years around the outbreak of the Second World War saw the beginning of a "revival" of the style of New Orleans jazz. This had by then declined in popularity almost to the point of being a purely local music, as it was originally. Some enthusiasts, surprisingly enough usually educated whites, felt, however, that, unlike yesterday's newspaper, yesterday's jazz fashion was not the deadest of news, and that more music should be created by the original musicians, who were now middle-aged, at least, before they became too old to play and the tradition was lost. It is a tribute to the talent of these largely musically illiterate men, who had thought themselves merely to be playing dance music, that their creations were highly regarded as art all over the world by many very cultured listeners, of whom one, the Frenchman Hugues Panassié, was greatly instrumental in beginning the revival. The importance of this from our point of view is that it helped in future years to form a climate in which the jazz influence could be assimilated. It did not create a new fashion at the time: the American listener has always expected each new generation to create its own style of jazz.

Thus at the same time, a new set of young Negroes, dissatisfied with the quality and associations of the older music and with the more and more commercial nature of popular music, and being also full of a desire to express musically the pressures which forced the American Negro into the position of a second-class citizen, evolved a new style, known as bebop, which was the first form of the style now known as modern jazz. The most influential member of the movement was Charlie Parker, an alto saxophonist, who began in 1939 to produce his own musical style. The movement cannot, however, be said to be the result of one man's ideas only, and so the trumpeter "Dizzy"

Gillespie, the pianist Thelonious Monk, and the guitarist Charlie Christina can be said to have been equally important in some respects.

The influence of the bebop movement on the general public has probably been exaggerated. Except for a very short period at the end of the War it was not accepted by the majority of people, who after some fifteen years of commercial music, which had conditioned them against any degree of difficulty in techniques, found the discords and rhythmic complexities of the music quite intolerable. On the other hand its influence on technical standards was great, in that even the most commercial records thereafter expected a standard of performance which left far behind the very "church hall" amateurish efforts of the majority of pre-war non-classical musicians, and enabled the jazz performers to be united with symphonic musicians on a basis which, technically at least, could no longer be patronising. The Second World War, the greater economic difficulties and the quite considerable lag between the standards of British and American musicians meant that the bop movement had much less effect in this country until after 1945.

Though, on the one hand, the country was exposed, because of the presence of US forces and the existence of radio programmes for them, to an unprecedented amount of American musical influence, it is significant that the most popular swing bands by far were the Glenn Miller Orchestra and the US Army Air Force Band led by him, both of which had a much sweeter sound than the bands mentioned earlier. This sweet sound may be illustrated in its extreme version by the tune "Moonlight Serenade" which was symptomatic of a great need at a time of stress for a highly romantic escape, epitomised by Vera Lynn. The direct influence of the bebop movement may perhaps best be measured by the fact that the most popular number in this idiom was the best-forgotten "Cement Mixer, Putty, Putty".

The only direct influence of the pure jazz follower was to encourage the Hot Clubs which were beginning to appear at that time, to assist the formation of Revivalist Trad jazz clubs, featuring such people as George Webb and Humphrey Lyttelton, and to introduce the public to boogie-woogie. This form was to suffer the fate of most such innovations and become, in the post-war period, the standard showpiece of pianists who wished to show off a lively technique, whilst demonstrating a complete lack of artistic understanding by playing suitably watered-down pieces at too high a speed in a very mechanical player-piano style, which lost all the feeling of the original Negro idiom. Typical was the most popular pianist of the early fifties, Winifred Attwell, who featured a great deal of boogie-woogie and ragtime, both of which were mistakenly performed in the style of the latter.

The forties saw the repetition of the phenomenon of an American singer captivating a British as well as an American audience. Bing Crosby, aptly known as "The Old Groaner", had done this in the thirties, but was now challenged by Frank Sinatra. This extremely boyish-looking young man made an enormous impact, on the younger generation especially. The type of publicity machine which had guided Benny Goodman to fame had polished its techniques and was now able to push a music of far less distinction with even more success than it had ever achieved before. Sinatra was aimed especially at the heartstrings and purses of young girls; he sang love ballads, mournfully, in return for the cash which these girls were earning, in un-dreamed-of amounts, in the war industries. His début was surrounded with ballyhoo: girls screamed (sometimes they were paid to), fainted (usually they were paid to), and in the mass hysteria which followed, attacked their idol in a mad scramble for the modern equivalent of a medieval relic.

The most interesting part of this phenomenon is the high degree of Americanisation which had taken place. English singers were forced from this time on to adopt an accent for singing and announcing which is known in the trade as "mid-transatlantic". At the same time, the need for a micro-phone was now unquestioned, as was the need to be "modern" and "different".

A disturbing result was that the young person was becoming daily less familiar with the old traditions, and more imbued with the new ones. Thus, after the War the violin had disappeared almost entirely from the dance band, and the louder saxophone/brass combination had taken its place. Similarly a new sphere of modern dancing was becoming clearly delineated. Despite the addition of the Samba in 1946, it was true to say that the average pattern of a "modern" dance was entirely covered by what is now known as ballroom dancing, that is, a combination of slow waltzes, quicksteps, fox-trots, with the odd Latin-American number for good measure. The dances of the pre-Great War period, and those of the twenties were almost equally dead, as was their music.

The eight or nine years following the Second World War continued in the same fashion. American singers, such as Guy Mitchell and Frankie Laine, sang or crooned their way to fame, and nowadays give us the impression of fresh young men in a nation victorious in war and prosperous in peace. Their styles of dress (the drape) and haircutting (the crew cut and the DA) were slavishly imitated by the youth of a Britain which had grown up in a period of stress, followed by a time of austerity, and saw in the American way of life a prosperity they longed for, and a manner full of confidence and free from inhibition, which contrasted with the traditional picture of the Englishman, a picture which was at that time largely discredited, if only because of its association with the failures and troubles of the past.

Musically speaking, it is of great interest that improved recording techniques and a far higher standard of technical and reading ability on the part of the "jazzers" enabled the recording studios to produce records with a "big" sound, using part or all of a symphony orchestra for effect. Thus public attention was directed, if only in a superficial manner, to a means of musical expression which had been neglected since the first startling popularity of the five-piece Original Dixieland Jazz Band. This situation continued, with its emphasis on sentimental songs, until 1954. In that year, the "Television Age" proper may be said to have begun, since the ITV programmes were added to an already rapidly expanding BBC service.

In the same year, two important events happened in the United States popular music world. The first was that a man called Bill Haley launched a group (the Comets) playing a crude form of the "Rhythm and Blues" style popular in Negro halls. The second was that an unknown lorry driver from Mississippi called Elvis Presley made some recordings in a similar style.

At first, these events went unnoticed, but after Haley had appeared in a singularly bad film called *Rock Around the Clock*, and had played the background music to a much better film called *The Blackboard Jungle* the promoters "discovered" a "new" style which they christened "Rock and Roll".

The effect of this was firstly, in the United States to give a nationwide popularity to a hitherto localised or even racial music, and secondly to give to Britain, and soon after to Europe, something little less than a teenage cult, the belief in which was encouraged by the horror of the older generation at various of its manifestations. The portrayal of the highly rebellious and anti-social spirit to be found in certain parts of the American education system, the association with speed, with a new style of dress, longer hair and riotous behaviour at concerts resulted in a classic example of how a suitable image, coupled with press coverage which, whatever its intention, only aggravated the tendencies, can produce a whole way of thought in millions of people. Actually, the success of the publicity is hardly to be wondered at if we examine its timing. The ever-present desire of youth to be different from its parents was added to an extreme suitability of moment. The young person in Britain was in full employment and likely to remain so; he was earning an unheard-of amount of money in both nominal and real terms; he was not linked to his parents by the common experience of unemployment and war. In fact, anyone born after 1934 outside of the most heavily bombed cities was unlikely to remember much of the War, unless they had undergone some very personal and violent experience. Significantly, Elvis Presley was born in 1935.

From this point on, the popular music business has gone from strength to strength; record sales have risen and TV appearances of groups have increased in frequency. The nature of radio programmes has changed markedly. The Light Programme has become much nearer in conception to Radio Luxembourg, which in turn imitates American commercial stations. The proportion of time given to popular music has risen, and various styles of popular music are played until 2 a.m. Commercial "pirate" stations also added an influence. It should be mentioned in connection with these, that though they have rightly been condemned for their abuse of the laws of copyright, their claims of superiority of programme in this field are largely justified. Not only does their choice of popular music keep that vigour, or even crudeness which is far preferable in this type of music to the politeness which the BBC's insistence on professionalism tends to infuse, but also the range of music tends to be wider, as on many Continental stations, and will include some jazz, and popular music outside the current teenage idiom (e.g. the songs of Frank Sinatra). Nevertheless, they help to create the satiation which results in a constant desire for novelty.[1]

The amount of money to be earned has risen to astronomical proportions, in that the Beatles in their first United States tour grossed $19,000,000 (official figures of the *American Journal of Commerce*), and the total takings of pop groups since that time have been about £12,000,000 from records and appearances. When one considers that car exports from Britain to the US brought in about £37,500,000 in the same period, we can see that the name "popular music industry" is far from inappropriate. The economic value to the country has been much discussed, and approved by the highest quarters: the controversial award of the MBE to the Beatles was justified by a Labour spokesman with the reminder that "we should only need 100 Beatles" to restore our balance of payments. There has been a definite tendency to allow this type of excitement to affect critical judgements, however, and some remarkable statements have been made. It is heartening to find that there is as yet no sign that Duke Ellington has wept in rhapsodic delight over "Twist and Shout".

The concluding years of this brief history show factors of far more interest

[1] It should be noted that since the time of writing the BBC have introduced their new format, with Radio One concentrating on popular music. This has remedied somewhat the situation noted mentioned above, but significantly, in a direction towards that of "pirate" programmes.

That Old-fashioned Mother of Mine. Etching by Sickert, 1928
A favourite of the Music Halls

Ball-room scene of the 19

to the musician than the merely financial ones. As was to be expected, the Rock and Roll craze resulted in a host of would-be Presleys in this country: typical was Tommy Steele, who has now become an entertainer, having found music too constricting a form for his talents. Such singers at first clearly owed allegiance to America, and imitated blindly (or should one say deafly), as they had done in previous decades. But at an early stage more definitely "British" products arose; the Shadows, for instance, managed to produce a softened form of beat music, which as a functional music made no worse an accompaniment to dancing than Mantovani or Joe Loss. The new sound of the Beatles and the Merseyside groups has been much commented upon in a most authoritative manner by many who are quite unqualified to do so, lacking, as they do it would seem, both experience and ears: it will be discussed in Chapter 10. For a period the "wilder" style of Bill Haley predominated, but the public soon returned to the type of thing that was sweeter on the ear, such as the songs of Adam Faith (behind whom violins were first used in this country for a "beaty" effect).

In the latter years of the fifties a wilder style returned, in the form of Traditional Jazz. In the early sixties this was followed by Rhythm and Blues, and later by Soul Music. Though in the last ten years the public seems to have maintained a more continuous interest in heat and beat, there nevertheless appears to be a cycle, alternating between wild and smooth music, presumably due to a public inability to sustain interest in anything for long. The two types are, of course, always present, but the proportions vary widely in the general direction, though not to the extent, indicated by the publicity.

The quality of popular lyrics also rose in the sixties, largely because of the influence of folk music; interest in all forms of this has been very great. Of considerable influence is the fact that when Bob Dylan left his folk style in favour of rock, he did not alter the quality of his lyric writing, as might have been expected. Instead he used a very popular idiom to communicate ideas beyond the wildest conceptions of earlier lyric writers.

A further development in the sixties was a series of interesting attempts at linking popular music with forms hitherto untouched by it, notably the use of the Indian sitar, of classical instrumentation, and of jazz. From these a new style has arisen, usually called "progressive pop", which is of such musicality that it has been heralded by some critics as a new form of art music. But it is true to say that despite its great virtues and considerable popularity, it is still far from being a mass music. Recent fashions, such as Ska and the Reggae, suggest rather that mass music is already returning to a period of greater rhythmic and melodic simplicity.

We now reach the present day, after an examination of nearly 1,700 years of music. The last chapter has been brief, possibly too much so, since there is enough material in the twentieth century to provide the themes of several books. What I have tried to do is to refresh the reader about the events of the past six decades, and perhaps to fill in the odd gap. Unfortunately, there is no authoritative and readable history which I can refer the reader to if he wants more information: this is not true of pure jazz, about which there are several good and reliable works. Here is a task for someone with more patience and love of detail than I have.

In my discussion I have avoided far more points than I have made. I have not, for instance, mentioned the quite remarkable popularity of Billy Cotton, whose music was undoubtedly popular and yet was the very antithesis of that of Frankie Laine or Elvis Presley. Nevertheless, I feel that my generalisations are fairly correct in that they sum up the main features of the period, and were probably numerically the most popularly followed. Billy Cotton was largely the manifestation of the interests of an older generation, less inclined to spend on records, and, of course, becoming a steadily smaller minority of the listening and paying public.

I am aware, too, that I have omitted to deal with the many nine-day wonders of the popular music world: the nonsense songs, the songs for special occasions, and so forth. Where relevant, I hope to discuss this at length later (Chapter 14). This also applies to many of the tendentious statements, especially the technical ones, which I have been obliged to make and leave for fear of digressing.

8 The Techniques of Twentieth-Century Popular Music

The percussion and the bass ... function as a
central heating system.
IGOR STRAVINSKY

I now propose to come to a brief examination of the technical characteristics of popular music, but before doing so it is necessary to clarify my position and fundamental tenets.

The first of these is that I accept the premise that the Classical tradition has provided a set of analytical techniques which, by and large, may be satisfactorily applied to any music of Western European origin or inspiration, and that proper application of these is, therefore, likely to provide answers about, or at least workable lines of approach to, a type of music over which much critical ink has been spilled. The reason for violent controversies and misunderstandings between the adherents of this and other types of music has, as I see it, been largely due to an incorrect, non-standard critical approach and to the faulty usage of language and technical terms, which have been understood differently by different people. It is, of course, true to say that, as in any sphere of art, there has also been confusion because of the claims (usually unsubstantiated) of extremists. Two or three examples will perhaps help clarify the above statements and the fundamental problems which underlie them and which have bedevilled the serious discussion of this music for many years.

An example of pure inaccuracy is to be found in the notation of the rhythm ♪, which was in earlier times miswritten as ♩♩. Though most musicians of all types are now aware of the historical nature of the mistake, and accept the difference as one of convention, such problems have not helped to bring about mutual respect.

A more serious example of the misapplication of standard technical vocabulary is seen in the statement by Benny Green, in his book *The Reluctant*

Art, that Charlie Parker "made the giant step from diatonic to chromatic harmony". To any Classical musician unfamiliar with jazz this would mean a change from harmonies formed only from the notes of the scale of a given key (diatonic) to harmonies using notes alien to this scale (*e.g.* the use of the major chord with added seventh built on the supertonic). This would be highly confusing to him, since jazz and popular music have used such harmonies from the beginnings. What Mr Green wished to say was that Parker made into an essential part of his harmonic language the higher discords built on dominant or minor seventh chords, the fundamental discords, such as the augmented chord, the various sixth chords (French, German and Neapolitan) and, most important of all, the phenomenon often known as "chromatic slide", *i.e.* the movement in semitones (usually descending) of the roots of chords which may, in themselves, be comparatively consonant.

The worst kind of statement, because it is merely one of an opinion which is not even based on the available evidence, is one such as the following, made by Douglas Hague in the collection of essays *Concerning Jazz*, edited by Sinclair Traill:

> Not only is jazz art, but it is also the only true modern music . . . There has been little change in the basic harmonies or theory of classical music; nor have any improvements been made on the trends of "Les Six", hence in all music jazz is the only new art contribution to the world.

It will be noticed that the comments made above tend to refer to jazz, and it may justifiably be asked whether this is really relevant to popular music. I feel that it is, for several reasons. Not only has "jazz proper" been popular at times, but it has also been a continuous influence on the creators of popular music. Most important, it is, as I see it, historically and musically demonstrable that jazz and popular music (of the sort that we saw in the last chapter to have risen to a position of supremacy over the traditional styles) are of the same stock. However much the purists of the jazz world may dislike the fact, the greatest separation which they can reasonably make is that popular music is an illegitimate offspring of the same family, that Glenn Miller and Count Basie may be different in quality but not in genus. They are clearly allied in a way that neither is, say, to Mozart or Stockhausen. Thus they can often, not always, be analysed in the same terms, and in fact popular music may frequently be said to be no more than a cruder version of jazz.

Finally it is to be hoped that it is unnecessary to say that this technical analysis is intended as an aid to understanding certain problems of an aesthetic nature, which have to be faced by the person seriously interested in art and which would be difficult or impossible to explain in any other way. It is not intended to suggest that praise on technical grounds, where it is found, necessarily carries with it any implication of an artistic commendation. Clearly, the quality of the music can only depend on other factors and on the composer's powers of conceiving and shaping his material in a way that, though analysable finally, after the act of creation, is perhaps rarely thought of in any very worked-out fashion during creation. Otherwise one is in a position in which one comes to the conclusion that a D.Mus. exercise is of necessity better than the efforts of many well-known composers merely because of a greater and more easily analysed technical facility.

The first element we need to consider is that of rhythm, and in order to do this we need to define what it is that we are describing when we use the word. In the first instance, we are talking about metre, that is the basic pulse pattern which underlies the music, and which literally keeps the various parts together. This in turn is, I believe, too simple an analysis, in that the basic pulse, describable by, say, a 4/4 or 2/2 time signature, is divisible into at least two parts. One of these we could conveniently describe by using the old word "tactus" to mean a counting of beats, as it was used in pre-seventeenth-century polyphony, but including for our purpose a further element, namely the division of this basic pulse into small groups, with a slight stress on the first of the group.

The other part of the rhythm may be termed the "subsidiary components", which distinguished the metre in the sense in which it is interpreted in standard works from the metronomic tactus and gives such a metre its particular form of "lift" and sense of progression. As an example I will continue the analysis of a 4/4 rhythm, because this has become more and more the rhythmic base of popular music in recent years. Continuing our line of thought we find that we can divide the 4/4 rhythm into its tactus component (a slightly strong 1 and 2, 3 and 4), and its "subsidiary component" of a strong 1 and 3 and weak 2 and 4. This might even be regarded as two bars of 2/4 metre superimposed onto one of 4/4. These combined produce four beats of which two are strong and two weak, but which all have different intensities—from strongest to weakest, 1, 3, 2, 4.

Diagram I overleaf will clarify this idea.

It may be suggested that such an elaborate exposition is not necessary in that the feeling of progression produced by this combination of strong and weak beats is easily understood and has been satisfactorily analysed. I would agree that this is true of Classical music and Classically-influenced popular music, but I feel that the component analysis method is both likely to be more effective, and in fact does give a more satisfactory explanation of the peculiar lift of the metres of jazz. These are in a 4/4 metre, it is true, and utilise the same system of notation as the Classical works, and are able to be so because all the relevant additions which are needed to turn a Classical into a jazz 4/4 are matters of the type of convention which any music has. Except for a stranger, it would be superfluous to notate them, even if a satisfactorily simple and manageable form of doing so could be evolved. It should be stressed at this point that I am not here trying to demonstrate some kind of superiority (whatever that might mean in this connection) for jazz because it has these "mysterious" and unwritten conventions. They are present in all music, and only become noticable when a stranger or an incompetent enters the picture: a good example of this is to be seen in the experience of Western conductors with Japanese symphony orchestras. I am told that these orchestras have a high degree of technical competence, but will often make mistakes of interpretation that few European amateurs would make, because they have not grown up in a circle which has permitted them to assimilate the unwritten conventions subconsciously.

	1	2	3	4
Tactus	x	x	x	x
1st component 2/4	x		x	
Extra stress making the basic group 1 × 4/4 instead of 2 × 2/4		x		
"Units" of stress	3	1	2	1

Note. Such a diagram does not show that in practice the stresses on 2 and 4 differ in intensity.

Diagram I

In the foregoing sentences, it will be clear that I have made an assumption that not everyone would be prepared to concede, *i.e.* that the metres of jazz are more complex than those of Classical music, at least in certain ways. If this point is not accepted, I am only able to advocate a fair amount of sympathetic listening, since the only evidence for my statement is in actual performances, there being, as I have just stated, no signs of this in jazz scores, where these exist at all.

However, assuming acceptance of this, we find that the word "rhythm" hides by its very vagueness several further facets of the essential metre which are nonetheless audible.

The first of these is most frequently described by jazz followers as "swing" and is a peculiar phenomenon which has a very lifting effect musically and an almost hypnoidal one mentally. The Count Basie Orchestra, for instance, is often said to produce a "rocking beat", which is a fairly accurate way of describing the simple but effective procedure of keeping the strong pulses, but also of setting up rhythmic counterbalances by the simple mechanism of accenting the off beat more strongly than usual. The word "syncopation" would not really be satisfactory, since it only describes a *momentary* disturbance of accent, whereas the use of the accented off beat in this type of music is so universal as to be a part of the basic structure of the pulse. Certainly the players feel it not to be a piece of exoticism but something quite fundamental, a prerequisite for the addition of a satisfactory personal creative effort.

The mechanism of the "rocking beat" (drummer's function)

	1	2	3	4
Top cymbal:	X (taking main stress)	x	X (taking secondary stress)	x
Hi-hat cymbal:		x (throw accent onto off beat . . .)		x

Diagram II

In practice, the rhythm is divided between the bass and the cymbals; the bass playing the pattern of Diagram I, and the cymbals playing the pattern of Diagram II.

In addition to this, this word "rhythm" incorporates the idea of strict regularity of tempo, *i.e.* that the time elapsing between one beat and the next is always exactly the same. This is no new feature of popular dance music; indeed it is an obvious necessity if the dance is not to degenerate into chaos. But I believe that it can be validly argued that the metronomic pulse has never before been observed with quite such rigidity, nor has the basic pulse been so carefully sought out and executed as an end in itself.

Initially, this springs from a difference of cultural concept, in that in Western European dance music the function of the pulse has always been only as a metronomic device to keep the dancers together, so that they might concentrate on the interpretation of the music, and the general sense of the words, if any, by previously planned steps, which in earlier music had a definite ritual element in them. Thus the country dance, with all its intricacies, was both symptomatic and symbolic of an equally complex pattern of social conduct derived from antiquity. All this necessitated a simple, easily followed, fairly regular basic pulse. This was not so of song or of any other type of music (e.g. for a church service).

In contrast, the aim of jazz players is, in one sense, to incite. The reason for this is historical, in that the best jazz is still largely a Negro product and contains a great deal of the Negro tradition, even where this is not consciously followed out. Now, the aim of African traditional music is to rouse the individual to a physical demonstration of his emotional responses at communal ritual gatherings. Africans, at least in their tribes, find the most satisfactory expression of such fundamental conceptions in physical release and especially in dancing. This is even true of times of sorrow. The South African musicologist, Hugh Tracey, mentions the comment of a Chopi musician—"We dance out our grief." Such dancing is a mixture of ritual patterns and improvised, very personal expression, which is often of great subtlety and dexterity. To achieve this, a subtler, more physically exciting basic pulse was evolved, which has been taken over in a somewhat changed form by the American Negro. This type of music, unlike that of the European dance, was used for all forms of musical creation.

The American jazz historian, Professor Marshall Stearns, has used the term "metronome sense" for the feeling for subtlety of this kind which has developed to a high degree in many Negroes, but it is necessary to reiterate his point that such abilities are not inborn, but acquired by living in a suitable environment.

The subtlety mentioned above is due to the extreme regularity of the basic pulse which also produces several other phenomena not found in a "free" metrical approach to music. The most obvious is repetition. By definition, the pulse is repeated at regular intervals, as are the superimposed components we have already mentioned. On the other hand, it is the very complexity of the components which gives the music just sufficient variety to make it exciting, rather than infuriating in the way that a dripping tap is. The fineness of the balance between repetition and variation is a fundamental factor in deciding the relative qualities of pieces within this idiom. For instance, such a difference goes a long way towards explaining the superiority of Count Basie over Victor Sylvester. The one achieves the peculiar effect of swing mentioned above, whereas the other produces a more sophisticated version of the dripping tap, owing to a cruder, less sympathetic handling of the basic pulse. The world-acclaimed "strict tempo", stripped of its brain-washing publicity, reveals itself as no more than the regularity which has been required in social dancing in Europe since the earliest times.

We have so far seen that the jazz rhythm contains several elements: the tactus or metrical count, the superimposed secondary stresses, strict tempo, repetition and swing. The latter is possibly due to a complexity of the basic pulse which can only be considered in a larger context than the single bar unit. Careful study of the music will reveal points of climax, which are evenly spaced, and which suggest analysis into further rhythmic components, which are separated by greater intervals of time than the secondary accents which occur in every bar. These give a sense of progression over a period of several bars (at least four, and perhaps several times this number). These numbers are nearly always even, unlike Eastern European folk dances, and the "irregu-larities" found frequently in Western European song. This fact has caused M. André Hodeir, the French critic, to use the word *carré* to suggest this concept of "squareness" in jazz.

To this is allied the fact that jazz pieces are almost invariably composed of multiples of four bars. Such repetition of the four-bar pulse patterns gives a definite feeling of expectation, which can be cultivated to a fine degree if one listens to the music fairly frequently. The mind gears itself to the regular climaxes, and so gains access to a most exciting aspect of jazz, the production of interest and excitement by breaking the expected pattern in some rhyth-mically acceptable way. The most frequently used method of doing this is the "break" or point at which the pulse is counted, but not played for a period (usually two bars) before the beginning of another rhythmic cycle. On paper a lifeless thing, it is, heard sympathetically, a most exciting musical experi-ence, peculiar to jazz, as the Classical composer denies himself the possibility in order to give himself freedom with the basic metre, tempo and length of musical period (see Diagram III overleaf).

Again, this discounts the fact that the 2nd and 4th beats differ in intensity, as do the 1st beats of the 2nd and 4th bars.

Theoretically, this process could be repeated over the period of a whole "chorus" (the standard jazz unit of composition), *i.e.* a further unit of stress would be found on the 1st beat of every eight bars, another on the 1st of every 16, and another on the 1st of every 32. In practice, the possibilities are likely to be much more limited than this, because of the difficulty of playing and hearing such fine distinctions of accent. The *carré* effect, which is undoubtedly felt, is most likely caused by the climaxes in harmonic move-ment.

Accents over a four-bar period

	1				2				3				4			
	1	2	3	4	1	2	3	4	1	2	3	4	1	2	3	4
Tactus	x	x	x	x	x	x	x	x	x	x	x	x	x	x	x	x
2/4 component	x		x		x		x		x		x		x		x	
4/4 component	x				x				x				x			
1st stress of two-bar unit	x								x							
1st stress of four-bar unit	x															
"Units" of stress	5	1	2	1	3	1	2	1	4	1	2	1	3	1	2	1

i.e. Relative intensities of 1st beats of bars = 5 : 3 : 4 : 3.

Diagram III

It will be noted that I have not so far used the term "syncopation" which I take to be a rhythmic discord or breaking of accent within the basic unit of one or two bars. Furthermore, syncopation is a melodic component, and not a purely rhythmic one, a point which brings to our notice the fact that the foregoing argument has been concerned only with the basic pulse of the music and that no mention has been made so far of the melodies which go over this pulse. It is to these that we now turn.

Wilfrid Mellers, in his book *Music and Society*, speaks of American music as indulging in the exploitation of a " 'harmony of rhythm', an interwoven texture of different rhythms which proceeding together make up a whole in the same way as different tones combine together to make a chord". Though written about American "serious" music, no better explanation can be found of the fundamental aim of jazz players. The melodic strands are more elaborate lines which combine with the pulse to give a "harmony of rhythm".

This is achieved in several ways. The first, well known in Classical works, is the changing of the metre of the melody while the pulse remains constant. The most common example of this is probably "double time", *i.e.* the melody moves at twice the speed of the pulse, but in more recent years, especially where the Negro element is stronger, there has been a frequent use of triple time in such a complex fashion that it must be viewed as something more than a mere "three against two" triplet. In slower music, a triplet component undoubtedly needs to be added, thus creating a form of 12/8 metre.

A second feature of melodic strands is the use of phrases which cross the normal accents of the pulse in that the strongest point will fall on a weaker pulse, or more frequently between two pulses. Known as syncopation and found in most music of value, the jerkiness of this feature of jazz melody appealed very much to some serious composers in the first quarter of this century, when they were seeking to escape from the traditional, mainly on-beat rhythm of the great masters. These exotic rhythms were found to lose their appeal and effect very quickly, in the way that a complex verse metre does, and were, therefore, not pursued as a line of experiment for very long. The fact that jazz has continued to use them has, in fact, been cited against it by some critics.

Such an argument falls down, however, because it fails to understand the position of such cross-rhythms in jazz. These cannot be regarded as mechanical or unnecessarily intricate, simply because they are not an assumed feature of the music. They are not a piece of exoticism which can be taken up, grafted onto the music and laid aside at will, for the simple reason that they are a fundamental and integral part of the jazz player's musical language. His concept of music is as intimately connected with and thought out in terms of continuous cross-rhythm as was that of Bach. The comparison is more than superficial: both types of music are a special form of polyphony in which superimposed rhythms are set against a simple basic pattern and need to resolve on it. The type of approach which condemns jazz for being "all in 4/4" may as well condemn Bach for the same kind of reason; the simple framework is a necessary foil, since one cannot have crossing of the beat without a beat. The composers of the sixteenth and twentieth centuries are concerned with a different kind of polyphony, in which irregularity may follow upon irregularity without any need for these to be contained within simple and prescribed limits. A similar comparison might well be made between the later poetry of Shakespeare (virtually always in a set framework) and the work of Eliot (using a free number of accents whenever required).

Jazz syncopation contains a further element which means that two phrases of approximately the same syncopated rhythm, and notationally the same, are made different and, therefore, acceptable by continuous slight variations of accent within the phrase. This is quite alien to the symphonic approach— it would be difficult to achieve this with two, let alone seventy people—which seeks an evenness of accent and tone production which is alien to jazz, in which the flow is constantly punctuated and broken up by these slight accents. As in classical music, such accents may be stressed or may result from the utilisation of suitably placed high notes which automatically attract attention, as illustrated in the following bass line:

Ex. 21

Clearly, there are at least five basic parts of the music in which variation of accent can be found: breaking the expectation of the metronomic pulse, of its additional components, variation of metre, syncopation, and accent within the melody. These produce a counterpoint of rhythm, continually clashing, yet moving towards and aiming at points of mutual accent and temporary "harmony of rhythm".

It may well be argued that the above comments complicate or even fly in the face of the type of rhythmic nomenclature hitherto used in Classical music. The reply must be not unlike that of the scientist who, when told that he is rejecting Newton, replies that the accusation is incorrect, since Newton's ideas are still valid, but not for all situations, *i.e.* his work really deals with special cases of a particular type of phenomenon. Similarly, the music which we always consider the greatest has, in order to achieve this greatness, and also for historical reasons, limited its materials in certain ways; these can be described in quite simple terms for all practical purposes. The newer type of analysis does not invalidate such conclusions; it merely re-phrases them, possibly in a more complex manner. But when we come to deal with other types of musical phenomenon, traditional ideas can help us very little. We need, for instance, to consider as metrical components factors which would only be seen in classical terms as ostinati, or as sequential use of ideas: any factor which is *constant* in its appearance must be regarded as helping to create an individual metre, and automatically imposes limitations on what may be superimposed; consider how unsuitable Viennese waltz rhythms would be over a Spanish bolero basis, even if all other typically Spanish elements had been eliminated. A parallel from poetry would be a form, such as the limerick, in which not only the number of lines and feet, but also the rhythmic pattern, and hence the verbal possibilities, are laid down (this is not to suggest that a fixed rhythm is incapable of serious use). This type of analysis is indispensable in discussing certain types of African music. Hugh Tracey has recorded various tribes whose music can be counted out in simple metrical groupings, but in which the musicians consider some particular pattern to be the metre. This directly affects the way in which the music is enjoyed and evaluated, since artistic skill is shown in the use of variation upon this pattern and in the playing of it with combinations of drums producing different tone colours. Another type of folk music in which traditional thought can lead us astray is our own folk music when it uses irregular groups, such as 5/4. This does not occur because the composer set out to write in an unusual metre, but because the melody line follows the lyric, without any relevance to an underlying fixed basis: words spoken or sung freely, without regard to regular counting, will obviously produce very complex rhythms indeed.

After such a lengthy exposition of the qualities of jazz rhythm, it may reasonably be asked what this has to do with popular music, since the previous chapter informed the reader that from about 1930 onwards jazz was a minority pursuit.

To answer this it is necessary to reiterate that popular music has become in the twentieth century less and less European (i.e. using the traditional rhythmic concepts, as in the waltz) and more American in nature. Furthermore, this American music, though lacking the subtlety of jazz, and crude at times to a point at which it could hardly lay claim to any of the merits of jazz, has nevertheless tended, generally speaking, to a more jazz-aligned style of performance. Of late, the process seems to have speeded up to a point where a jazz critic of the stature of Nat Hentoff (not a man to give praise readily to commercial music) feels that the records of the Rolling Stones are comparable to and nearly indistinguishable in subtlety from those of Negro rhythm and blues players. Though, having heard the Rolling Stones in the flesh, a pleasure so far I believe denied to Mr Hentoff, I am inclined to doubt this, the fact that the possibility can even be seriously discussed is significant. It would not have happened ten years ago.

The results of this influence so far have frequently been of appallingly bad quality, but the implications of it are nonetheless far-reaching. It suggests that the "metronome sense" of non-American players and of non-Negro players is rapidly becoming more acute, and that perhaps the popular musician is becoming so immersed in the idiom that instead of imitating it, he thinks in it. In other words, the whole musical approach is altering, for the first time, not only to that of a different country, but to that of a radically different culture. The effects of this are inestimable, both in the extent to which it will further the understanding of that culture, and to which (ominously) it will lessen the understanding of traditional culture.

A few examples will help to show the increasing subtlety towards which popular music is tending, and also some of its deficiencies.

The basic metre of even ten years ago was often very little more than the Victor Sylvester type of 2/2 time, with strong off beat. Nowadays much popular music is conceived of as being in 12/8 time (*i.e.* a compound of 4 and 3 beat metres) or in 8/8. Even casual listening to the 8-in-a-bar rhythm of many popular records will convince the listener that the 8 beats are an organic part of the metre, and not mere quaver ornamentation. Another rhythm which has become widely used, and reappears in some subtly transmuted forms, is the 3-3-2 division of 8 quavers, *e.g.*

Ex. 22

(basically the same as the old Charleston and Rhumba rhythms).

Even the simplest forms of beat are now being treated with greater subtlety. For example, a common feature of the present-day style is to use only four beats in a bar, or a heavy off beat. The off beat effect employed by Bill Haley would have been of little credit to a self-respecting steam engine, and the four in a bar of Dave Clark's "Bits and Pieces" was reasonably crude. Yet these effects have been used with great success by certain jazz drummers, notably Art Blakey; as we have seen the off beat in jazz is an organic part of the metre. What then is the difference? The answer lies in the *exact placing* of these accents. The jazz drummer has realised that monotony can be avoided, and a sense of drive added if he anticipates the "tactus" or basic count. Two musicians often combine to obtain this effect. Thus Ed Thigpen, of the Oscar Peterson Trio, will sound the main beat, and keep the tempo constant, whilst the bass player Ray Brown will "race" him, and give the impression that the music is speeding up. The effect needs to be heard, but may be notated approximately as shown in Example 23. To the listener not accustomed to this type of music the effect may not, at first, be fully obvious (though I believe the intense excitement and drive will be felt at once), but any jazz musician or listener will attest its existence. Recent popular records are showing awareness of this effect. We see that with popular music (as with any other), one criterion of excellence is subtlety in handling materials.

Ex. 23

(a) hi-hat anticipates beat

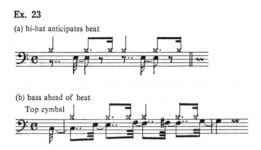

(b) bass ahead of beat
Top cymbal

A typical fault of the popular musician is a failure to appreciate the limitations of a given technique because of some immediate attractiveness. Of such a type is the 8/8 rhythm mentioned earlier, in the forms in which it was first used.

Ex. 24

8/8 beat

The effect of this is to smooth out or even conflict with the sinuous motion of the original metre, and to emphasise the off beats. But nothing further is added. The extra notes do not lead us on, as in the jazz cymbal rhythm:

Ex. 25

Jazz cymbal rhythm (as written)

The off-beat accents add nothing to what is already there. The quavers add a rather jittery or chugging effect to the basic pulse (though it must be admitted that above a tempo of about MM 130 this rhythm can create a certain type of relentless drive).

The busy nature of the rhythm also tends to restrict the range of possible melodic figuration: too many quavers become monotonous, semiquaver movement is too brisk, and crotchets or longer time values move too slowly to be sustained for long. It is significant that the nearest jazz equivalent, boogie-woogie, had only a limited influence, despite its great popularity in the late thirties and early forties. The players also preferred a "dotted boogie" (so called because of its appearance in notation) to a "straight eight".

Ex. 26
(a) "straight boogie"

(b) "dotted boogie" - as written

(c) "dotted boogie" - as played

In the dotted form, the metre takes on a triple component, making it a form of 12/8: this clearly offers greater possibilities. Recently, however, beat musicians have developed new possibilities of the 8/8 metre. Inspired by Soul music they have reduced the tempo, thus making the eight component slow enough to be considered as a superimposed double tempo beat. Its relation to the basic pulse is reinforced by stressing the 3rd and 7th quavers, since these coincide with beats 2 and 4 of the pulse. At the same time the 8/8 beat is used as a starting point for characteristic syncopations, even in the bass part. We thus have three layers of rhythm. This is an expression of the beat as complex and jumping as much of jazz, and is symptomatic of the rapid advancement of popular music in the past few years. Certainly this Soul/Tamla inspired form of music is the most complex, sophisticated and pulsating rhythmic experience ever to be widely popular in this country; musicians can undoubtedly feel that British popular music has at last grown up.

A direct result of the emphasis on rhythm, in all the senses mentioned above, has been the introduction of percussion instruments to a degree unprecedented in previous European music. Furthermore, not only their number, but their function has altered. We are all familiar with the use of percussion as colouring instruments—even down to the use of the anvil and the whip—in serious music, but the percussion has rarely played an integral part in marshalling the metre and even in creating it, outside of the military band.

As far as can be seen, such uses of it as there were in earlier times, *e.g.* in pipe and tabor music, is likely to have been very primitive in nature.

In contrast to this, African music is predominantly a music of percussion instruments, especially of drums, with the result that the Negro has developed a feeling for the subtlety of effect obtainable even from a piece of stick or bone (*viz.* Brazilian instruments) which has in Europe reached only an embryonic stage, at best. Such composers as Bartók have reached out towards this, but have not found this side of music of more than passing interest in their attempts to extend the range of acceptable instrumental and orchestrational techniques. There have also been considerable problems of notation, and of the interpretation of what has been written, for under the generic term of, say, cymbal, there is as much variety as under the term violin.

Though not, as yet, equalling the complexities of African music, jazz has taken over at least some of its approaches, and no jazz (or popular) drummer would now consider his equipment adequate unless he had at least a bass drum, side drum, tomtom, two cymbals, and a hi-hat (pair of cymbals clashed together by the operation of a foot pedal), as well as a pair of sticks, a pair of wire brushes, and a pair of tomtom sticks. With this expansion of percussion has gone a rapid development of technique, to a point where the "one man—one note" approach of the Classical orchestra now seems ludicrous to jazz drummers. A very advanced technique has been evolved, not only for the playing of single rhythmic lines, but also of independent lines (most commonly two in popular music and three in jazz), played by one man's hands and feet, in much the same way as an organist.

Moreover, the presence of percussion has influenced all the instruments to incorporate something of the percussionist's concept of music into their own technique. It has become essential for instruments to emphasise their percussive aspects. Instruments which are by nature difficult to play in this way (such as the clarinet) have dropped largely out of favour. The strident nature of the sound produced by many jazz or popular music ensembles, often commented upon by people who prefer a smoother tone, is in no small measure due to a forceful production of sound, or "attack", which results in heavy accents and the predominance of the harsher overtones. Typical of the process and very much favoured by popular groups at present are the recent developments in guitar structure and technique. The Spanish guitar proper, with its gut or nylon strings, played by the fingers and thumb, gives, even at its most harsh, a tone which always has a slightly rounded or even dull edge to it. It was found that a much more incisive and percussive sound could be obtained by using steel strings, and that these effects could be heightened by using a tortoiseshell or plastic plectrum (or pick). The popular world has found in recent years that the requisite amount of tension and forcefulness can only be obtained by playing near to the bridge, which cuts out the lower overtones to a large extent, thus giving a more "treble" sound, and it also acts on the vibrations of the strings in such a way as to strengthen the effect of the more discordant overtones.

It will thus be seen that one fundamental change of conception causes a chain of other effects. We are now considering not rhythm but tone, or the nature of sound, even when produced by a front-line instrument. Other important differences are also to be found because there are further forces acting upon the popular musician which tend to drive him further from the traditional approach.

If we are fully to understand these it is necessary once again to go back to Africa. There we find that there are many quite basic differences between West African and European languages. In the latter, though a rise and fall of voice is an important part of language, it is rare that it is of great importance in the communication of meaning. It is certainly almost never indispensable. In contrast to this many African languages (such as the Nigerian language, Ibo) become meaningless unless the correct pitch is used: the vowels and consonants themselves are not enough. This phenomenon is known to linguists as a "tone language", and has a direct influence on music in that an indistinctly heard sentence can often be reconstructed into a sensible pattern, provided that the pitch changes are clearly heard: the clarity of vowels and consonants are in such cases of small importance. Thus any mechanism for producing the right pitch changes can be made to "talk": hence the "talking drums" of Africa.

As far as I know, little of this survived the enforced move from Africa to America, where the use of English became vital; the aim has only been to show the intimate connection between language and music in Africa, and so to lead to another point arising directly from this.

It is clear that if meaning is so closely dependent on pitch of voice, then many of the means of expression of emotion in speech which are used by Europeans are not available. To circumvent this problem the African has evolved a whole series of expressive techniques based on the alteration of the timbre or quality of tone of the voice. This has directly affected Negro music, both African and American.

To describe these effects in the space we have available would be impossible, and the only and best way to understand what it sounds like is to listen to the records of celebrated Negro singers, such as Bessie Smith, Mahalia Jackson, Muddy Waters, Ray Charles and Jimmy Witherspoon. I am aware that there are important differences between the approaches of these people and that "purists" may well suffer an almost apoplectic fit of rage on reading the above list, but such readers must bear in mind that it is meant for a reader uncertain of the true Negro style (as distinct from the highly Europeanised "spiritual" style), and not for those who have an already considerable familiarity with the music.

The lover of a pure European tone will be horrified by the sound produced, with its growls, falsetto cries, glissandos and so forth, and is, at best, likely to describe it as "unpolished". Certainly, the liberties taken with tone and pitch could under no circumstances be countenanced in any serious interpretation of a "classical" work of any period. On the other hand, more careful listening to the best performances will reveal not chaos, but a definite set of guiding principles, which, though unformulated in the way that those of European music are, are nevertheless there and, I submit, combined into a highly expressive whole. The restriction of much of the music to a repeated theme or theme and variations form, the predominant use of a non-European scale form of which the main features are a lowered third, fifth and leading note, and the pitch freedoms taken with these notes are the very limitations, which, though apparently appalling to the Western listener, allow greater variability, both in rhythm, as mentioned above, and in tone. This in turn allows, in some ways, a far greater element of intimate personal expression, which is made the more personal by the fact that its complexity dictates that it cannot be imitated and repeated by a group with much accuracy.

This type of approach to tone is pretty near universal among non-Academy-trained American Negroes, and was (and still is) one of the features which gave jazz its peculiar style. For the reasons indicated above, it was not easily or successfully imitated, especially by those who were trained as symphonic players, since the idiom was not only unfamiliar, but at times quite definitely unpleasant. It was thus possible for those who were able to acquire the knack to rise rapidly to a wider popularity and a greater wealth than men with years of training. Bing Crosby has pointed out this fact with reference to his own success.

This "Negro" approach to tone steadily permeated the popular world, and again the process has speeded up of late, as the idiom has become familiar. It is now extremely difficult, without considerable experience, to decide the origin of a given group, especially where American and British *white* singers are concerned. The Negro still has some tonal distinctions, as well as a greater flexibility and sensibility (as is to be expected) in handling the techniques of emotional expression outlined above.

In the twenties, the Negro tone was described as "hot", where white singers were said to produce a "sweet" sound. Popularly known as "crooning", the sound has to be heard to be understood (and believed). Until recently, the most popular singers have always been "crooners" though now such a mixture of techniques is found (as in Elvis Presley) that the labels are no longer apt. This style, too, seeks to express feeling, though it is difficult not to use the word "sentiment" rather than "emotion" in this context.

Some of its features are commonly found in non-symphonic music. In particular, one must mention the control of sound from the throat rather than from the diaphragm, with a resultant lack of "roundness" and volume. The latter deficiency necessitates a microphone, especially when the singer is in competition with percussive instruments. This point has received much criticism, as usual, by those who did not understand the problems involved. The reader will by now be clear that in order to create music using the concepts so far outlined, the use of the microphone for a singer was an inevitable consequence. We should also bear in mind that this type of voice production is common in folk music of good quality, apart from the fact that the ability to make a loud noise is not necessarily of itself a virtue. In closing, it should also be noted that this type of singing has, in common with folk music, the widespread restriction of range to one octave, or a little more (the voice keeps within its natural range and is not pushed to its extremes).

Why then is the "sweet" popular tone so widely condemned by music lovers (both "Classical" and "pure jazz") on grounds of being syrupy? The answer is, I feel, that the emotional impact of the tone is one of sentimentality, due, among other things, to the systematic elimination of any aspect which might be disturbing, or even mildly unpleasant. Like the wallpaper of the average popular listener, it tries to crowd pleasant experience upon pleasant experience, under the mistaken impression that two such must give twice the pleasure found in one. Furthermore, to the serious listener, who expects more from his music than a mere lulling of the senses, it has a more important deficiency. Without the roundness and sturdiness of the symphonic and operatic tone, of the intentional harshness of Negro music, without extremes of ranges with their attendant tension, or the intentional, carefully handled freedom of pitch of the blues singer, the "sweet" tone of the popular singer can only succeed at best in being pleasant and must, therefore, appeal to a very limited musical and emotional spectrum. At the same time these emotional trivia are given an over-dramatic type of presentation which wrings the last ounce of emotion from every phrase. It is symptomatic that the style is most popular with teenage girls, whose emotions we criticise, not because they are not deeply felt, but because they have an element of self-righteousness based on inexperience of mature life and an unwillingness to look at the realities of life before thinking, feeling and acting. Musically the tone of the pop singer is equally escapist—he neither can nor will face the implications of a more realistic emotional approach, and it is for this reason that all serious-minded musicians and listeners much condemn both the style and its listeners, as being, in this sense at least, immature. Though there may be some argument about its value as "audible wallpaper", it cannot be accepted as art, and should certainly not be given the recognition or serious discussion of inner meaning accorded to works of art. Only the work of a serious artist, created as a result of years of experience, study and effort, is worth being regarded as if it were on an equal plane by the intelligent person (in pop music, crudeness of performance alone should dictate this to those who hold that one of the hallmarks of great art is subtlety). It may be analysed as an unfortunate phenomenon, like juvenile delinquency, which has to be investigated, but as nothing more.

The peculiar nature of the popular sound is due largely to the mixing of the "hot" and "sweet" tones and the opposition of jazz fans tends usually to decrease towards any given pop star in direct proportion to the amount of "hotness" in his tone. It is gratifying to find that even the general public seems to realise to some extent that "sweetness" or polish, in the sense of a removing of rough edges of tone, is generally neither so satisfying nor so sincere. They do not accept half so willingly a product in the idiom produced only under commercial pressure by a competent musician and played in a very professional manner by, say, a BBC Show Band, as they do the rougher products of people who were at least in the beginning sincere and whose musical techniques can only entitle them to the name of amateurs. The sincerity (this word I shall examine again later) of the average beat player and his comparative faithfulness to his originals come through in this way, despite the frequent hindrance of a slight technique. It is perhaps in its simplest form a striking example of the answer to the perennial problem of choice between technique and feeling.

Before leaving the question of tone it is necessary to mention that the influence of the singer has affected the tone of instrumentalists, especially players of the guitar and the saxophone. The guitar has achieved its effects largely by electronic means, though some Negro players (and the Rolling Stones) have obtained a great deal of flexibility by using a bottleneck or a "steel" such as that used by Hawaiian players. The steel is slid lightly along the strings instead of using the left hand to finger the notes: thus greater possibilities of legato and pitch alteration are available. The short-lived fashion of a few years back for a "rocker arm" (to alter the tension of the strings and thus the pitch of notes) was another attempt to obtain this flexibility. Another recent development has been the use of strings at very low tension, and very high amplification.

The saxophone has needed none of these devices, being an instrument which is by nature very flexible in tone. Popular players, such as Rudy Vallee before the War, attempted, like Eddie Calvert on the trumpet after the War, to produce a very sweet sound, but its most successful use has been by jazz players, who have found it to hold immense possibilities of passionate expression. Even a cursory listening to records by, say, Stan Getz and John Coltrane will illustrate what a diversity of tone is possible.

Before passing on to the more traditional technical aspects of popular music it is necessary to say something about improvisation. Here again the Negro influence is the cause of its existence. Negro music was, almost by its very nature, not written down but composed spontaneously, and it was both natural and necessary (because of a lack of sufficient education to get to the state of advancement needed to express what they could invent) to transmit the main ideas orally and to improvise that which was not memorised.

In jazz, improvisation has two main forms. The first of these is the one to which the most attention has been drawn: the improvisation within the limits of the idiom and of the piece being performed, of a variation upon the original theme derived from the harmonic basis, rather than by using the melody as a starting point. This is no new idea to Classical musicians, but it is nevertheless not so familiar, in that the variation form has tended to use either a process in which the melody is the starting point (*i.e.* allowing changes of harmony or accompaniment) or variations in which so much liberty is taken that the variation is almost a short development section (*i.e.* the length is not rigidly fixed).

This "free" improvisation is not only an important part of jazz, but its main aim. However, in popular music it is far less important, except in the creative stage, since the audience demands a known comprehensible tune, and thus even improvised solos used to fill out a piece must, once created, usually be repeated note for note: they become set pieces.

There is, however, another side of improvisation. In addition to this "creative approach", there is also what might be called "utilitarian" improvisation. By this one means that though the various points of the arrangement are fixed in the main, there is also some limited scope which goes beyond what may reasonably be called "interpretation". Thus, in a drum part, or a part for a chord-playing instrument, only an outline of what is required is given: the player uses his initiative to fill in the details.

In the case of harmony the "chord symbol" system is used; this has been compared to the figured bass system of the Baroque era. The comparison is not a very good one, in that the chord symbol system gives only the name of the required chord, whereas the figured bass system gives the bass, and hence the inversion, with consequent limitations of part movement; usually the melody is given as well.

In this case, the pianist has chosen to voice the chords with a very open spacing, for a fuller sound; the rhythm is entirely a matter of choice. The bass player selects notes freely off the chords, whilst bearing in mind that the simple triads will be most effective, and that roots and fifths will tend to come on the strong beats. The drummer plays the commonest jazz rhythm on his cymbals, but has added interest by creating cross-rhythms on his other equipment. The drummer's part has been put onto two staves for the sake of clarity: it is, of course, played by one man.

In Example 28 (overleaf) the difficulties and advantages of the two systems can be seen.

In 28a (i) we see a typical given part of figured-bass notation; there is little more that could be done than to play 28a (ii). The same progression in chord-symbol notation would be written as in 28b (i). This might legitimately be played as close to the figured-bass version as 28b (ii). But it is equally likely that a pianist would choose to add the seventh on the C chord, and alter the rhythms and voicings to produce 28b (iii). However, the comparison is useful in that it draws attention to the fact that such systems are only of use in a kind of music in which the development of the melody alone (and not the inner part movement) is specified in detail, and which is based on a fundamentally simple harmonic scheme. Thus, the approach of later centuries, with its attention to fine detail and development of complex harmonic systems (*e.g.* chords built on fourths) is rejected; this is equally true of the concomitant conception of the sacredness of the work of the artist, and of the idea that a work of art should be the unaided work of one man.

Ex. 28

This acceptance of the idea of much more group effort explains in part the usually derided fact that a pop tune frequently has two or more contributors. In such cases this is merely an acknowledgement of the fact that usually all members of a group will make amendments or additions to a piece. I say "in part" since one has to recognise that the named authors are the ones who receive performing rights, which bring in such a commercial incentive that it is not unknown for unscrupulous persons to offer to "push" a work, if their name is included in the credits.

When commercial elements are less dominant, as in a good jazz group, the result of this collaboration and improvisation is a highly personal expression. This is well illustrated by the fact that though the music of Duke Ellington is generally thought to be perhaps the finest and most "classically" acceptable of all jazz composers, it is never seriously reperformed by others, in the way that the music of Beethoven is. Though re-orchestrations of some of his most popular melodies are used, it is generally accepted that it is probably impossible to produce a worthwhile imitation or reproduction of the band's music.

The melodies of popular music would be the next obvious topic for this chapter, but they are so important that I propose to devote a separate chapter to them later. I shall, therefore, turn at once to discuss popular harmony. In one sense there is little that can or need be said, but I do find it essential to dispel a few still reiterated illusions and fallacies.

Firstly, popular harmony is nearly always what may be called "natural" harmony, in the sense that Dr Andrews uses that term in his volume of the *Oxford Harmony*. This may also be termed "expected" harmony, in that harmonisations are basically of the sort which might be found in any standard period work of "Classical" music. On the other hand, where a change from this is found, it is always in favour of chromaticism, so that popular harmony may in some senses be described as "Victorian", both in period, and in emotional implication. Generally speaking, these chromatic effects are heightened by frequent transitional modulation, as well as by a real modulation, frequently to a remote key, in the "middle eight". This type of harmony has become so standard that it is widely applied to melodies which have a definite chromatic movement, and also to ones which are strictly diatonic in structure.

Nonetheless, it is of great importance to be aware that, generally, the harmony does not "advance" beyond this stage of development. Thus, chromaticism of the kind adopted by many composers with varied success after Wagner is almost non-existent, and "modern chords" built on non-tonal principles are unheard of.

Since the War there has nevertheless been an increasing use of "discord" in the standard classical sense, so that in both jazz and popular music the added 9th and 13th are commonly used, both in their major and minor forms, and the chord of the dominant 7th with augmented 5th (analysable as such, and not as some skeleton form of 13th chord) has been commonly used since the twenties. A less frequently used, but not unknown chord is the chord of the "flattened 5th" (or "French 6th", as it is known to Classical musicians).

On the other hand, it must be added that these chords are used in a very definite and limited way, so that the voicings are always the most consonant ones and rarely exploit the possibilities of tension available in such complex chords. For instance, notes are never a semitone apart, except in a handful of standard cases.

The only genuine and forceful harmonic contributions are to be found in pieces of a strongly blues origin, where the original "nineteenth-century" harmony is influenced by the blues scale. This may take the form of an alteration such as the changing of a perfect to an augmented 5th in a II (maj)⁷ harmony, or it may take the form of a superimposition, such as the addition of a minor 3rd (or flattened 10th) to, say, a chord of I⁷.

Ex. 29

(a) Normal progression   (b) with altered " blue " harmony

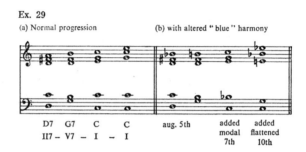

A very popular version of this is to be found in the penultimate phrase of the Beatles' "You Can't Do That"—"I've told you before". However, as has been said, these advances are few, limited and largely confined to jazz and Negro music, if only because they are, generally speaking, beyond the amateur's range on the guitar.

One should perhaps mention at this point the added 6th chord on a major (or sometimes a minor) chord, with no sense of this being a II⁷ discord, which became a notorious feature of popular harmony in the period after 1918. This is still used and has become so fundamental a unit of harmony as not to be thought of as a discord. This is also true to a great extent of the other standard harmonies mentioned above. It suggests that people are becoming acclimatised to discord to a degree unimaginable in years gone by, and to such an extent that for many people popular music without this type of chord is like meat without salt. Another feature of the added 6th has been to blur, even to many musicians, some of the distinction between major and minor usage in that I⁶ and VI⁷ are frequently accepted as being interchangeable.

We must, therefore, accept that, given the exceptions mentioned above, popular harmony is not only static but stagnant, and most important, is unadventurous. If we condemn harmony merely because it lacks "modernity", we shall condemn much fine music to the scrapheap; Sibelius and Vaughan Williams would be among the first to go. What we seek is not the invention of new harmonic combinations (Ravel pointed out that the practical possibilities had probably been exploited by 1930), but a freshness and vigour of conception in making these old materials the means of expression of a new message. Popular harmony fails partly in this but mostly in that it is geared to "sweetness", and the avoidance of harshness. This does not necessarily make it totally without value, but gives it only a limited sphere of experience which it can possibly succeed in expressing. This is clearly against its interest musically and is, moreover, unnecessary since there is no reason why popular music today, as in the past, should not express a diversity of basic emotional experiences, often at a deep level.

In view of this, it is of interest to note that the "new wave" of pop stars have tended to return to the more simple diatonic progressions (not always because of technical inadequacy) and feel the chromatic style to be somewhat cloying. At the same time, there has been an increasing tendency to use progressions, such as VIIb maj–I and IIIb maj–I, not, as they have sometimes been used in the past, to conjure up a quasi-religious atmosphere, but for the rather static but forceful sound which they have; perhaps best illustrated in Appalachian folk music or, Classically, in Vaughan Williams.

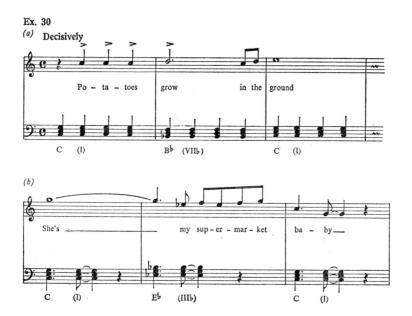

Wilfrid Mellers has commented upon these facts in a recent article (*New Statesman*, 24 February 1967):

> The Beatles' early numbers indeed betray, in their instinctive pentatonicism and modality, many features in common with medieval music and with primitive folk cultures, and very little in common with the harmonic practice of the eighteenth century and after. "A Hard Day's Night", for instance, has no conventional tonic-dominant modulations but a distinctively plagal, flat feeling, and is riddled with blue false relations and oscillations between the triads of the tonic and flat 7th comparable with those in the keyboard music of Gibbons or Farnaby.

The reason for this can be derived from Professor Mellers' statement. Such techniques are different from those of the "standard" period of music (Classical and popular) and have been adopted precisely because of that difference. Debussy and subsequent serious composers rejected the language of the Classical period because they felt it had been fully explored, and because it was felt to have overtones of emotions of a type incompatible with the vision which the modern artist wished to express.

The popular musician has at last reached this point, though for slightly different reasons. He feels the old chromatic language to have been explored as fully as possible *in this type of music*. There is, of course, much more that could be done (*viz.* the harmonic resource of the early Schoenberg). But this would require considerably more competence than is the present norm. More particularly, it would turn popular music in a direction which, for the time being at least, it is incapable of taking. The emotional climate which would be needed to permit the use of such an intense language does not exist. The popular musician has, therefore, needed freshness without complexity: his answer clearly lies in the modes and folk techniques. The other side of Professor Mellers' argument, the emotional implications of such a change, will be discussed later.

A final, but most important point, is that it is not reasonable to judge part-writing in popular harmony as crude, because it does not conform to Classical conventions, any more than one would expect Beethoven to conform in this respect to the standards of Bach. Though definite unwritten rules can be deduced, there is little or no concept of part-writing in the way it is understood by "serious" musicians. Harmony is necessary because the solo singer without accompaniment produces a sound which is quite outlandish to the popular audience. At the same time, it is of the kind specified earlier, for emotional reasons. It cannot be too diatonic, as this is considered old-fashioned, nor can it be too modern, as it would be too tense. Even if it is theoretically possible to use the twelve-note system for lullabies, it is unlikely that the popular listener will ever accept the fact. Outside of these considerations, the chord is thought of as an entity and not in terms of inversions and voicing. Thus, almost any block voicing or chord cluster will do. This ignores the subtleties obtained by some jazz players, but by and large it is so. It should be remembered that jazz needs called into existence the chord symbol system but not the figured bass system (which implies part movement). There are, however, some practical needs for this approach, in particular in the matter of orchestration, where it is found that more "punch" can be obtained by a close "block" voicing of wind instruments: furthermore, the melody predominates, and five instruments can be made to sound like one strong one.

Another important point is that the bass part is very limited. A line will usually move from root to root, or if the harmonic movement is too slow, from root to 5th, then on to the root of a new chord. The idea of an independent bass line with its consequent inversion of the chord is rare. Popular music is thus a striking example of the Rameau idea of a "fundamental bass". The foregoing statements only need modifying in two cases: first in modern jazz, where the bass-player is expected to move fairly freely through the chords, even to the point of using discords, and secondly in Boogie-Woogie and Rhythm and Blues in which an ostinato pattern is imposed, with exact transpositions to fit the other harmonies of the tune. Again, the first note of every new harmony is almost invariably the root.

From what has gone before, it is easy to see that terms, such as "Wagnerian" or "Debussyish", which have often been applied to this music are highly inaccurate and, by association, misleading. The harmony does have various late nineteenth-century features, but cannot be compared even to the average drawing-room song in that its guiding principles are even more limiting, especially with regard to part movement. Furthermore, there are features in the modern music which would be quite anachronistic in any past idiom. Those of us who are more concerned with the accurate analysis of popular music, rather than with expressing prejudice based on a lack of knowledge by the use of emotionally loaded terms, would probably do best to use the term "chromatic tonal harmony".

Form, in the sense of architectonic structure, is easily dealt with in considering popular music, since almost without exception, it consists, as it always has, of the immediate repetition of a tune several times. Nowadays this is done sufficient times for the piece to last about three minutes. The reason for this is derived originally from the problems of recording music, since the standard medium was at first a 78 rpm record which played for about this period. Now, however, though tunes could be longer, they are not, since public taste has become conditioned to the length and will rarely accept "long" pieces of four minutes or more. This is much less true of "progressive pop" in which flatulence has become a virtue.

The tune which is repeated is usually known as a "chorus" as a result of an evolution from a form of verse-chorus-verse-chorus etc., to one of verse-chorus-chorus etc., and finally to the omission of verses altogether. Nowadays, it is quite rare for a tune to be written with a verse at all, and the same strophe is repeated several times. The length of this strophe is generally 12, 16 or 32 bars, or alternatively some multiple of 8, even though the basic unit of composition is of two-bar length, as we shall see in a later chapter. Tunes of "irregular" length (*e.g.* 10 bars) are known but are exceptional, and such is the extent of tradition that these are a cause of considerable trouble to amateur musicians, and feel strange to many professionals. An introduction (usually 4 bars) and sometimes a "tag" or coda (again 4 bars, often repeated several times in records ending with a "fade-out") are usually added. The tune is repeated, with slight, generally melismatic variation, though on more modern records there is an increasing tendency to give some time to a free variation, played by a solo instrument, as mentioned earlier.

Finally it is necessary to look a little at orchestration, as it is in this side of popular music that much interesting work has been done.

In the earlier days of the modern style of popular music a first and most decisive step in breaking away from the traditional idiom was made by the introduction of wind instruments, rather than strings, as the backbone of the orchestra. The reason for this was both practical and aesthetic. It was a practical matter in that in a large hall, particularly if there is much conversation, clinking of glasses and other extraneous noise, not only the beautiful tone, but even the sound itself of strings is lost. The trumpet and trombone had an easier job, and the formation of bands of the modern type was completed when, in the twenties, the saxophone, which had much of the fluency and less of the technical difficulty of the more traditional clarinet, took the place of the symphonic woodwind. A further musical reason for the use of such instruments was that the new stress on drums, which are, physically speaking, much louder than any other instrument, demanded instruments with a sufficient reserve of volume to carry over them. In addition to such practical and theoretical considerations, it seems that the generation which was growing up in a world of unprecedented clamour, first of guns, and then of machines and automobiles, sought refuge, not in quiet, but in greater volume. The modern demand for background music seems to be based on a similar tendency to find relaxation in all-pervading sound. The stridency of the music has been frequently noted also by some observers as echoing the tensions of the age.

While the change to this new format was still in progress, and band arrangers wrote happily for cellos and saxes, another development took place, because of the rapid expansion in applied electronics. The microphone became widely used though it gained no respectability, and still has not done so, despite the immense possibilities which it opened up.

To begin with it answered the needs of the singer, who was unable to compete with the new volume, and also of any quiet instrument, such as the violin or the flute. It thus presented new possibilities of balance. One flute, for instance, could balance against not one but several trumpets, given appropriate amplification. At the same time, it offered new possibilities of subtlety, since sounds scarcely audible even without accompaniment could now be made available to the orchestrator. Any abuse of this does not, of course, invalidate the general line of the argument.

Perhaps part of the resistance of "serious" musicians was due to the comparative crudeness of the early techniques. However, now, great fidelity of reproduction is possible. Furthermore, many arguments against amplification are made on the grounds that the instrument "does not sound like the real thing" (this is very true of the bass). This is surely only to state the obvious and through mere prejudice not to allow the replacement of traditional instruments by an adequate substitute, when it is not practicable to use the original. This type of approach also has a worse effect in that it denies the writer the chance to increase the range of orchestral possibilities on which he can call.

Another interesting development has been the introduction of new methods of producing sound, either by taking notes and altering their quality electronically (as in the case of the electric guitar) or by producing the notes themselves by electronic means (as on the electronic organ). The latter instrument I am inclined to regard as "mechanical" and, therefore, inferior in the sense that any mechanical instrument is, *i.e.* that it does not permit the subtle variation from note to note of pressure and note production with subsequent variations in the overtones produced, which are to be found in traditional instruments. As I understand it, it is certainly difficult if not impossible to produce electronically the type of subtlety which can be obtained cheaply and effectively from a string. On the guitar, however, notes are reproduced as faithfully as possible before "treatment" and the interest lies in the striking effects that can be produced by cutting out overtones, or by adding a vibrato or tremolo (an experiment tried in a more complex form, as I remember, on the Baroque organ) and by the use of "reverberation" and "echo". The echo chamber, of course, far from being a glorified public lavatory, is in fact a small tape recorder, on which a loop of tape records and plays back almost at once, to give the echo effect.

The tape recorder has brought, both here and elsewhere, another possible dimension into music, and already successful experiments have been made in which, by multi-recording, a singer can sing in harmony with himself (doubletracking) or, on at least one occasion to my knowledge, a skilled musician ("Tubby" Hayes) has accompanied himself as virtually a one-man group.

The possibilities opened up by recording techniques have been increasingly exploited recently, especially by the Beatles. The Indian sitar, for example, has enjoyed a sudden surge of popularity because of its use by them and other groups, whereas it is far too delicate an instrument to have any possibilities used acoustically, with a beat group. In recording *Revolver*, for instance, electronic resources have been used in a way which Wilfrid Mellers feels to be reminiscent of *avant-garde* serious music. Like him, I am excited by the results, and hope that his analysis of the situation may prove correct; he suggests, if I understand him rightly, that they are opening up new worlds for popular music both in terms of sound ("a new sonorous experience") and in depth of artistic perception (" 'Penny Lane' brilliantly recreates everyday life in a state between sleeping and waking"). I must admit to a certain degree of pessimism, however, as the public have all too often responded to new ideas, especially when accompanied by intense publicity (*viz.* the numbers of records sold before the date of publication), but in a way which was superficial and was attracted by novelty, rather than by new possibilities.

These experiments can of course only be carried out in a modern recording studio (this is equally true of modern "serious" electronic music, such as that of Roberto Gerhard) and have, therefore, led to a new concept of the way in which performances can be made and enjoyed. It is rapidly becoming accepted that records offer an artist new possibilities and are another valid aspect of his music; there is no doubt that there are virtues in hearing a record, as well as in attending a performance live. The latter will be more conducive to excitement and will have the tension which is only possible when the value of the performance is as yet unknown, and also (in jazz) when creation takes place, but the former method offers perhaps a greater satisfac-

Demonstrations of the
Tango and Rockn'roll

Humming Birds—or a Dandy Trio. Etching by Cruikshank

Bill Haley and his Comets

tion to the person who wishes to listen undistracted by other noises (dare one mention the concert-hall cough in this context?) and when the appropriate mood is upon him. As far as popular music is concerned this is definitely so. In view of the overpowering din which is to be heard at a Beatles' concert, it would appear that the *only* way to hear them at all is on record; the advantages of records for "mood" music need no extolling—fornication has never been a really feasible pursuit in front of a seventy-piece orchestra.

There are dangers in recording in that the standards of performance may become *too* high. Because of skilful editing of tape in the studios it is possible to buy a performance so polished that even a virtuoso is unlikely ever to equal it in a live performance. In popular music it is well known that there are many players who cannot match up in the flesh to the comparatively polished product which they can turn out by making repeated attempts in the studio.

On the other hand, the pressure of the commercial world for new sounds has forced the arrangers of popular music to seek out many byways (and perhaps highways) utilising the resources mentioned above and it is certain that some of their effects are striking, both in their novelty and, I suggest, their brilliance. Some of the "nameless" commercial arrangers may be minor artists, but they are masters of the craft of imagining new sound combinations. It may well be that some future musicians may look back into the long-forgotten arrangements of popular tunes and find some inspiration.

9 The Effect of Popular Music on Serious Music

My orchestra was modelled on those of Harlem
and consisted of seventeen soloists. I used the
jazz style without reserve, mingling it with a
classical sentiment.
DARIUS MILHAUD,
speaking about his *Création du Monde*

The closing ideas of the last chapter lead me directly to the consideration of influences which have already taken place on "serious" music.

The extent of this topic may be judged by the fact that I have long considered it to be a profitable theme for a book. It is, therefore, clear that anything attempted in a work of this size and aim must be of the most cursory nature. Nevertheless, I think it worthwhile to outline the main developments so that those who are unaware of the influence of this type of music may become so, and those who are, may be reminded and perhaps persuaded to hear the relevant works again and to rethink their approach to them. I feel I must stress from the start that there is no intention in this chapter of trying to perpetuate the jazz-classics arguments of many years' standing, or to offer jazz as some panacea for the problems of the twentieth-century composer. My only aim is to point out in general terms, and without the subtle expansions and qualifications which are really necessary in analysing the artistic creations of any great man, the general attitudes of certain composers at certain times to the new wave of popular music, and to the use of musical techniques consequent upon these attitudes.

It is of interest to note that whereas the academic world has only just begun to admit of the possibility of American-styled popular music as being a serious study of any sort, the practising composers were quick to seize upon it as a new mode of expression. The experiments made from an early date in this century by serious composers were a symptom of a grave dissatisfaction with the possibilities of the contemporary Classical tradition.

While the new Ragtime was still only a craze of some of the young, Debussy's pastiche *Golliwog's Cakewalk* was followed by Stravinsky, who started to use elements of it in his composition and continued to do so for some years (*e.g. Ragtime for Eleven Instruments, Piano Rag Music, Histoire du Soldat*). Great interest was also shown by the members of Les Six, and in particular by Milhaud, who after experiments in his piano Sonata of 1916, produced in 1920 *Le Bœuf sur le toit*, and soon after, *Le Création du Monde*, a work for which the author attributes the inspiration to New Orleans-type polyphonic improvisation. It should be noted that each of these composers sought something different from Ragtime, and that none attempted to reproduce it exactly or to create within its limitations. Debussy, for instance, having originated a style which broke free of traditional limitations of melody, harmony and rhythm, took an interest in this aspect, whereas Stravinsky was interested in the creation of rhythmic patterns which defeated the very square nature of much of the music of the eighteenth and nineteenth centuries. But he abstracted aspects of this rhythm and did not use the elements in it which are most important to lovers of it, such as the reiterated patterns and the "pull" against a very rigid metrical base. In contrast to the more mathematical working out of patterns which attracted Stravinsky, the jaunty syncopations which disturbed the mind and gave the music a rather puppet-like quality appealed to composers such as Milhaud and Walton (in *Façade* and *Portsmouth Point* especially) who were attempting to react to the strain of the War and the intensity of many of their fellows (Schoenberg in particular) by seeking the bizarre. *Façade* is an excellent illustration of the desire of many post-War composers to poke fun at everything, to parody, to escape, and to do so by the use of startling, novel material. It is, in a sense, Dadaism in music.

These remarks may lead the reader to conclude that the interest of serious musicians in jazz and allied forms was mainly for the technical possibilities it suggested. Though there would be a great deal of truth in such a conclusion, it is necessary to keep in mind that the motivation of Milhaud and Les Six was also very emotional. Speaking for them in his *Le Coq et L'Harlequin*, Jean Cocteau expressed their interest as being in the "stimulation of primitive masculine energy" in place of the "old-fashioned decorative paganism of the nineteenth century". Readers familiar with the painting of the period will see obvious parallels.

Unfortunately, Milhaud's involvement with his cause tended to cloud his critical faculty. Consequently, though *Le Création du Monde* has received much critical acclaim, in particular because of the "jazz fugue" it contains, it is, to many listeners (especially those aligned to jazz), rather dated and unconvincing because of its use of the clichés of the period. Stravinsky's *Ragtime* or Walton's *Portsmouth Point* are, as I see it, much to be preferred: they need no apologetic prefacing remarks because they have "flirted with the dance hall". The reason for this is that the composers used jazz only as a starting point: they made the materials they took up as abstract as possible (*cf.* the use of still-life by Cubist painters), and avoided any attempt to utilise the power of jazz to create instant excitement. Milhaud, on the other hand, did use it for this purpose, and for its barbarism; he was thus obliged to bring into his music the other connotations that inevitably go with this, whilst losing the conviction that only an original performance can have in this music (a Louis Armstrong solo on paper, or played by someone else can be quite banal: the subtly personal inflections which Armstrong gave on a particular occasion are what make a solo great). The latter fault could perhaps have been avoided in time; within jazz Fletcher Henderson showed, at about the same time, how to organise a band of ten or more pieces, using written arrangements, but playing music that was indubitably good jazz. The former mistake, however, is fatal in a serious artist. Manner must suit matter; but Milhaud tried to use slang to write an epic.

Despite the excitement they caused at the time and the success of certain of the compositions mentioned, perhaps the most important influence of jazz and popular music at this period (it would be an unenviable task to decide which it was that really influenced Milhaud) will appear to later generations to be that of the introduction of certain tone colours, particularly among the brass. The saxophone was taken up from time to time, but has retained a "juvenile delinquent" association, and the Ragtime use of the piano had little to offer to men brought up on Chopin and Liszt. Jazz percussion developments have caused interest, but rarely imitation, because the use of dominating percussion tends to be alien to the fundamental concepts of the Classical composer. However, the work of jazzmen and Louis Armstrong in particular drew the attention of composers to the fact that the potential range and velocity of the trumpet was higher than was thought. Furthermore, Negroes used various effects, many of them produced by mutes, in order to obtain from the instrument a greater proximity to the sound of the singing voice. White bands realised the gimmick value of these devices and exploited them, thus from these two sources the "serious" musician developed the idea of changing brass timbre by muting. Thus, in later years, John Ireland was able to use in his piano Concerto fibre mutes, up till then only found in dance bands, instead of the old pear-shaped brass ones, and to include Chinese blocks (used by New Orleans drummers) in a work which has no musical relation to jazz: this was, by then, possible without a sense of incongruity.

It should be borne in mind though, that for every composer who flirted with jazz for a few years there were many who at most gave it some signs of respect, but used it rarely or never. Thus Ravel, who shows jazz influence in the *Trois Chansons Madecasses* and in the *Piano Concerto*, and during his visit to America visited night clubs to hear Negro players, can by no means be described as a jazz composer, for his greatest works (*e.g. Daphnis and Chloe*) though sensual in nature, are still based on a concept of the beautiful which is far too ethereal to be linked with the primitive earthiness of Bessie Smith.

It was, therefore, not surprising that by the late twenties real interest in jazz had largely ceased, perhaps in some measure owing to the conservatism of audiences, who were less able than Ravel to accept a challenge to their basic ideas. For it is essential to accept that jazz and "Classical music" are based on quite different world pictures, which are as far apart as, say, Christian and Marxist ethics. They can coexist, and indeed one hopes that the antagonism of past years may cease altogether, but so far few men have successfully linked both in an even mildly satisfactory manner: works mixing the two approaches either lack jazz feeling or are deficient in formal Classical techniques.

This antagonism was very marked when the music first appeared, and an article by Neil Leonard in *Jazz Monthly* of June 1958 shows very well how much more royalist than the king were many of the lovers, performers and teachers of Classical music. Thus Fenton T. Bott, head of the (American) National Association of Masters of Dancing, said "Jazz is the very foundation of salacious dancing." Such a comment today would only cause amusement, but the comments of John R. McMahon, writing in the *Ladies' Home Journal* of November 1921, that "If Beethoven should return to earth and witness the doings of such an orchestra, he would thank heaven for his deafness", is not so far from those of Beverley Nichols, writing in an English women's magazine over forty years later, that "it might not be a bad idea for some teenagers, when they are being 'sent' by a piece of jazz to ask themselves where the music stopped and the sex began and vice-versa"; he adds that some "young ladies give me the impression that their brains would be unable to function unless assisted by a trio of trumpets played fortissimo at a range of not more than three feet".

Such views may well represent nowadays only an extremist minority, but however much they may criticise the terminology and inadequacy of thought of such commentators, many people will feel some sympathy still with the idea of another writer of the twenties, Frank Patterson, that popular music shows a "disregard for the self-contained and self-restrained attitude that has been prescribed by the makers of the rules of social intercourse". Even more people would feel that Elise Fellows White, in the *Musical Quarterly* of January 1922, was quite near to the truth when she said of Classical music that it "demands much time and thought" and that it is "the music of artistic cultivation, of humble ambitions, prayerfully and earnestly followed; of obedience to teachers; of self-denial, renunciation and sacrifice; of the worship of beauty and the passionate desire to express it". Such a quasi-religious view of musical (and other) art, epitomises not only the views of the nineteenth-century romantic, but also those of the present-day musical public. Despite surface changes of technique, it is clear that to most followers, practising or lay, of Classical music, the experience of music is predominantly an almost mystical quest for elevation of the spirit, in which the composer holds the position of little less than an inspired voice or prophet. Critics may suggest that their terminology is not meant to be interpreted so literally, and is merely part of an effort to convey something of the effect of a piece on a sympathetic mind: I would reply to this that it would be better in that case to find some other vocabulary which does not have such great possibilities of ambiguity. In contrast to this, the world of jazz and pop, though irritatingly addicted to hyperbole, remains largely rooted in a more basic approach to art: the attitudes of the jazz listener are closer to those of the music lover of the pre-Romantic era, and might well find themselves expressed (with the obvious modifications) by the comments of T. S. Eliot on poetry, that it is "a superior amusement" and is "excellent words in excellent arrangement and excellent metre".

We must now turn to those who, in contrast to the purists of either side, strove to find a synthesis of the two musics on a deep and satisfying level.

Perhaps the most well known of these is Constant Lambert, who both composed such jazz-influenced works as *Rio Grande* (1928) and wrote much valuable criticism. He felt of jazz that "it is the first dance music to bridge the gap between highbrow and lowbrow successfully", and that "Ellington, in fact, is a real composer, the first jazz composer of distinction, and the first Negro composer of distinction". Nevertheless, we should not be carried away by these comments as jazz critics sometimes are, since Lambert frequently makes such qualifying comments as those that Louis Armstrong had "a restricted circle of ideas" and that jazz was a "half finished material in which European sophistication has been imposed over coloured crudity".

The meeting point at this time was in the "symphonic jazz" movement, at the centre of which was Gershwin, a composer who still arouses more heat among both jazz and classical music lovers than anyone else, except perhaps Webern.

It seems to me that Gershwin has been overrated as a jazz composer and underrated as a symphonic composer. For instance, the defenders of his jazz side often like to cite as examples of his jazz quality tunes such as "I Got Rhythm" which are not as competent or as stimulating as the work of almost unknown composers such as Gene de Paul (composer of "I Remember April"), let alone the songs of well-known composers such as Jerome Kern and Cole Porter. On the other hand, *Porgy and Bess* is a magnificent synthesis of Negro and conservatory techniques. The melodies are technically well constructed—"I Got Plenty of Nothin'" contains some striking but successful chord movements—and at the same time combine most satisfactorily some aspects of the yearning of Negro melody with ample opportunities for the beauties of Classical operatic tone and expression to come through: they are products of a far greater musical depth and maturity than, say, the "Classical" experiments of Stan Kenton or Pete Rugolo. Similarly, *American in Paris* is an excellent piece of ballet music, tactfully and more than competently orchestrated, showing a distinct feeling for the more luscious type of harmony and the power to combine these into a satisfying and romantic whole. We should remember though that Gershwin was a composer who still felt the pressure of the European symphonic tradition so much that, despite his jazz origins, he gave up the central and most important feature of jazz—the pulse. In doing this, and in rejecting much of the Negroid expressive system, he produced a result in which, though strange to conservatory-trained ears, he managed to pick out certain features of jazz to adorn and inflect his music in such a way that he may be described as the last of the Nationalists.

However, as has been mentioned, by the time that Gershwin appeared, jazz was a dated fashion among the serious composers, and was thereafter much less used, partly because of a change in intellectual climate, partly because of the increasing influence of composers who had found a modern development of technique from within the tradition instead of importing one from outside, and partly because of the increasing desire to divorce jazz and popular music from the techniques and standards of classical music. Those who could see possibilities in Ragtime were much less happy with the Swing Era.

Before leaving the twenties, it is necessary to mention the influence which serious music had on popular forms: this was most fully seen in the work of the Paul Whiteman Orchestra.

Nowadays, a Whiteman record will usually only provoke hilarious laughter in any type of listener—classical, jazz or popular. The only other reaction (on the part of critics) will be angry comments about commercialism. But a careful listening will reveal many good points among the undoubted faults, for Whiteman valued quality. This may be seen in the fact that he employed good jazz players when he could (in fact, he paid for the convalescence of Bix Beiderbecke). Similarly, he bought good arrangements from Henderson, and paid well for them ($100 apiece). The result was great technical proficiency (illustrated in "New Tiger Rag" of 1930). This in itself did a great deal towards obtaining some kind of serious recognition for a music in which faults of technique and intonation were all too common. It also raised the standards of the public.

At the same time, Whiteman tried to raise the level of composition and arrangement in popular music by incorporating more advanced harmonies, more careful part-writing, more varied orchestration, variation of tempo, and to some extent "Classical" forms (contrasting sections, return of accompanying themes, passages built upon ideas derived from the song, but developed on classical lines). A good example of this is his "The Man I Love" (1928).

Many records of the period show some sign of such influence, if only in bridge passages of "unorthodox" harmony. Fletcher Henderson, for example, attempts in *Queer Notions* to use augmented chords as an integral part of the structure, instead of just as passing chords derived from a blue inflection of the melodic line. This kind of experiment was not repeated until the early years of the Second World War. Bix Beiderbecke's "In A Mist" is well known because it contrasts Ragtime and Impressionist material.

The reasons for the failure of Whiteman's experiments were varied. One was undoubtedly a faulty understanding of what was essential and proper to each kind of music. Varied tempo and orchestration, which are an essential part of a classical outlook, tend to militate against the production of good jazz. The formal experiments, on the other hand, fail because of the weakness of the writers. On paper, any classical form is a very mechanical business—it needs skill and talent to put life into the bare bones: only Gershwin was capable of this. Duke Ellington was a man capable of doing what Whiteman could not, of taking a large number of talented but very individual performers, and disparate and sometimes banal musical elements (*e.g.* the "jungle" music) and welding them into a unity.

Perhaps most important, Whiteman's music suffered from a common fault of the period—sentimentality. We are very aware of the modern elements of the period, but forget the still strong influence of Victorian attitudes, reflected musically in the chromaticism. There were many people who wished to put back the clock to the time before the catastrophe of the First World War. There were many more who were profoundly disturbed by the disintegration which the intellectuals were causing, and sought some fixed points. One such, in an age of a rapidly changing position for women, was the highly idealised Victorian concept of romantic love. Anyone trying to keep this unaltered was almost inevitably doomed to failure, for it was the decadent phase of an artistic movement. To create well, the artist had to see beyond the need: one such was Scott Fitzgerald, the American novelist. His *The Great Gatsby* studies an extreme form of the romantic dream, and shows its fantastic and impossible nature.

Only one thing need be added to the above; a comment on our own tastes. Whiteman's band was internationally popular: his musicians were paid three-figure salaries per week, and he himself became a millionaire. Nevertheless, he was able to offer as part of his repertoire works of a semi-classical nature—for instance, Gershwin's *Concerto in F*. This is a credit to the abilities of the band, and to the standards of its audience. Can we imagine such a situation today?

The most important figure of the decade before the Second World War, from this point of view, was Kurt Weill, who in his attempts to popularise music by using pop influences reflects again the fact that jazz seems to be a kind of Shangri-La for all manner of musical eccentrics. Finding fault with their musical world, they seek the remedy in jazz. Thus the left-inclined writers saw jazz as the music of an oppressed people, or, more rarely, the popular world as the true voice of a population who could find no satisfaction in the middle-class music of the concert hall. In view of this, it is quite fascinating that from time to time, in communist countries at least, the same music becomes the instrument of American oppression, a kind of opium, and a symptom of a decadent, sensation-seeking, escapist bourgeois world. Nevertheless, Kurt Weill remains one of the few composers accepted by the concert hall who have been really accepted by the popular music world. "September Song" and "Mack the Knife" have remained popular to the present day. Both have an authentic ring about them, without being mere imitations of the style.

In the years between 1930 and 1950, interest in jazz seems to have declined steadily, partly because the classical musician did not feel that it offered him any solutions, and also because, being at root a commercial music, jazz did not make the formal and harmonic advances which could have made its assimilation easier. The crudeness which was initially exciting became wearing as, to "Classical" ears, the primitive essence was smoothed out, and harmonic advance allowed only more sugary harmonies, still strongly rooted in tonality.

American composers, in particular Aaron Copland, were the most influenced by it, as might be expected, but continued in all essentials to follow Europe. Copland has frequently stated that though he is interested in creating music of a distinctive American character, he soon came to reject jazz except as an occasional colouring. He finds it too limited in its range of expression, which he feels to be confined to either the slow blues type of number, or to the highly excited, quick swing number.

Stravinsky continued to maintain an interest in jazz, but rarely to use it. Thus his *Ebony Concerto* of the forties, written especially for the Woody Herman Orchestra, is far less rhythmically dominated than his ragtime pieces, and though containing themes which are at times distinctly reminiscent of Negro music, is primarily a piece of experimentation with the sonorities obtainable from a jazz orchestra. Stravinsky has never been ashamed to accept inspiration where he found it and says of the flugelhorn playing of Shorty Rogers, "Hearing Mr Rogers play this instrument in Los Angeles last year perhaps influenced me to use it in *Threni*." He is fully aware of the real nature and aims of jazz—"The percussion and the bass ... function as a central heating system." But he accepts that though "jazz patterns and especially jazz instrumental combinations did influence me forty years ago" he was not affected by "the idea of jazz", because "this is a wholly different kind of music making".

Since about 1950, some writers in the United States have made another attempt to link the two musics, since the advanced jazz players have more and more rendered the glaring differences of technical ability and advancement of approach between the jazz and classical groups a thing of the past. Nowadays, John Graas, the French horn player, finds jazz a challenge, and Dizzy Gillespie plays, on occasion, with symphony orchestras. André Previn has acquired considerable standing in both spheres, as has Lalo Schiffrin. Leonard Bernstein's activity in both camps is, of course, world famous. The same is true in Britain, and thus Ray Premru, the brass player, is acceptable to both circles. The abilities of Dudley Moore are well known; those of Patrick Gowers are unfortunately less so. Of particular interest and importance is Gunther Schuller, the American French horn player and composer, who has, in his efforts to link the two types of music, become perhaps the most respected writer of what critics have now labelled "Third Stream music". He feels that both spheres have much to offer, and that now the time is becoming ripe for a union. Stravinsky has commented on the time it took even for experienced orchestral players to cope properly with modern works of great complexity and novelty of idiom. Such difficulties have always been more pronounced in the case of jazz. But Schuller feels that the commercial necessities which have forced jazz and classical players to co-operate in popular recording sessions have bridged this gap and have given both sides sufficient understanding of each other to permit serious attempts at a combination. It is certainly true that it is only in the past few years that classical strings could have achieved the type of relaxation needed to produce the swing found in the Nelson Riddle Orchestra backings to Frank Sinatra. Film and television work are rapidly dictating that the composer who can use both idioms successfully is the most likely to make a living. A notable example of this is the American composer Henry Mancini, who wrote the score for the film *Breakfast at Tiffany's* (the melody "Moon River" from this became popular in the widest possible sense). Elmer Bernstein (*The Carpetbaggers*) is another example.

This situation is beginning to obtain in Britain. Perhaps the first swinging use of strings was as a backing to the pop singer Adam Faith, but more serious attempts have also been made. Though it has not achieved the popularity it deserves, the work *Improvisations*, written jointly by Johnny Dankworth and the late Matyas Seiber, is one of the few combinations of jazz and classical music which neither sound like an ineptly orchestrated symphonic backing to a jazz band, nor an equally inept addition of second-rate unswinging jazz musicians to an average symphonic piece of fairly early twentieth-century idiom. Another composer who is certainly competent, though not to my mind so successful artistically, is Ernest Tomlinson. His *Symphony '65* uses not only jazz but avowedly popular elements. Such comparatively isolated experiments are now beginning to have their influence, and less ambitious uses of a mixed idiom are beginning to be heard frequently; thus a BBC Third Programme production of a modern translation of Aristophanes' *Festival of Women* used a mixed idiom in an attempt to catch in music the racy and contemporary flavour of the original Greek.

In concluding this brief summary of the influence of jazz-type music upon symphonic composers, it is necessary to stress again certain points, to draw a few conclusions and to make some predictions.

As has been said earlier, the influence is limited, and has been so much so that a reasonable collection of the masterpieces of the age might well contain no work with a jazz influence. This, as I have said, is due to the differences of aesthetic ideal between the two musics. This in turn may be based on some physical factors. The various physical manifestations which jazz arouses are common topics of criticism and sarcasm, although, as we have seen, they are to be expected. In the previous chapter I mentioned the element of physical incitement. This certainly explains the fact that the music appeals especially to young people, with their naturally greater physical energy, and comparative lack of rigidly formed habits of social conduct. I am convinced that this must be at least in part the reason for the extremely violent hostility of earlier generations of parents to jazz and popular music. Pure musical logic is far too intellectual a thing to have been so aroused by such a crude phenomenon; financial envy is a much more plausible explanation. The quick and easy fortunes made by popsters must have caused a great deal of acrimony. But it seems likely that an inability to respond physically, because of habits long formed by strict social conventions, combined with an instinctive realisation of the threat implicit in yielding to the influence of the music must have caused much of the vehemence that is always to be found when a man's basic pattern of life is threatened. I have used the word "threat" here because I am sure that to "give" to jazz meant allowing oneself to give to the music in a way which was utterly alien to and impossible in the European, reared as he was to a tradition of self-restraint, and the enjoyment of music in a spirit of meditation and contemplation. Moreover, though the hackneyed picture of violent debauchery with loose women as the inevitable concomitant to performances of this type of music is clearly more tickling to the fancy than true to life, there is no doubt that the music is also overtly erotic, in many cases. We only need to mention the name of D. H. Lawrence to recall what a storm this type of attack on conventional sexual behaviour patterns will arouse.

It is, therefore, of interest to note the increasing responsiveness of young people to this music. Does this mean that we can expect two streams of influence and creation for some time? (For, contrary to the beliefs of some educationists, not all those who are captivated by Dizzy Gillespie, or even by the Rolling Stones are senseless morons.) Alternatively, can the process work in reverse? It can definitely be argued that jazz and its allied forms need a type of response which inhibits, or even precludes, the closest type of contact with symphonic music. In fact, there are many intelligent and sensitive people who find little or no satisfaction in classical music. This decade has seen a rapid acceleration of the process. The cultivation of traditional jazz, because of its integrity and expressiveness, in the period after the war, was followed by an interest in modern jazz which was founded upon the assumption that such music was as valid as modern serious composition. These minorities still exist. The youngest generation of intellectuals, however, has gone much further, and has carried the revolt against parental standards to an unprecedented degree. Not only *avant-garde* jazz, and folk music, but also blues and popular music as such, have become rallying points for this revolt. Newspapers are expected to run pop columns, and disc jockeys are increasingly expected to take up a pseudo-philosophical stance. Popular music (especially of the type produced by the Beatles, the Doors, Jimi Hendrix, and The Who) is seen as a subject as fit for both experience and debate as Classical music, even by university students. In fact, some see it as more important, because more alive, and refute the difficulty and abstraction of Classical music in favour of the greater directness and emotional impact of popular music. Horrific though such a prospect must appear to some, the suggestion of a decline of classical music is by no means ludicrous; one has only to observe the decline of polyphony in the seventeenth century to see how quick and extensive such a change can be, even eliminating consideration of the commercial pressures which can always aid an expansion of popular music.

Such factors are, if anything, likely to encourage any tendency towards a new type of art music. In his book *Death of a Music*, the American critic Henry Pleasants put forward a very convincing argument that a jazz-based music will be the serious music of the future.[1] As he sees it "Classical" music is in decline, and must continue to be so since the classical composer has opted to cut himself off (by the difficult idiom he has adopted) from the majority even of the serious concert-going public. In contrast to this, the very perceptive French musician and critic, André Hodeir, feels that jazz may already have passed its greatest point. Though this would not preclude the development of a new music, containing elements of both, I feel that the flaw in Mr Pleasants' book (which all lovers of any type of serious music should read) is that most Europeans are likely to feel for many years, as M. Hodeir does, that even if they like jazz, they would feel the sacrifice of the enormous amount of music which the European tradition has produced, to be far too high a price to pay. As M. Hodeir points out, though jazz has new and exciting experiences to offer which classical music must by its own limitations deny itself, there are enough experiences in European music alone to keep a man busy for a lifetime.

[1] Since the time of writing Mr Pleasants has extended his theory, to include mass popular music, in his book *Serious Music—and all that Jazz*.

10

The Effect of the
American Style on
Traditional Folk Music

It is internationally comprehensible and yet
provides a medium for national inflection more
convincing than the very modified and occasional provincialities of Boyce and Grétry.
CONSTANT LAMBERT,
on American-style popular music

A few years ago, Humphrey Lyttelton suggested that jazz was becoming the
new folk music not only of Britain but of the world. It is the aim of this
chapter to examine this idea.

Despite the efforts of workers such as Cecil Sharp, folk music in the traditional sense died a century ago in this country. Sharp himself commented on
the sudden and amazing decline which took place about 1840, due mainly to
the cumulative effects of the Industrial Revolution. He pointed out that much
had already been lost owing to the deaths of the singers of the old style, and
how the work had only been started just in time to save any substantial
amount of music. The First World War completed the process. Since that
time, despite the extremely laudable and energetic efforts of the English Folk
Dance and Song Society, the keeping alive of such music has been due almost
entirely to them. The popular taste has moved away completely from the
traditional tunes and though the schools have tried hard to instil a love of
them, only a minority of people now listen to and play them—the picture of
the guitar-twanging student singing scything songs, or something of that
kind, is already a standard one in popular humour. The result is that popular
music and folk music (in the sense of music popular among the majority of
ordinary people) are now one. Folk music in the sense meant by Cecil Sharp
—an anonymous product arising spontaneously from a society and polished
by unconscious communal effort—is now dead. Instead, despite the paradoxical increase in the sale of musical instruments, and especially the guitar,
society has divided into two groups—the musical few, and the much larger
non-musical group. As a consequence, the twentieth century has seen the
culmination, musically speaking, of the spiritually stultifying effects of an

industrialised society, living in drab surroundings, working at tedious jobs of soul-destroying monotony, with a life offering little or no creative pleasure taken at social gatherings of a truly communal importance.

I am aware that such views are unfashionable at the moment, and are associated with the idealistic outpourings either of Marxist critics attaching blame to wicked (now reformed) capitalists, or to William Morris-type over-artistic families who will only drink from handmade cups. Nevertheless, I maintain it to be true, and state that we are living in a musical desert, which even the most cursory examination will show to exist and which a detailed survey might well confirm the existence of with figures of appalling magnitude. Leave the grammar schools and try to find young musicians in the secondary modern schools. Or leave aside the high level work in Technical Colleges and look at the Craft Apprentice courses. The vast mass of people have accepted passive entertainment, with its subsequent implication of a division between those who can and those who cannot, between the talented and the untalented. This in turn gives a false impression of the nature of musical talent which, like all others, is a continuum and not a rare quality possessed in entirety or not at all. This creates a vicious circle, breeding ever more extravagant praise for second-rate creation among those who, not being participants, have no standards to judge by. To my mind this is a far more serious long-term problem than the very ephemeral phase of pop star hysteria which some teenagers go through. The latter is a manifestation of high spirits combined with the need for an ideal both physical and mental, but, whereas on reaching maturity this passes, the lack of critical power does not diminish, and so the feeding of second-rate material can go on.

This situation seems to be spreading wherever Western culture goes. Even the most casual playing with the tuning of a radio will give one the same sound, though in a different language. It is true that in many countries the folk and traditional elements continue to be very popular—*e.g.* French accordion music, Greek folk tunes, Indian music and Portuguese *folklorico*—but I get the impression that these are losing ground and are becoming unfashionable with the young, who associate them with the older generation.

In this respect, England seems to have achieved one of its customary lifeless and bloodless states. Compromise and a middle-of-the-road position, which so many Anglophiles take a pride in, spell death to music which thrives on virile positive attitudes. Thus, the European mainland can continue to draw upon its traditions for a little longer, and America, if only because of its large coloured population, continues to receive a continuous injection of the most basic rhythmic Negro music which has hitherto given American popular music its quality. England, on the other hand, has lost tradition (its roots to use the fashionable term) and can only accept American products second-hand, and so has tended to produce a music lacking in the vital elements of either. It remains to be seen whether the type of spontaneous creation which is going on in rhythm groups will really form a basis for a new tradition, in the way that one could envisage a new working-class tradition of literature based upon writers such as Alan Sillitoe and Bill Naughton. (It may be argued, of course, that such literature is based on a background of an already vanishing Britain.) On the other hand, the rhythm groups tend to an ever-closer approximation of the American sound (*viz.* the Rolling Stones) and already the Beatles' work, with its distinctly folky progressions, is being seen as a flash in the pan, and appears to have no real successors.

Perhaps the reason for this is that modern popular music is so advanced technically in comparison with all previous popular music, that a considerable degree of musicianship and/or talent is needed to permit an artist to think up a worthwhile development, and those who are capable of this tend to dissociate themselves from the popular world and to apply themselves to the more demanding problem of jazz creation. Thus a situation arises in which the majority of upper- and middle-class people do not create, and those who do usually go into classical music. A now substantial minority break away into the more fashionable jazz world. Similarly, among the working and lower middle classes the majority do not create, but some find their way out of this and produce either popular music or, in a minority of cases, jazz.

It is because of this association of jazz as being either a more progressive form of composition than classical music or a superior art form to popular music that I feel that Humphrey Lyttelton is wrong to consider that pure jazz is the new form of folk music. Jazz composers (writing or improvising) will tend to find their audience among serious listeners and to become increasingly associated with serious musical creation. The increasing stress on the extremely advanced music of the *avant-garde* shows that, if anything, jazz is moving even faster away from the fundamental simplicity of the dance hall.

In the past two or three years the further creative possibility of 'progressive pop' has arisen. This has produced a stream of music parallel to, but in competition with jazz, though there is some prospect of a union at certain points. In its first stage this movement resulted in creations of real quality: following the example of the Beatles and the Beach Boys, groups seemed to be able to draw upon the best of all worlds. But the awareness that they were creating music of real value seems to have given the musicians the desire to move towards "art". Thus, as happened much earlier in jazz, there is an increasing insistence upon the need to tax the musician technically. Complex time signatures and lengthy solo improvisations have been introduced, together with increasingly dissonant techniques. To the musician and to the more intellectual listener this is a very exciting situation, but it seems fairly clear that the popular audience, with its permanent demand for entertainment, is not likely to find this attractive. Moreover, it is likely that the audience for popular or folk music is never, and perhaps should never be, made up of serious listeners of the type that jazz is more and more coming to require. It would appear that the qualities which we value in a good piece of folk music are not sought out consciously, and are really synonymous with the talents of the composer as demonstrated in his ability to handle more successfully than most the materials at his disposal within the limitations which the entertainment of the audience lays down.

Thus, all popular music of any period will be a reflection of the society from which it springs and its quality will, therefore, depend on the quality of the attitudes of its audience. If we do not value the attitudes of the listeners, it is unlikely that we shall value the music written for them. For popular and folk music are definitely written for their audience, and not at it. The popular singer rarely, if ever, views himself as educating and elevating man, whereas this is a role taken on by the serious artist and even expected of him. We have, of course, to bear in mind such didactic material as the broadsides, but I am inclined to feel that these were written to reflect a widespread discontent and not to stir one up. Thus, even in this context, it is possible to argue that the popular artist is likely to be most successful when he is most representative.

From the foregoing paragraph, it is clear that the types of comment made about present-day popular music—that it is debased, banal, sentimental and pornographic—are in fact a criticism of the values of the bulk of our society. The same argument applies to the popular newspapers and the Sunday "Sexsationals". Clearly, this argument makes no allowance for the fact that, like all mass media, these things not only reflect taste, they form it. This problem will be examined in a later chapter. But clearly the criticisms of tastelessness in the general public still stand, at least in part. On the other hand, we must bear in mind that trade figures alone would be sufficient to demonstrate that popular music really is the music of the people, and being thus rooted in reality has the double advantage of comprehensibility and soundness. It may, therefore, be that out of this will develop a form of music which will have as many virtues as the much admired folk music of the past. If the people have moments of spiritual fineness, their music must show it. None of us, however, can ignore the Orwellian note of warning or can help wondering if the production line and suburbia are really going to produce the beauty comparable to that which was the result of an exaltation of the spirit which was to be found in the harvest field and the small close-knit communal and family life of the village.

Much more difficult to assess is the folk music boom; I find a particular difficulty here, because I am living in Cambridge, a town whose moods and fads are not those of the average English city. My work at the Technical College, for instance, gives the impression that a substantial minority of teenagers wish to learn folk guitar; on the other hand, I am fairly sure that this is an illusion created by the fact that our students come predominantly from a limited (middle-class) social range. I would expect to find that in Manchester, or a similar industrial area, the demand would still be for guitar as used in the Top Twenty.

There have clearly been many changes over the last fifteen years. In 1954, Reginald Nettel could write:

> Long playing records present a problem. It takes a collection of songs to make up a disc, and there is still apparently a suspicion that folk songs alone will claim only modest sales. The way out is thought to be by mixing other songs with folk songs and offering the whole as a recital of the songs of England, or the British Isles.

A visit to any record shop will show how much this situation has changed.

One could argue for a long time about where and how the revival began, but I think with reference to the *present* boom we can trace the beginnings in the interest in blues singers, and to the songs of Joan Baez. The one linked up with the Rhythm and Blues movement, and the other claimed popularity by its sheer quality. Probably the next important figure was Bob Dylan. Among intellectuals, his songs first attracted attention as being competent imitations of conventional styles, such as those of Jack Elliott, or Woody Guthrie, but this type of singer has only become known to the mass audience *since* the popularity of Dylan. Dylan really began to achieve a following, however, as his subsequent records began to show the emergence of a very sensitive and individual talent. His singing, for instance, sounded at first hearing to be rough and amateur; but more careful listening and comparison with the really amateur efforts of the average popular singer showed that his style was full of subtle inflections, inspired by, but not merely imitative of the

Negro blues singers. Moreover, his lyrics had poetic qualities not, to my knowledge, to be found in any other type of popular music, folk, blues or pop. His imagery and metaphor were more intense, and more sustained than anything previously produced. The average lyric is direct, and is built upon a small number of ideas. Dylan's style is oblique, and is so full of perceptions, that only several listenings will begin to create an understanding in the listener's mind: in this, his lyrics had the qualities which one normally associates only with poetry which is written without relevance to music.

Dylan first made an impact on the general public with his record "The Times are a Changing", at the same time that groups such as The Seekers were beginning to gain a success with a "Folky pop" style, which contained elements of both. The startling fact about Dylan's record, apart from the quality of the lyric (not his best, incidentally), was that it was made entirely by one man and a guitar, *i.e.* it rejected the group, and treated the beat much less rigidly. Folk clubs experienced a rapid increase in membership; The Seekers club in Liverpool, for instance, had something in the region of 2,000 members, I am told. Similarly, promoters could put on folk shows in the Festival Hall, where the hiring fee alone is a matter of £400.

The amazing thing, which still remains unexplained, was that Dylan, a man well known for his uncompromising attitudes, and world famous on the basis of a pure folk style, then issued records on which he was accompanied by a rock and roll group—and not a very good one at that. The effect artistically was disastrous. Dylan's style is intensely personal, as I have said, and despite its hard-hitting nature, is fundamentally delicate. Group work of any type is likely, by its nature, to be far too crude by comparison to be a suitable foil. Furthermore, group work requires a ranting, shouting type of delivery. This has its virtues, but it does not permit of delicacy of delivery or subtlety of lyric. The contrast was heightened by the fact that the LP which contained these "beat" tracks had on one side "The Gates of Eden", which expressed a philosophical vision of a rare sensitivity.

Dylan's actions though have indicated the way for a whole line of popular music. The folk-music purist, finding that American styles were both inimitable for foreigners, and were also constantly in danger of commercialisation because of the close relationship between the pure and pop styles (*viz.* the fate of the blues singer Ray Charles), has turned to more esoteric forms. An exciting development has been that of the English guitarists Davey Graham and Bert Jansch. Both are excellent technicians and have tried to link hitherto contrasting elements on the instrument. Davey Graham has experimented with the linking of Near Eastern and jazz techniques with folk styles, whilst

Bert Jansch has created what are virtually instrumental fantasias, based on Appalachian modal music, but using finger-picking styles so far only used in other areas of American music. Both have been deservedly popular, though it remains to be seen what influence they will have on folk music as a whole.

Much more widespread has been the move towards traditional English folk music: the heart of Cecil Sharp would indeed rejoice at the amount of chorus singing and ballad singing which is now taking place in folk clubs. It might be ventured that for the purist at least, the popularity of American styles is on the wane. The interest springs from the deep-seated needs which any audience has. They wish to create, but may not have time or inclination to acquire instrumental technique—vocal music clearly does not present this problem. Secondly, people wish to let go, as they always have done, in communal singing: there are times when to be entertained is not enough, one wishes to join in. Finally, the range of subject and vigour of treatment are more in accord with the wishes of the modern young person. Comment has already been made on the limited emotional range of the popular song—we are probably more inhibited today than were the Victorians. But the climate of opinion daily grows more favourable to the directness of the ballad style. It may therefore be that this type of club will make an important and valuaable change in our popular cultural life.

There will, however, need to be changes in attitude on the part of the originators of the movement. The type of purism that will accept only unaccompanied song, or songs of attested antiquity can only result in fostering the image of the traditional folk singer, as an eccentric singing, with eyes closed and finger in ear, of the three-field system or the defeat of the Spanish Armada. To attract the people, folk music must be felt by them to have relevance to them, and to be directly reflective of their lives and aspirations. Lines such as the following (from "Come Fill Up Your Glass", by Peggy Seeger) are only likely to impress a certain type of intellectual:

> To the ploughmen and shepherds and all men of worth
> Whose joy is to harvest the fruits of the earth.

Something on the lines of the following by Stan Kelly is what is needed; real-life situations and experience:

> I wish I was back in Liverpool, Liverpool Town where I was born
> There isn't no trees, no scented breeze, no fields of waving corn.

> But there's lots of girls with peroxide curls and the black and tan
>   flows free,
> With six in a bed by the old pierhead, and it's Liverpool Town for me.

Another problem of the folk singer, up till now, has been his political commitment. This is obviously a matter very difficult to discuss without offending some readers at least, but I hope the following analysis may prove acceptable even to those whom one would expect to be most hostile to it.

I believe, in the first instance, that a political song must have immediate relevance. The type of singer who insists on singing large numbers of Irish rebel songs not only drags up a past which is best left to be forgotten, but does not talk about modern problems (at least when singing in England—I am unable to comment on the situation in Ireland).

The bulk of the "protest songs" are nevertheless about current problems; many have enjoyed considerable success in the folk clubs. Karl Dallas' "Strontium 90" would be a good example. Yet I think that even the most ardent advocate of this type of song would have to admit that the success of such songs has been minute in comparison either with that of the Beatles or even of the Dylan records. Why should this be? Before answering, let us look at an example, from Alex Comfort's "St Pancras Day":

> Come all you tenants skint
> Pay heed to my narration
> I'll give you all a hint
> On dealing with inflation.
> The Tories were returned,
> Decided on a flutter,
> We'd pay them what we earned,
> Or we'd wake up in the gutter.

I have already, in connection with Northumbrian song, suggested a theory that conviction (artistically) only comes with total involvement, as distinct from sympathy (Alex Comfort is a doctor). Perhaps the rather old-fashioned diction of the opening is likely to put off a modern audience, too. But though the problems of housing in London are well known, and I suspect that my solution to Rachmanism would be just as violent as Dr Comfort's, many people do not have these problems (e.g. persons already with a house, and unmarried teenagers). And it would seem to be inherent in human nature that most people can only get very excited by what is very close to their lives; the defence of Europe holds far more interest for the average Englishman than war in Vietnam. I am not sure what the solution to this problem is, for the writer who is deeply critical of aspects of the social order, which are tolerated or even supported by the majority of the population. His sense of duty prompts him to attempt to convince people, yet his frustration at the refusal of society to accept the obvious tends to make him fall into a deep bitterness which comes out in his songs, and seems to make it impossible to create well, let alone to achieve popularity. For it is the tone of "St Pancras Day" which would put most people off. I am not happy with generalisations about the innate gentleness of the Englishman's character, or about his good humour, but I would suggest that in the following song, "Cheering the Queen", Cyril Tawney manages to win us over to his viewpoint far more effectively by using humour than he would by direct criticism. He slips under the guard which most people set up when they hear Royalty attacked, by merely letting the absurdity of the situation speak for itself

> When we saw the signal boys, it made our innards freeze:
> On the order ONE, you hold your hats at forty-five degrees,
> At forty-five degrees, m'boys, that's what their lordships said
> On the order TWO you wave your hats three times around your heads.
> . . . But when we reached the moment, boys, that every skipper dreads,
> A swarm of gnats as big as bats descended on our heads.

This is exactly analogous to the work of the TV satirists, or to Peter Sellers' approach in films like *Heavens Above*. It would seem that we find it uncongenial to have a moral stated directly: we seem to prefer to work it out for ourselves.

Whatever the future for the more purist type of folk music, there is no doubt that popular and folk music are interacting to create a style of their own, in a way that is certainly to the advantage of the popular style. The range of subjects, and the possibilities of diction and imagery are being extended by the influence of the folk style. And, as we saw in the chapter on techniques, the musical language is being given a freshness of style by the influence of the folk (modal) scales and harmonies. It will be interesting to see if guitarists will tend to leave the present plectrum style, with its necessity for a division of labour between melody and chord players, in favour of a finger-picking style of the folk sort. Existent idioms have only *begun* to utilise the possibilities. It would also solve one of the perennial difficulties of popular musicians—the lack of technical challenge in the music, once a certain stage of competence has been reached. Until now, the only way out of this impasse has been to turn to music which abandons popular values to some degree (for example, jazz).

On the other hand, popular music has brought about fundamental changes in the viewpoint of the folk artist. Most obviously folk music, to be popular, has had to acquire a regular beat, and to assimilate the metrical advances which popular music has made since the First World War. Changes of aesthetic approach are also to be found. Pop has attracted not only by the nature of its singers, but by its accompaniments. An attractive accompanying phrase, or a pleasing trick of orchestration has often been a vital factor in selling records (*viz.* the Burt Bacharach arrangements). This interest in accompaniment for its own sake has gone over into the new folk-pop idiom. The records of Dylan, even before his move into a beat style, are often thought to be simple in their accompaniments. Technically this is so, but in their content and conception they are far from the strummed "three-chord trick" of the amateur. By a selection of particular voicings of chords, or of effects of resonance caused by altered tuning, Dylan is able to set up an apt emotional climate into which he will insert his lyrics (*viz.* the accompaniments of "Masters of War" or "North Country Girl"). The twelve-string guitar is particularly appealing to audiences with this interest in sonority.

Perhaps the most important factor, and one not so pleasing to those who desire a communal culture of the sort described by Cecil Sharp is that such folk singers, and their audience, have accepted the idea of individual creation. In so doing they will naturally keep alive the type of situation which has been evolved in urban civilisation, in which the entertainer, however in touch with his audience, is still a man apart. The folk-pop man may be "like us", and be apparently informal and spontaneous in his manner, but in the last analysis he is credited with superiority, and he is known to be able to live in a style to which the ordinary person cannot aspire: he is still a dream figure, as Sinatra or Cliff Richard were. This is probably a situation which will now always be with us. The constant demands of the mass media for new material and higher standards exclude the amateur from seriously trying for success in popular music: one becomes totally involved in the industry, or one remains of no importance. The existence of a mass culture must also inevitably mean that the artist who succeeds will become extraordinarily rich: if one takes the public fancy at all one's markets are so great that one is bound to earn large amounts. Moreover the demand to make contact with the artist is bound to be so great (autographs, etc.) that he is forced to cut himself off in order to make life at all tolerable. Like the overcrowding of holiday resorts, this seems to be a problem which is inevitable and insoluble in a population which is increasing both in numbers and affluence. For this reason, the type of folk culture found at its height in the Anglo-Saxon period can probably

never exist again: it is a phenomenon of small societies, primitive in organisation, in which the number of tasks to be performed is limited, and of immediate relevance to everyone. In Anglo-Saxon society, despite the social
stratification everyone was involved in defence, and in tilling the land, even
though functions differed.

It is extremely dangerous to predict about a form of music which changes
so rapidly. It is perhaps better therefore to attempt to do so no more and
move on to our next topic.

11

The Attitudes of
Popular Musicians

I feel pity for those artistically dedicated types.
JOHN BARRY

A great deal has been written about classical musicians and their views, but little has been attempted, outside of jazz magazines and one or two bad novels, to explain the attitudes of popular musicians. This is a pity, because the two have very different outlooks.

However, the difficulty of making valid generalisations is made greater here by the fact that within the popular world there are some quite sharp divisions. To begin with, those connected with the production of popular music may be divided into three categories—the businessman, the "craftsman musician" and the pop player.

In the first group come agents, publishers, recording managers and disc jockeys. These people may be musically trained (like George Martin, who arranges the Beatles' recordings) or they may have no real connection with music at all (like the late Brian Epstein, the Beatles' manager). However, their attitudes have much in common.

The overriding factor is that for all of them music is quite clearly a business, and is, therefore, to be run on business principles—investment is to be made at as low a rate as possible in that which is likely to be most saleable. This may not be by any means the most musically desirable approach, but it is the only one which the musical businessman can allow. These attitudes have to be applied to a highly fragmented type of employment, in which the employees are very individual and tend to have a high resistance to organisation; as a consequence, though there are unions, there is nothing to enforce collective bargaining like the strong unions of, say, steelworkers.

Thus a situation most resembling the classic Marxist picture of capitalist exploitation is to be found. I should stress here that I do not automatically imply illegal practice. In fact, most marketers of popular music seem to have realised that this generally brings more trouble than it is worth. Only a disreputable and unknown publisher, for instance, will steal material. But probably the tendency to favour one's own is more marked here than anywhere else in the commercial world. Thus a disc jockey will be unlikely to receive a bribe to put a certain record on his programme, but he will be remembered when lucrative "perks" are being handed out (*e.g.* a TV appearance, a crate of whisky at Christmas, or expense allowances). Similarly, although a publisher will not steal material, it is difficult, despite the "rags to riches" legends which are fostered, to get even an honest consideration of one's work, let alone a publication, unless one is already in the circle. Also, when a work is considered, there is still the shameful situation (also found in the world of literature) in which a company can and does buy up the whole rights of it, keeping all the not inconsiderable profits of a successful piece. Of the same type is the payment of a fixed wage to a pop star, frequently at a rate of as little as £15 to £20 a week, even when the star is earning thousands a week. Naturally all the arguments about supply and demand, sound business practice, and the need to cover investment and risks will be brought forward by people wishing to justify this state of affairs. To those to whom these "ethics" are acceptable as a moral and aesthetic code, and do not seem to make nonsense of many of our artistic claims, I can say no more. It will already be clear that I cannot share the opinion that Brian Epstein was doing a kindness in taking a mere 20 per cent of an artist's earnings as a reward for his skill in answering the telephone.

The second main type of producer of popular music is the "craftsman musician", from whose ranks come most of the songwriters, arrangers, studio musicians (*i.e.* for film and TV work) and a fair number of the backing groups for artists other than the top names. By "craftsman musician" I wish to imply a highly trained man of all-round competence, who can be called upon to play anything but virtuoso pieces at sight in any idiom. The most obvious need for this type of musician, rather than a slightly gifted amateur such as Paul McCartney, is found in the business of accompanying singers. For this a player is needed who can quickly and easily produce a suitable backing, irrespective of key, speed or style. This clearly needs a definite standard of musicianly attainment, which may have been obtained at a music college, or under a private teacher, together with a considerable range of practical experience in dance bands.

It is not surprising, therefore, that to these musicians pop music is a job, and a means of earning money, rather than some exalted form of existence.

Thus at least one famous trumpet player is obliged to earn much of his income by making vocal noises behind pop records. The craftsman musician, therefore, has a concern with skill, correctness and the idea of doing a job properly. Steve Race was typical of many when he said that he tried to play anything that was required, as well as possible, and took a pride in doing this properly, no matter what his artistic opinions of the music were.

It is thus to be expected that such players are very scathing about groups of a low standard, and prefer to listen to pure jazz or to symphonic music. Many have played in pure jazz groups and enjoy the occasional "blow". Others, not having the improvisational talent, prefer to listen with admiration. They are also bitter about the increasingly youthful age of many stars. But by the time that a man is really competent and experienced (say, in the early to mid-twenties) he is already ageing by pop standards, and while still young is completely out of the question as a player in a big "name" group. Consequently we have the farcical situation that fine guitarists such as Dave Goldberg, Ivor Mairants and Bert Weedon, being "old" men of thirty and upwards, have to work hard to set a little money by, while guitarists such as John Lennon can earn enough to retire upon in a few months.

On the other hand, the craftsman musician can be over-critical and even unjust. In setting himself apart from the popular world, he often falls into a worship of technique rather than of true musical quality, with the result that bad Chris Barber may be considered better than good Manfred Mann. Thus my own preference to listen (if compelled to do so to either) to Elvis Presley rather than to Victor Sylvester would be a distinctly unpopular one.

It is worth explaining the fact that I include songwriters in this bracket. The reason for this is that, except where the group produces its own material (quite rare outside of "progressive" groups), the job is too difficult for amateurs. Again a wide range of technical competence is needed. When groups have written "originals" they have rarely been the most memorable of their recordings, and the bulk of submissions to publishers rarely rise even to competence, let alone to above mediocrity. I have only met one untrained songwriter (Ann Bevan-John) who produced songs of much worth; unfortunately she wrote in the wrong style to be popular with the adolescent market. When groups produce their own material, the compositions seem to be the result of the commonly found period of adolescent creativity, during which two or three good works are produced, to be followed by silence or sterile repetition, because the talent is not deeply enough rooted to continue into maturity.

The final group of pop musicians to be considered, probably the most interesting sociologically, is the pop player (that is, the player whose talent is confined to this type of music); with him may, perhaps, be linked, in apparent contradiction to what has just been said, the jazz player. The main link between them, other than the musical ones outlined earlier, is that they are both members of a definite social type, a minority group with strong characteristics, conventions and attitudes of its own. They have an argot or group slang, though it is a source of amusement to the "hip" jazzman that the slang of the popster was "dead" twenty years ago. Similarly, as in many minority groups there are set conventions of dress. Thus the modern jazz men wear suits, and look smart to affirm the professionalism which comes with the high level of technique needed to play their music, while tradmen prefer a casual "unaffected" look; popsters want something to make an impact and Rhythm and Blues men prefer rough (dare one say unwashed?) appearances.

For all of them, music is not just a pastime but a way of life, a life of informality, hours that are irregular by conventional standards, and interest in the pleasures of the body as well as of the mind (for the attitude towards musical problems is one of the greatest concentration). This emphasis on music and the rejection of day-to-day convention produces a definite arrogance towards the audience, paradoxically reinforced in the case of popsters by their popularity. Nevertheless the popster seeks fame and fortune on the grand scale, the immediate popularity and standing with girls which joining a group brings, overcomes many an adolescent problem, and the "bingo" get-rich-quick mentality finds more likelihood of a fortune in music rather than on the pools. After all, even a poorish group can earn several hundred pounds a year from "gigs" (casual engagements).

Such similarities as there are tend to be very superficial though, precisely because of this interest in money. Naturally, the jazzman likes to earn, as do we all, but he has a concern in the quality of his music which is lacking in the popster. He takes a great pride and interest in achieving technical proficiency and in understanding his art, whereas the popster is more concerned with his equipment than with the musical result. There seems to be a common belief among them that the better the guitar, the better the player; this has induced manufacturers to raise prices to unheard-of levels. An illustration of the power of publicity may be seen in connection with this, since the dearest guitars are solid (*i.e.* have a solid body with no soundbox). Now every string player knows that the biggest single factor in determining quality on an instrument is its soundbox, and the wood and skill of construction which have gone into it. Nevertheless, pop guitarists will maintain stubbornly in discussion that a solid guitar costing £200 (more than a baby grand piano!)

sounds better than a solid guitar costing half the price. It never seems to dawn upon them that the sound is electronically produced, and that it is the quality of the *amplifier* and *loudspeaker* which determines the quality of the resultant sound.

Another basic difference between the two types of musician is that though both believe in their music and each distrusts the other, the very technical proficiency which jazzmen strive for and condemn the lack of in pop makes jazz too complex to be satisfying to popsters. It is, however, necessary to accept that *both* are intensely excited by their music and that strange though this seems to the critical listener, the beat player believes in beat music and finds it and its lyrics meaningful and expressive of emotions which correspond to something inside him. This important point is too frequently missed: that despite the shallowness and commercial nature of the rulers of the pop kingdom, it is for the average player a real and genuine form, a music in which he is being sincere, even if his technique is too crude to express this sincerity, and furthermore it is usually the only form of music which he really knows. It is his only real culture.

This final point is true of the majority of both jazz and pop players, and is one which those who wish to propagate good music and musical discernment must face, unless they are prepared to try to dodge the realities of life.

We have to accept that, musically speaking, we are two nations, and that these are more distinctly divided, generally speaking, than the two nations of C. P. Snow, or than the North of Stan Barstow is from the South. There are those (a minority) who, after adolescence, have little or nothing to do with the popular or jazz world and there is the large group which, after they leave their last school music lesson, leave classical music alone and listen to nothing but pop or jazz. The result is that the popster speaks a language and accepts a set of basic musical values which, by and large, the classical musician neither understands nor accepts, and that the classical follower lives in a world of which even the most obvious monuments and landmarks are unknown, even by name, to pop listeners. As I mentioned in an earlier chapter, these include a steadily increasing proportion of the highly educated; one hears with horror of the formation of university beat groups, some of whom actually believe in the artistic value of singers such as Adam Faith (one Oxford group is on record as saying this).

The dangers of such a situation, from the cultural point of view, hardly need stressing. They are aggravated by the fact that classical music has always been a middle- and upper-class pursuit. This division by class is heightened by all kinds of factors great and small (such as the fact that symphony musicians play in evening dress), and is the most unsatisfactory aspect of its image. For the health of music of all types it is essential that this should be altered quickly. Otherwise serious music is in danger of becoming a steadily ossifying, ivory-tower pastime in which the great works become more and more of historical interest, and the modern composer remains a weird outsider producing for coteries which are too small to support financially the continuous creative activity which is necessary for strong and vital music to be produced.

12

The Attitudes of the Popular Music Audience

The whole stinkin' commercial world insults us
and we don't care a damn.
ARNOLD WESKER, *Roots*

The first and most important factor about the audience of popular music is its size; this has meant that a market of vast proportions has grown up in which the financial reward can be quick and immense. Thus the Beatles became millionaires in a space of time during which many a businessman would still be collecting capital.

The result of this has been that the vendors of popular music have come to use the methods of the soapflakes manufacturer to push their wares. Big advertisements, glossy magazines, souvenirs and judiciously timed radio and TV appearances are the stock-in-trade of the agent. At the same time a study, formal or otherwise, of public taste has given the musical businessman a sense of the importance of an "image". Thus television producer Jack Good is quoted in Royston Ellis' book as saying:

> . . . the star we really created with "Oh Boy" was Cliff Richard. . . . I knew that here was someone who could be built into a new idol the teenage public would go completely mad over. . . . For the first six months I dared not put him in front of the cameras without hours of rehearsal. . . . Cliff was moulded into someone totally different from his real self . . . [he was] a sex bomb who was a cherubic faced infant. . . . That was how people saw him and wanted him. The image had to be kept for people to believe.

Similarly, in the sixties there was the careful concealment of the marriage of Paul Jones of the Manfred Mann group, so as not to spoil the image. Such doctoring of facts, together with the propagation of complete inaccuracy or vague (and unbelievably wild) statements such as the one that "the vitality of Liverpool beat music was due to its proximity to America and to the fact that sailors arrived with the latest records before they were released in this country", shows that the art of publicity has come a long way since the days when girls were paid to "faint" at Frank Sinatra's concerts.

The terrible fact about this situation is not so much the tailoring of propaganda, but the fact that the public so crave a world of glamour that they will accept it all and will refuse to look critically at it. To the best of my knowledge, popular artists before the First World War were admired for their talent and envied as having access to the luxurious life of upper-class society, but they were not regarded as superhuman figures. I have been appalled again and again by the statement by teenagers that "you must have an ideal and some-one to admire", coupled with the unquestioning acceptance of the value of such groups as the Rolling Stones, who rose to fame in the eyes of the public for their "individuality" of music and appearance, and to notoriety in the eyes of the entertainment business for their unique ability to be arrogant. The suggestion that a great doctor might merit more admiration is usually put aside as being just not acceptable.

Concern for money is one of the most saddening features of all, especially when found in the young. I have met many musicians, classical and jazz, and many students whose merit, despite the many adolescent factors in it, was their rebellion against what they considered to be false ideals, their unwilling-ness to accept without question, and their desire to do what they thought was right even if it were unpleasant. I had assumed this to be the commonest feature and indeed the privilege of youth. It, therefore, came as a great shock, when I began to go into the popular music world, to find that the first answer to the question "Why did X make this record?" was not "Talent", or "He had to do it", or something of that sort, but "Money". Such an acceptance of the commercial nature of popular music, without an accompanying critical faculty, is to me most disturbing. Further discussion showed a very wide-spread acceptance of the profit motive to the exclusion of artistic considera-tions, and of the idea that people will push a product and use questionable methods to make sales.

It is not surprising, therefore, that with this attitude comes a taste for gloss and for novelty. The former is manifested in the manner of production of television shows and films, with high speed, a "galaxy" of talent, costing sums that make a symphony musician's heart bleed, and, as mentioned in the last chapter, in the instruments used. The laudable desire for better equip-ment has led to the exploitation of the ignorant by the crafty use of a coat of varnish or a "modern" design, and to the placing of the more knowledge-able in a position where even if they can see the tricks, they are obliged by

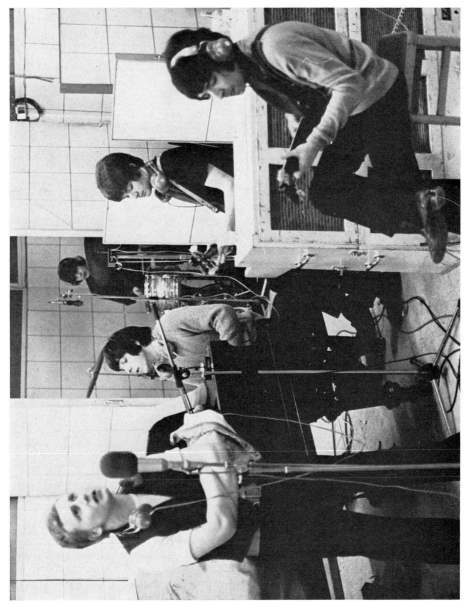

Recording session by The
Love Affair

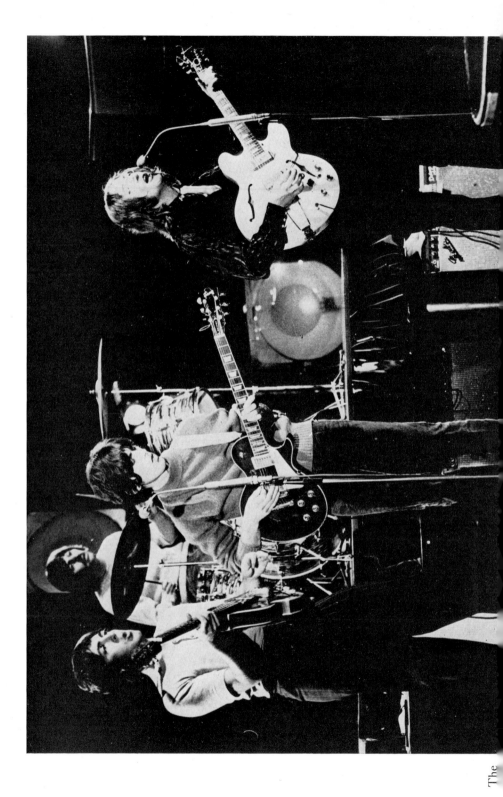

public taste to obtain equipment of the right appearance, at, of course, a higher cost. Thus, whereas any self-respecting electronics man can build an amplifier which is all but gold plated for £50, the "in" amplifier of the moment costs £200 and there is a steady sale of ones costing £300.

Slick presentation coupled with a desire to "plug" as many records as possible leads to the ludicrous situation in which only a part of the record will be played. This leads to the very dangerous musical state where the repetition of a record induces a craving for it which is in turn satisfied by the stimulus (to steal a psychological term) of the opening bars: the rest of the record thus becomes redundant, and a habit of inattention is formed, under the influence of which it is unnecessary to listen to more than this, and impossible to listen to anything beyond the standard length of a record. For this reason a record of only five minutes' duration is felt by many teenagers to go on interminably (so much for Mahler's symphonies!). Since it is true that for many centuries works by masters of much complexity and depth only lasted a few minutes (*e.g.* Bach fugues), no one would claim that length is an important factor in the production of good music (indeed, much popular music is too long by three minutes). Nevertheless, it would seem that the fostering of an inability to concentrate musically, which like any other concentration is acquired, is helping to widen drastically the already great gulf between the popular and the serious listener.

At the same time, the commercial emphasis on novelty is resulting in an ever-increasing pressure of demand upon the market for new records, and a proportionate lack of interest in the past, with obvious effects for classical music, which at present has a view which is diametrically opposed to this. I soon found, as a teacher, how dated someone was considered to be who thought he knew something about this type of music but was not up with the latest fashion. Most of the names in this book are already unknown to teenagers. Music three months old is "out", a year old is definitely "dated" and three years old—if remembered at all—is regarded with awe as "classic". When this is added to a natural adolescent desire, aided by publicity, to establish their own world with its own fashions as apart from that of all others, and especially that of the older generation, it is obvious why older people who attempt to be "with it" are regarded as figures of fun. They are seen to be missing all that is really important.

It is, of course, true that the following of fashion is an eternal characteristic of human behaviour (it was, for instance, a frequent topic in Restoration Comedy). But there are, today, new dangers, I feel, in that mass media puts a pressure upon the individual to conform to fashion so great that, unlike in the Restoration plays, the highly fashionable figure is not made a figure of fun, but a desirable model. The pressure on unformed minds to accept these ideas and the implicit values is immense and tends towards a distinct stifling of individuality and critical judgement. Furthermore, the Restoration period had a great advantage, at least in music, in the widespread nature of practical musical acquirement among those adults who had leisure to listen to music at all. There was a consequent sharpening of sensibility towards good music, so that Pepys, for instance, who could make "barber's music" for the Admiral with cittern and candlesticks, also had serious musical interests and played and listened to good music by the best masters.

One of the results of the cult of novelty is the increasing demand for sounds and effects, such as the wobbleboard and the echo chamber, rather than for that which is truly musically valuable (technical proficiency, tone and pitch control, form). By such standards a fugue for harpsichord can only be interminably dull and a Haydn symphony little better.

Paradoxically enough, the need for novelty in popular music, as administered by record player or radio, seems to be counteracted by a very definite conservatism in taste in such areas as film music. The composer of music for this purpose knows that he dare not experiment, when writing for a mass audience, and that muted string tremolos when the villain enters show that in the fifty years since the cinema pianist enjoyed his heyday, the popular audience have only accepted a refinement in techniques and not in basic emotional approaches and their musical representation in the cinema. It would seem that for any given situation there is a set type of musical accompaniment, which has become a ritual element, or perhaps one should say a bad habit, like the *Messiah* at Christmas. This is found at its worst in the TV Western, where even the dialogue and ordering of incidents have become highly predictable. Perhaps the element of predictability with its attendant feeling of comfort in the presence of the familiar explains somewhat the increasing positive need for popular music, which seems to be directly linked at the same time to a diminishing attention to it. Such tendencies are aided by repetition.

The media through which popular music is presented in their desire to cash in on the demand for any given record miss no possible opportunity of bringing in yet a little more profit. To hear anything so frequently (and for the average teenager listening to Radio Luxembourg an average of four times a week for upwards of two hours a night the frequency is high), leads to a familiarity which encourages the lack of attention already mentioned. This alone would explain the high turn-over of records in the Hit Parade. But this is aggravated by a new factor, the all-pervading presence of popular music.

It will soon be true to say that it can be heard everywhere except the public library and the mortuary. The transistor radio is largely responsible for this, though the tendency was in evidence thirty years ago; Constant Lambert commented on it, and the appalling popularity of music quite soon after radio had become firmly established. As a consequence, it must be true to say that in the twentieth century, for the first time, music has ceased to be organised and created for the sole purpose of listening. It has now become for many people a necessary background noise for all kinds of activity. It is now essential for tedious work (this has been exploited more and more since its value was first found in factories during the War), and now the Musak people have produced long-playing tapes of sounds for public houses and hotels which are carefully selected for their unobtrusive and innocuous nature. I have heard one at least once while paying a bill at the local Gas showrooms!

Far worse, for the young person, is the increasing need for music to fill in the gaps of conversation, the result of which is that one does not have to force one's mind to learn how to do so. At a time when, because of earlier maturity and greater freedom, teenage problems have increased in number and complexity, there are not a lot of signs that the majority of young people have learned how to verbalise them and how to seek the aid and advice of others; unmarried mothers, particularly, illustrate this fact, and many seem to be unable to comprehend what has happened to them. Less important than this, but still unclear as to its effects is the fact that many of the young people find background music an essential accompaniment to study—they say they cannot concentrate so well without it. Personally I find it hard to believe that anyone can really concentrate to their utmost *with* it, but it is a widely held opinion: whatever the truth, it is a habit which is unlikely to help one in a public library.

The universality of music has widened the audience of popular music to an unprecedented extent; since 1918, this had largely tended to be adolescent. Now, the claim of the Beatles' publicity, that the group appeals to dukes and dustmen, is in fact true. The debutante and, more sad, the university student have fallen prey to the music. It has also widened the age range to which it caters. Unfortunately, the scope of the lyrics has suffered a proportionate decline, as we shall see later. Affluence and changing parental attitudes have meant that young children are now familiar with it to an extent unimaginable twenty years ago, in fact the 12 to 16-year-old market is a very large one.

At the same time the older person is not only interested in it but appears to prefer it. I was most surprised to find, when playing in a group which specialised in playing beat and ballroom dance music (the Soulstirrers), that audiences over the age of 25, which one would expect to want a majority of waltzes and quicksteps, would, once given beat music, demand it all night. This state of affairs only appears to change markedly in the over-40 age group.

The phenomenon may be partially due to the enormous stress which is given to youth and to its activities in the USA, and, increasingly, here. The exhortation to stay young and "keep up to date", which is laudable enough if it encourages people to stay mentally alive, seems to result in a frantic and rather pathetic attempt to put the physical clock back and to pretend that a large part of one's life and experience has not happened. A particularly dangerous situation, as I see it, is the acceptance of what are fundamentally adolescent (and thus by definition immature) attitudes to life in general and to love in particular. I cannot see that a retreat from Victorian prudishness to an adolescent fantasy world, in which the realities of personal relationships are not faced, is any great gain to society.

Musically speaking, the omnipresent nature of popular music presents great dangers, if only because any stimulus, too often repeated, becomes cloying. It is conceivable that music itself could become wearing, though it is more likely that the situation will encourage an attitude which regards music as a necessary adjunct to all activity, but not as something to be concentrated upon. To this must be added the tendency to debase any remaining sense of standards, by the frequent pushing of inferior material. (The Chris Montez record "Let's Dance" was a good illustration of the margin of error in pitching and all-round competence which was tolerable in a hit record.) A lack of sensitivity to the finer points of even this very simple music is also going to be encouraged if the staple diet of its audience is the very poor reproduction of the transistor set. Live performance is at present of no help as a corrective, since guitar groups are prone to obtain maximum volume (and so maximum distortion) from their equipment.

It is, therefore, clear that the public attitude to this music already leaves much to be desired, and is in considerable danger of further decline, to the detriment of all music, since in any mass industry, the lowest common denominator which is acceptable will be offered for sale before long.

13   A Modern Dance Hall

We intend to wage a fight against this worm
wiggle.
THE MIAMI BOARD OF REVIEW

It is possible that many of the readers of this book will never have been near
a beat dance and will, therefore, have only a hazy idea of what one is like.
For this reason, an attempt to describe one may not be out of place, since it
may help the understanding of the popular musical mentality, which is after
all the aim of this book.

The hall itself will vary in splendour and decor according to fashion and
area, but it is generally true to say that the dancers prefer a smallish place in
which people are crowded close together; they feel "lost" in a big hall. Low
lighting adds to the atmosphere.

Into this come the dancers, who divide broadly into two main groups—
those aged 13–18, and those aged 18–25. An older face is rarely seen, except
at "village hops". These age groups tend to have quite definite characteristics
of their own. All give a false impression of maturity, so that one may easily
mistake a 14-year-old for 18. This is, I think, one of the factors accounting
for increased promiscuity at that age, since generally the older man avoids
the younger girl, if only for fear of the law. The younger group tend to wear
the more extreme modern fashions, but have only a surface affluence, because they are earning little or nothing. Any hall owner knows that it is the
older group which will pay ten shillings or more entrance fee, and will buy
a great deal of alcohol.

From both groups one gets a great feeling of solemnity—a strange thing
to find in a dance hall. Caused partly by the fashionable way to act and partly
by social ineptitude, it results in the audience's standing around in small
groups waiting for the music to begin.

The music comes, of course, from the bandstand, upon which there is a growing tendency to have a turntable, often in a booth resembling a cashier's desk. From this the latest records are played during band breaks, or for the whole night on days when takings do not warrant the expense of a band. This is another point at which taste has changed, since a decade ago record sessions were usually a flop. Now, the prestige and popularity of recordings is so great that many people are happy to dance to them all night.

When the band comes on, it begins at once. The equipment used is not only impressive in appearance but also so complex that it has to be set up and well tested before the start. The band attracts attention and there is always the inevitable gaggle of young girls who walk to the front of the bandstand and dance there, often all evening, to attract the attention of the players. To me, as a dance musician used to being thought of as a kind of glorified waiter, this aspect of the music was startling (and not unpleasant!). Membership of a group, no matter how humble, gives one an unbelievable stature in the eyes of "pop"-minded girls. Singers, of course, are the most popular. On the other hand, the typical middle-aged person's impression of screaming uncontrolled teenagers must be disposed of at once. This type of wild treatment is reserved for top groups only, and usually at concerts. Their attitude to all other groups is far more restrained, on the surface.

This comment is also fairly valid for the dancers' attitudes to each other, as well. While it is undoubtedly true that outside of the dance hall, sexual relationships often take place on so casual a basis that it has been known for people to ask each other's names after intercourse, if at all, there is little sign of this inside the hall. Most modern dances are performed with the partners completely apart, apparently dancing by themselves, and not touching, and frequently the partners are both girls. The looks of the dancers are most intense, and show little apparent enjoyment. Men do approach the girls, but with results so varied as to confuse the onlooker as to the purpose of the operation. Frequently the girls will refuse in a most obviously disdainful manner, for no clear reason, whereas on other occasions two men will walk up and with a complete lack of courtesy "break up" a pair of girls, who will then continue dancing with their new male partners with as little show of emotion as if the change had not taken place.

The lack of sex is found also in the fact that there is comparatively little kissing and cuddling by those around the edges of the floor; less, I am inclined to think, than ten years ago. This is certainly not due to any lack of interest or ability, since at the average teenage party the same people may well be found in positions of abandonment which, if described, would make *Fanny Hill* seem like a nursery tale.

The reasons for this I am not psychologist enough to suggest, though I am certainly prepared to offer the idea that for the younger group, dancing is the last stage of the expression of childhood high spirits. This impression first came to me when seeing 16-year-olds dance the Beatles' number "Twist and Shout", in which a scream is emitted at certain critical points. Far from being a hysterical expression of sexual excitement, this reminded me for all the world of the screams of 13-year-olds playing Musical Chairs. This impression of high spirits and physical release is reinforced by the tremendous effort which is put into a dance such as the Shake, which is the greater since the audience expect and usually get non-stop music. Gaps for conversation, relaxation and social mixing of the older style of dancing have disappeared entirely.

In the older group the sexual implication of the lyrics and of the dance are more clearly realised, however, and one sees a distinctly conscious attempt to indulge in erotic display. Even here, I am doubtful that the average popular listener is anywhere near as conscious of the erotic ambiguities and implications of the lyrics as are the more literary-minded critics who draw our attention to them. Such criticisms are much more true of those who write the lyrics, who as I have said before, follow a very clear-cut commercial attitude. The average teenager tends to be very simple-minded in many respects, and I think that teachers agree (as they do so rarely) upon their sincere and openhearted attitude.

It is sad to have to record that despite the fact that the dance spots are, generally speaking, far less iniquitous than some older people would believe, and far more moral and healthy in atmosphere than many a hotel bar, there is nevertheless a substantial minority of socially inept, uncouth, belligerent youths. For this reason most halls hire "bouncers" to remove troublemakers, but incidents still occur. To be fair, I must admit that it is possible to go the whole evening without actually noticing such an incident—they are usually confined to two or three individuals of the same type. But few dances go by without a fight, and one of the most striking differences I noticed while playing beat music was the much higher incidence of unruly behaviour at such dances, presumably due to the fact that the older style no longer attracts the immature and rowdy element. Certainly, in ten years of dance playing I had never seen or heard of an incident in which a band was involved —there seemed to be a sort of unwritten law against it—whereas in a few months of beat work I experienced three such incidents, one quite serious, which was provoked by the throwing of a glass of beer at the well-known Nottingham singer Dave Turner. Professional groups usually hire a "road manager" for this purpose, since it is quite common for louts to hang about afterwards so as to "duff up the band".

Another feature peculiar to the halls of our time is the apparently insatiable craving for volume.

After hearing the 22-piece Stan Kenton Orchestra at close quarters I thought I was ready for anything, but I soon realised my mistake, when I found that the main aim of beat groups is to produce as much volume as possible. To this end an average group will have four amplifiers of 30 to 100 watts power each. At the same time, the drummer plays as loudly as possible (literally) and certainly at a volume which would render most dance groups inaudible. It is felt that the bass guitar should actually vibrate the floor and a sound which will make an almost visible "whoof" in filling a hall is greatly admired. There is, therefore, some case for the idea that the dancers are excited by the actual physical vibrations set up. All this is a new phenomenon though volumes have been steadily rising since the advent of Rock and Roll (and, indeed, since 1918). Thus, a 15-watt amplifier which I bought as a most up-to-date model ten years ago, and which was quoted by the firm as filling the Dominion Theatre, London, is now completely ineffectual in even a poorly equipped beat group.

It is perhaps worth stating that I do not see volume in the way that it is received by some traditionally minded critics. Not only is volume an observable feature of the music, and enjoyable within limits—it seems to command one's attention and so to force one into an exhilarated state—but I believe it may even be considered as a formal element, in the sense that it is vital to the music.

In the first place, the percussive nature of the music almost implies volume: it is virtually impossible to use percussion at a very low volume level (compare the practice of Classical composers). Moreover, any accent not caused by length of note (quantitative) must be produced by stress (qualitative), that is the emphasis of one note relative to another. Certainly it is a fact that a beat group cannot play at low volume without losing its impact. I have been present on occasions when the goodwill of the neighbours depended upon the beat group reducing volume to something like that of a lounge pianist; the groups inevitably protested vigorously, and from a musical point of view with good reason: their impact was reduced to nothing when this important component was taken away. It is also true to say that conventional dance bands and jazz groups are in a similar position, though to a less extreme degree.

The big bands of the forties used to specialise in the use of volume in the form of crescendo, but paradoxically enough neither this nor accelerando seem to be vital to popular music. A given tune will usually begin at a fairly high level and not alter markedly. There are, of course, slight changes, and on occasion, especially in the last chorus of a tune, there may be a marked increase, but the constantly fluctuating use of volume and subtle interpretation of the Classical musician are not idiomatic in popular music, and are, by and large, irritating. In this there seems to be a link with the lack of variety of orchestration, tempo and form. This need not be a condemnation of the music; it merely needs a different approach in the listener. Some parallel may be traced in serious music of the pre-Classical period (the Mannheim Orchestra became famous for its "invention" and exploitation of crescendo).

Though the taste for the high volumes mentioned above is not incompatible with musical value if the sound is controlled, it takes little imagination to realise the dire effects of amateurs playing at that volume. The sound becomes a blur, in which nothing is distinguishable, except perhaps a thudding from the bass. The words are part of the jumble and the danger of feedback is ever present. Thus, a performance by an amateur group will be punctuated by roars, hums, screams and howls of the most excruciating type. Unfortunately, this is rapidly becoming accepted as an inevitable feature of existence, even at the highest (?) level. The Rolling Stones, whom I heard at the notorious Magdalen College, Oxford, Commemoration Ball in 1964, produced a performance full of such noises, interspersed with a sound which might have been recognisable as music had not their amplification been so turned up that there must have been at least a 50 per cent distortion.

This, then, is the sound track to the so far silent picture I have given of a dance hall. I feel it to be an honest attempt to describe a feature of twentieth-century life with which few older people are familiar, and yet which is the centre and generating plant of a very substantial amount of adolescent thought. As a teacher, I have never ceased to be amazed at how important popular music is to this age group, and how much of their time and energy it takes up. In fact, I have not hesitated to use this and to draw upon the great admiration which is given to anyone who can play the guitar in their style (no difficult task) for wider and more liberal educational aims.[1]

For better or for worse, this is the situation. Perhaps later writers will see it as a symbol of the pulsating vitality of the mid-twentieth century. I only offer it, as I do all the other information and ideas in this book, for the reader's enlightenment, and, I hope, stimulation.

[1] For further details see my article "Using Fashion for Education", *Journal of the Liberal Studies Association*, June 1965.

14   The Melodies of Twentieth-Century Popular Music

I believe that one must be vulgar to be lyrical.
LIONEL BART

Since, in the last analysis, the essence of all popular music is melody, and it is upon the quality of its melody that a given era will ultimately be judged, it is time to consider this most basic of all aspects in some detail.

Technically speaking, the popular song, with the exception of the 12-bar blues form, which is enjoying an unusual popularity at present, is built up of 8-bar units. In fact, until recently a 12-bar form was almost a clear indication that the music in question was not "popular".

This statement about 8-bar units is the one most commonly made, but needs qualification, since a not insubstantial number of tunes (e.g. "How High the Moon") are built up of sections which can only satisfactorily be analysed as two 16-bar units. Furthermore, though in practice 8- and 16-bar units are the normal length of comprehensible sections, or "sentences", the fact that the fundamental unit of popular musical composition is really 2 bars becomes important in considering exceptions. Thus, "Moonlight in Vermont" (6–6–8–8) breaks down into a pattern A–A–B–A+2 bars (see Ex. 31.) The B section is standard in length but the A section, though beginning with a 4-bar phrase, as though it were a standard 8-bar sentence, "goes wrong" by the addition of a 2-bar unit. Such additions account for the structure of "Stormy Weather" (8–10–8–10) and "I Got Rhythm" (8–8–8–12). This type of exception is too frequent to support the commonly found statement that "Pop tunes are all 32 bars long."

Popular tunes are sometimes condemned for being written in a limited range of keys. In fact, *G, C, F, B♭* and *E♭* and *A♭* are regularly used. *D♭* is found, but rarely ("Body and Soul"). The sharp keys are less used except in music of a Spanish or Latin American character and in "beat music". Both of these favour *G, D, A* and *E*.

Ex. 31

Moonlight in Vermont

It must be admitted that there was a time when the average dance musician was less technically proficient than his classical counterpart, though this is no longer true. Thus, earlier music tended to favour the less remote keys. But the real reason for the use of the keys listed above is quite simple and justifiable, and it is that they bring out the best tone and sonorities of wind instruments, especially the saxophone and the trumpet. The "Spanish" and "beat"

interest in sharp keys is similarly related to the guitar, which is easier to play and most effective in those keys. It is, of course, generally accepted by musicians that an orchestrator of any style will attempt to utilise the best sonorities of the instruments at his disposal and will choose his keys accordingly.

A great deal has been said about modulation in popular music, and again much effort has been wasted because of the faulty use of terms.

In the first place, it is essential to distinguish between "transitory modulation" as a form of harmonic colouring in passages which are quite definitely in one key, and structural modulation, in which the essence of the listener's experience is that the music is moved into a different key for a substantial period, during which the satisfactions of harmonic movement physically heard in that key are given a second dimension by the mind, which retains the impression of the original key and so appreciates pulls towards and away from it. This type of experience can take place both within the piece, and between the sections of a larger work such as a symphony.

Large-scale "architectonic modulation" of the latter type is, it will be clear from our earlier comments, not found in popular music, and is likely to be by nature alien to it. At certain points there have been periods of a vogue for the performance of the final chorus in a different key, but such changes have always been rather disturbing, largely because they were managed in a very crude fashion, often by the simple expedient of transposing the piece bodily into the key a semitone above, without so much as a bridge passage.

When we consider the "structural" and "transitional" forms of modulation within one piece, however, comparison can be made with similar classical works (e.g. the nineteenth-century song). For a critic seeking "advancement", the popular song will offer nothing more striking or complex than the works of serious composers of that period. In this sense popular music is completely derivative. On the other hand, if our criterion is the successful use of the available techniques, as distinct from either a lack or an excessive or unsatisfactory use of them, some popular music of this century can claim a considerable degree of success. Pleasing or even beautiful tunes have been written with an interesting and successful use of key changes. Furthermore, it is much to the credit of composers that they have produced a result that, though technically quite advanced, is undoubtedly popular and comprehensible. In the case of the popular audience this is especially interesting, when we consider the nature of earlier popular music. The serious composer of the nineteenth century had the advantage of building upon two centuries of experiment, whereas the folk idiom, being modal, was by definition denied even the simplest possibilities of modulation. Even the middle-class idiom used, generally, the most simple movements to related keys. To arrive at a stage where harmonic movement was possible even to the most remote keys, while at the same time using quite strong discord (7ths, 9ths and 13ths) meant that the public's ability to accept a wider musical language had increased beyond recognition. This can only be to the good; the fact that more possibilities are not used and exploited is more due to the businessman than to the musician.

Examples of the type of tune under discussion are "Body and Soul" (modulates in the bridge passage from D♭ major to D major, through D minor to C major)

Ex. 32

Body and Soul

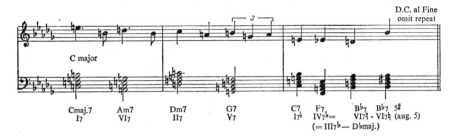

D.C. al Fine
omit repeat

C major

Cmaj.7	Am7	Dm7	G7	C7	F7	B♭7	B♭7 5♯
I7	VI7	II7	V7	I7♭	IV7♭=	VI7♮ - VI7♮	(aug. 5)
					(= III7♭— D♭maj.)		

and "Moonlight in Vermont" (see Ex. 31, changes from C to E major, thence
to F major, before returning to C), and "I Remember April" (G major
changes to $B♭$ major, back to G major and by means of a suggestion of E back
to G). Clearly, not all popular tunes have such workmanlike and advanced
changes. The move into the subdominant key, returning by means of II
(major)⁷–V⁷ progression to the original key is a cliché of the style.

I use the term "transitional modulation" to mean modulation as springing
directly from the introduction of chromatic notes, which thus give a distinct
sense of key-change not found in diatonic harmony. This is especially true of
chains of 7ths. Thus, a progression such as III min⁷–VI min⁷–II min⁷–V⁷,
a cliché of the eighteenth century, is rarely found in twentieth-century
popular music and is generally used for "pretty effects". Depending on the
melody line, one or more of the minor chords will be made major. When the
chord affected is VI, there is a transitory sense of passing to II minor, and
when III and II are also affected, we obtain the "chain of dominant 7ths",
a phenomenon used in earlier periods for its disturbing and discordant
nature, which is easy enough on the modern ear to be the harmonisation of
many a tune for 8 bars (*e.g.* middle 8 of "I Got Rhythm"):

Ex. 33

(a) old form   (b) popular form   (c) chain of dominant sevenths

The common feature of all these harmonies is that they last for a short
period only and are used within a sub-section of 8 bars which begins and ends
clearly in the original key.

A different type of thing is done in tunes such as "All The Things You
Are" and "Laura". In these the frequency of changes, though effective, is
such that the effect can only be described as one of "disturbed tonality". The

pieces are clearly tonal—they are too short to be anything else—but they only reach a point of rest at the end of the tune.

"All The Things You Are" is excellently constructed in that it begins and ends on the note *A♭*, in which key the piece ends:

Ex. 34

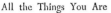
All the Things You Are

However, the first chord is that of the relative minor, and between it and the last bar the keys of *C, G,* and *E* are clearly touched upon. It moves first from the *F* min by a chain of 7ths into a IIb⁷--V progression establishing *C* major. The second eight bars begin with a change to *C* minor, and then echo the harmonic structure of the first eight to end in the related key of *G.* This key is then established firmly by the use of a II–V–I progression and then the II chord is used to move to *E* major. The fifth of the *E* major chord is raised and the resultant augmented chord is used enharmonically to return to *F* minor. The same procedure of a chain of 7ths is used in the last section, but the ending is different. An ambiguous chord is used which turns out to be IV min and leads naturally to the point of rest in *A♭.*

The aim of the above analysis is not, of course, to claim for the song anything which it is not, but merely to point out the degree of craftsmanship, which is not merely competent but attractive. The aim is also to point out the continually moving nature of the harmonic changes.

A similar analysis can be made of "Laura", which shows an even greater sense of harmonic restlessness:

Ex. 35

Laura

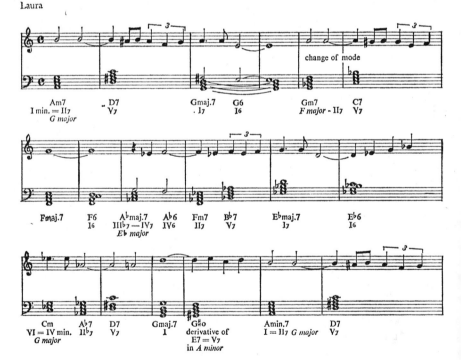

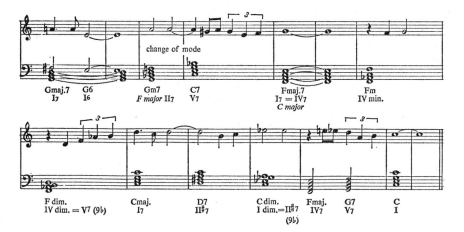

The piece consists (with the exception of the movement to $E\flat$) of a series of simple V–I progressions in different keys, the V chord of each being preceded by II min or IV min, balanced against more complex movements round the dominant seventh (of G and C) at the end of each section. The whole is skilfully linked to give a feeling of satisfactory movement.

It is clear, though, that however interesting and subtle the modulation of a "popular" tune may be at times, its melody and hence its melodic construction are its most vital features. Here, three distinct aspects of the melody may be studied: the intervals used, the rhythms used, and the combination of these in the construction of the melody.

The first is easily dealt with, since though, on the one hand, most intervals are used at some time or other, the use of the augmented 4th is rare (but not unknown, *viz.* the openings of "Bali Hai", from *South Pacific*, and "Maria", from *West Side Story*): I cannot call to mind a use of the major 7th. Nevertheless, popular music is created predominantly of scale passages and simple consonant arpeggi, which give it a pleasant character. Moreover these are indispensable for the untrained listener and singer. As a consequence, it denies itself all the shades of tension and dissonance found by the use of much more frequent dissonant intervals in serious composers.

At an early stage, however ("Alexander's Ragtime Band", 1911), the new type of popular music had adopted rhythms rare, unknown, or even impossible to earlier musicians. The free speech-like rhythms of the older folk music denied it the possibilities (or need) for the syncopations available in a stricter metrical form, and the music of the nineteenth century sought a rather square, on-beat style. The rhythm of modern popular tunes has tended, however, to incorporate, even in its simplest forms, all manner of syncopated rhythms. This tendency has become strongly pronounced in recent years. Thus a tune, such as "Happy Days and Lonely Nights" (published 1928), is 32 bars long and contains syncopation of some form in 20 of them. As much has already been said about the rhythm of popular music, and space does not permit a more detailed consideration, even if that were desirable in the present context, I shall press on at once to the consideration of the combination of these resources of harmony, interval and rhythm.

The standard view of this is very gloomy indeed. The very sound critic Francis Newton calls it "assembly line" composition and, in the collection of essays called *Discrimination and Popular Culture*, Donald Hughes claims of hit tunes: "Given the opening phrase, any average composer could finish the tune and the result would be very much what is eventually published." This might be true of the second class of popular material, but Donald Hughes is talking about "hits", so I am bound to challenge this.

In the first place, the selection of striking, easily memorable and pleasing phrases is not as easy as might be thought; there is a definite knack in it, as anyone who has tried to write a good pop tune will have found. Though many flatter themselves that they could do as well, few seem able to persuade publishers of the fact. This applies even to the continuation of a tune. It is disputable that an average composer could do this; he would, for instance, have to invent new material for the middle 8. I suspect that the type of composer Donald Hughes is thinking of is a man not of the highest standing, but known to his own national classical music public: such a man must be, in the twentieth century, a man of considerably above average ability, because of the immense difficulties of obtaining a performance of one's work at all.

The faultiness of the "assembly line" type of generalisation struck me finally when, tending to accept it, I came to look for examples. Then I found that rhythmic, though not intervallic monotony was to be found in tunes such as "Memories" (built largely on one rhythm), and "I'll See You In My Dreams" (minims almost throughout). "Making Whoopee" followed closely behind, with three rhythms, if one includes a slight variant. Perhaps the most close approximation to an assembly-line method which I found in my admittedly not exhaustive search was "Laugh Clown Laugh" by Ted Fiorito (1928) (see Ex. 36.)

Here, an opening phrase is repeated a tone lower. A new rhythm is introduced and repeated a tone higher. The first phrase returns, with its repeat, plus an added two notes. The second phrase returns, but the ending brings in a new phrase instead of repetition.

Ex. 36

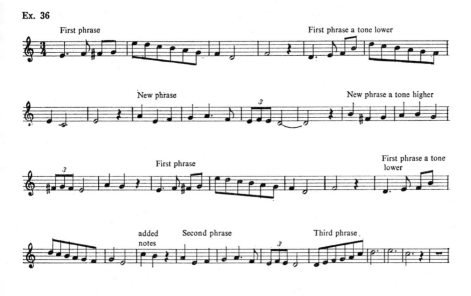

On the other hand, the regularity of shape found in this type of tune undoubtedly gives it a strength not found in works containing more ideas. It may, in fact, be argued that it would be both unreasonable and unsound musical practice to introduce much more material into compositions of any style and of this duration which are not of a very profound type indeed. There is probably a limit to the degree of complexity which is artistically satisfying. The essence of the better type of popular music seems to be to take a couple of basically simple but strong ideas and to submit them to subtle alterations. This can be rhythmic, as in "Moonlight in Vermont", in which the second main idea is used sequentially in the middle of the tune, whereas the opening idea, though repeated three times, is never exactly the same; both repeats change in pitch and one changes in rhythm. "Memories of You", on the other hand, keeps the same rhythms but changes in direction of melodic movement, so that the falling second half of the phrase balances the rising first half, and monotony is also avoided by balancing rises of a tone with falls of a third:

Ex. 37
Memories of You

Another attempt to use a limited number of phrases is found in the Beatles'
tune "Love Me Do", in which two basic phrases, which are repeated, are
made more interesting by the insertion of a third phrase which contains a note
which is held long enough to disturb the normally expected rhythmic pattern:

Ex. 38
Love Me Do

One of the elements of the much-vaunted Beatles' "freshness" was this breaking up of the regular and expected pattern of popular music. However, this
was true of only a few tracks and does not seem likely to inspire imitation even
in those who might be capable of doing so. It is of interest that this feature
again points to an attempt in melodic construction to compose according to
the criteria of jazz, rather than of classical music, which again indicates the
degree to which this idiom is becoming assimilated.

Some tunes have melodies which could under no circumstances be described as "assembly line", unless we are prepared to concede the organiser of
the line a greater than average ability to make large-scale plans and to deal in
greater lengths of time than the basic 2-bar phrase.

Thus "Tangerine" (Victor Schertzinger, 1942) is built up from a sentence
of 8 bars, which in turn is constructed out of four 2-bar phrases:

Ex. 39
Tangerine

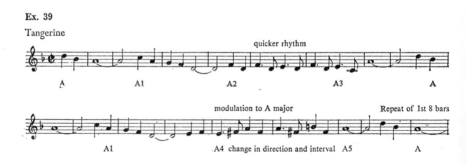

All begin with the same rhythm, but this is concluded in different ways. A quicker rhythm is used in the second repeat to avoid monotony which might occur through the frequent use of long notes in the tune. This whole 8-bar structure is used twice more, but in the first repeat the modulation to *A* major is accompanied by a change in the direction and intervals of the melody, though not in its rhythm. All three sections end on the same note (*A*). Variety is achieved by making substantial changes in the last section. A new rhythm, built upon the opening three notes of the tune, is repeated sequentially. The fall in pitch brought about by this is countered by a rising figure in the last four bars which successfully continues the tune (it may in fact be analysed as consisting of the mirror inversion of the opening phrase, followed by an augmented form of this, but such an analysis implies a degree of conscious composition which I would not care to postulate).

A similar degree of complexity is found in "All the Things You Are", which was analysed earlier for its harmonic content. This tune has as a basis the typical A–A–B–A pop-song structure, but the tune is so much more subtle than this that such a description can only be applied loosely.

Songs of this quality are undoubtedly the exception rather than the rule, and in fact it is often suggested that they are representative of a period of popular composition which has already disappeared. However, I am not sure that this is true. The Beatles' song "Please Please Me", for instance, is an example of a song which, formally speaking, is not just repetitive and factory-like (see Ex. 40).

It starts with a phrase which has three clearly distinct rhythmic elements— a three-crotchet lead in, a dotted crotchet-quaver-two-crotchet bar, and two minims. There are three melodic elements also: the scalar fall, the alternating between fifth and sixth, and a figure consisting of the rise of a fourth and a fall of a second. This whole phrase is then repeated exactly. A contrast follows since there is a syncopated and rising phrase which contrasts with the opening on-beat falling phrase. It is followed by a new phrase, suggested by the first in that it is scalar, and in that it uses the dotted rhythm mentioned,

Ex. 40

Please Please Me

but nevertheless quite distinct. The whole section is then repeated. It is to be noted that the section is a clearly developed 16-bar (not 8-bar) idea. This unusual length for pop music is followed up with a 10-bar middle section, which contains new livelier and contrasting material. Built on quavers, and a hovering phrase using chromatic notes (the first in the piece), which rises sequentially, it ends on the same notes as does the first phrase of the piece. Very unusual is the immediate repetition of this, so avoiding the gap which one customarily finds at the end of every four or eight bars in this type of music. The middle section continues with the repetition of the first two bars, but then further variation is brought about by the use of a new idea, a leap upwards to the highest note of the song, followed by a scalar fall related to the first figure, but in the quavers of the middle section. A two-bar rest to allow the accompaniment to stand out is followed by a repetition of the first section, which ends with yet another variation in that different voices take up the final phrase, each starting before the other has finished, in a rather stretto–like fashion, so as to prevent the tune from coming to rest at the expected point.

The above attempts at analysis are in a sense unsatisfactory, in that they do not catch the life and spontaneity of the songs, and because of their technical nature appear to ascribe too much thought to an art form whose practitioners would recoil in horror from such an approach. Nevertheless, I hope that it gives some idea of the possibilities and limitations of the idiom, and at least gives some factual basis upon which the reader can make his judgement. This has been far too rare a situation in this type of music up to the present.

Having done this, I now propose to proceed to some more general considerations about popular melody. For this purpose I believe that it can be divided into several arbitrary categories. These are not always clear cut or distinguishable from one another, but have some general validity.

The first type that should be mentioned is one that has never been very important until recently, and may be labelled the "blues type" of melody. In this category falls such a tune as the Rolling Stones' "Little Red Rooster", and a large number of Rhythm and Blues tunes. It is true in a sense to say that they are poor melodies, and that the music has no tune, judged by traditional standards. This is because, whether consciously or not, they take their inspiration and conception from the Negro blues, which has generally been a melodically simple and repetitive form—deliberately so because the real interest is in what the artist can do with this by using the type of Negro expression discussed earlier. Tunes of this type must, therefore, stand or fall by their "expressiveness" (most will fall) and not by their ability to catch the ear with a certain type of beauty.

Another type of melody which is strongly jazz influenced in conception though not always in melodic turn is the "rhythmic melody". By this I mean that the tune will consist of a simple melodic phrase based upon a short and usually syncopated rhythm ("Jeepers Creepers", "Who's Sorry Now?", "Mountain Greenery" and "Blue Room"). Such tunes are generally joyful in lyrical content, and are very much designed to stimulate dancing (e.g. "The Charleston"). They may on paper look monotonous, but before condemning them it will be necessary to hear them at the correct tempo and properly played, to see how far this repetition does in practice approach the jazz balance between stimulating and tedious repetition.

In contrast to this type of melody is the type, nearly always slow, which may be called "quasi-classical". This type of tune is particularly used for the "serious" moments of popular music, which are eternally liked by the general public, which has an almost Victorian love of wallowing in sentiment and tears, provided that these are stimulated by self-pity. This type of song is also used for songs known in the business as "religiosos", a title which is both self-explanatory and apt, in that it makes a useful distinction between this and the genuinely religious folk song.

Such songs are to my mind the very nadir of popular music, though it is the tunes of the two types so far mentioned which tend to come in for criticism on grounds of banality. The reason for this is easily found—often the "quasi-classical" tune is better constructed by traditional standards, more melodious, and more complex and varied in harmonisation. Nevertheless, they are the very antithesis of what I accept as good art in that the "dance" tunes fill a legitimate function satisfactorily, even if this is a light and shallow area of life. The religioso, on the other hand, fails because it attempts to deal with a serious topic but cannot rise to the occasion. Two explanations may be offered for this. The first is that deep subjects require considerable artistic skill to present that illusion of sincerity which is vital to all great art, and without which a person who is undoubtedly sincere at heart is unable to convey this because he lacks the techniques which give conviction to his work. He will tend to fall into clichés which give a sense of insincerity.

However, a sterner criticism may be offered, which is the one that the failure to achieve success is ultimately because the songs have a smoothness which may well be suited to some aspects of romance, but which is not suited to more profound problems. Thus, the composer uses techniques which, though impressive, always aim to please and never to give offence—the atmosphere of the Technicolor perfume advertisement must be kept. This is because the audience does not wish to be shocked or even forced to think or feel. Thus songs on such topics in the older folk idiom are convincing because they are based on a profound religious belief closely linked to an awareness of death amidst life to which religion is intimately and fundamentally bound. The modern Englishman, generally speaking, lacks such belief, and death is removed quickly and quietly, is kept from the eyes of children and is not spoken of. The modern listener seeks from his religious songs a vague comfort, rather than outspoken conviction. He wants a musical aspirin which will take away the feeling of despair which occasionally he has to come up against, rather than give a sense of strength to face up to and overcome such gloom. On the other hand, he dare not give such comforts up, any more than he can give up a church burial service—"just in case". In this way the popular arts are again weak because they mirror the attitudes of an age which, in this at least, lacks strength.

An example of the kind of tune just mentioned is Richard Rogers' "You'll Never Walk Alone" (1944), which has the significant direction: "Refrain (with great warmth and like a hymn)." Though written in 1944 it is still of interest in that it continues to enjoy the highest popularity, even among people who were not even born at the time it was composed. It became a great hit due to the efforts (quite strenuous at certain points) of Gerry and the Pacemakers. Technically speaking, it follows the fashions of fifty and more years ago:

Ex. 41
You'll Never Walk Alone

* 'chromaticism':

It has a more complex form than the average pop song, and a steady rise in tension brought about by a rise in pitch, the use of high notes at points of climax, and chromatic harmony such as the diminished chord (for once not overworked), the minor chord on the subdominant, the French 6th and the augmented chord. But the high notes give the impression of being put there for display of the crudest kind, and the chromaticism is never anywhere near as thoroughgoing as in, say, Wagner. With the result that it falls into that cloying titillation of the senses which eschews the simpler harmonic patterns of an earlier age but does not risk the offence which more advanced possibilities of chromaticism might give. At the same time, the tune contains an unusual number of minor chords used in rather weak progressions (called "churchy harmony" by studio arrangers), heightening the weak and sugary effect.

The peculiarly sentimental effect given by the use of chromaticism mentioned above leads up to the consideration of another type of melody which is peculiar to the twentieth century, songs containing the "pop whine". Some well-known tunes of this type are "Mistakes" (1928), "Carolina Moon" (1928), "Side by Side" (1927), "Happy Days and Lonely Nights" (1928) and "Have You Ever Been Lonely?" (1933). (See Ex. 42.)

This type of sound is found especially in songs of self-pitying or in ones in which the dominant feeling is one of smug self-congratulation. The effect is brought about by the use of various Victorian emotive tricks, particularly the sequence of dominant 7ths, usually in the form I–VI⁷–V⁷–I (see Ex. 43), the use of fundamental discords (9th and 13th), and of other chromatic chords, especially the chord containing an augmented 5th (often this is the melody note).

The melody itself contains a large number of discords, accented passing notes, and chromatically inflected passing notes, especially the movement from a note to the note a semitone below and back, and the linking of notes of a chord by means of the chromatic scale.

It will be observed that these tunes all date from the inter-war period, but this is no obstacle to the consideration of modern tastes, as they are still known and popular, and are frequently rehashed as new versions of "good old oldies".

This period was the one in which there was the strongest Victorian influence. This is clearly visible to us, though such a suggestion would have horrified the bright young things of forty years ago. This is equally true of "traditional jazz", which has been and still is hailed as being a new and revolutionary sound in music. It is strange to think that these compositions which are so much in the tradition except for their rhythmic aspect should have appealed to serious composers as pointing the way to a break with tradition.

Ex. 42

Mistakes

= discord resolving

Ex. 43

It is fair to add at this point, since I have been so critical of this type of song, that I accept the charge of prejudice against them. Anyone who takes the trouble to look will quickly see that, judging by the standards which I have hitherto used to decide the merit of popular tunes, a tune such as "Memories" has as much quality as most of those I have so far named. On the other hand, I have to admit that, in common with many people of my age, I retain a personal distaste for them, perhaps for reasons of upbringing and environment; I continue to find them corny and oversentimental.

It is perhaps, therefore, fair to accuse me of equal prejudice when I praise my final class of popular song, the "modern American ballad" (to use John Lewis' phrase), into which category I would assign such songs as "Stardust" and "I Remember April".

The overall sound of these songs is sometimes called "Impressionist" and this is a useful label if we do not press it too far. The music is not impressionist in the sense used by classical critics—its harmonic resources and freedom from tonality are too slight for this—but there is an attempt to catch an atmosphere of vagueness and romance in something of the way that this is done in film music and in pieces such as *Daphnis and Chloe*. Thus it is not surprising to find that certain tricks are used which are typical of such "romantic" music.

Harmonically speaking we find the introduction of mollifying progressions so that the older II^7–V^7–I progression becomes VI min^7–II^7–II min^7–V^7–I (see Ex. 33). The introduction of the minor 7th chords adds a distinct softness to the progression. Furthermore, the chord of the 6th is also used as is the chord with added major 7th; the 9th is frequently added to both of these. They are no longer seen as discords but as pleasant atmosphere-producing sounds in their own right; the discords are not always resolved and certainly not always according to earlier rules. The dominant chord will frequently have its 9th and 13th added, or be substituted by Ib^7 (9). Finally modulation tends not to be the more common movement to the subdominant, or through the cycle of 5ths starting on III^7, but to the remoter keys, especially those with a tonic of III or IIIb.

Melody follows similar tendencies, so that movement over the 6th or major 7th chords is common and the major 7th itself is found frequently with very ornamental resolutions or none at all. In "Stardust" a major 7th is held over a minor chord in bar 3, in "Everything I Have Is Yours" a 9th is held over VIb^7 in the second bar, "Star Eyes" begins with a 9th over a major 7th chord and "Laura" abounds in unresolved 6ths and 9ths. Another interesting tendency is that of melodies to diatonic movement with chromaticism only being introduced as diatonic movement after modulation. One of the beauties of these songs is that their simple and singable melodies make complex relationships with the harmonic progressions below them.

Finally, the rhythm of the melodies tends to become more complex so that though the basic two–bar units remain to dictate the harmonic movement and main points of rhythmic equilibrium, the melody tends to be less analysable satisfactorily in terms of two–bar units stuck together.

A particularly good example of this is "Stardust" which contains a larger number of basic rhythms than usual. These are fitted into a traditional framework, but within the four-bar sections there is much variety. At the same time, the melody tends to be divisible (especially when played) so that two widely separated lines appear, each with a distinct movement (examples of this are to be found in bars 10 and 24). "Stardust" thus shows all the signs of being a very musicianly and carefully composed melody.

In summing up this type of melody I am again aware of the dangers of partiality, of manufacturing the evidence, or of drawing too many conclusions from too little evidence. Yet they do seem to me to be more complex examples of composition that we found in the other types of song. Perhaps this is because they do not imitate old material, or "hot up" the nineteenth-century style, in a way similar to the detestable practice of "jazzing the classics", but generally use more modern material. Furthermore, they are not merely simplified versions of jazz, but are a valid idiom of their own which combines complexity with singability. I thus find them evocative and convincing in their attempt to put over a certain type of approach to love. This, of course, assumes that one can accept the value of this, which may not be so for many readers. Its value will be discussed further in the next chapter.

15 The Lyrics of Popular Songs

The sentimentalist is one who would enjoy
without incurring the immense debtorship for
the thing done.
JAMES JOYCE

Of all the aspects of the popular song which have come in for criticism, none
has perhaps unleashed quite so much vehemence as the lyric. I propose to
begin by examining the less contentious material, *i.e.* the surface content and
prosody.

Not the least interesting facet of twentieth-century pop songs to future
generations is likely to be the social setting and the reflection of the life and
customs of the period. Indeed, this is so commonplace to us that we tend
to overlook it and its value. Thus, when Johnny Burke wrote:

> My very good friend, the milkman, says
> That I've been losing too much sleep . . .

and

> Then there's a very friendly fellow, who prints
> All the latest real estate news,
> And every day he sends me blue prints
> of cottages with country views . . .

we are inclined to forget how strange these lyrics would have seemed less
than a lifetime ago. Both are reflections of a city life in which everyday things
are easily obtainable, and yet from which most people dream of escaping—
hence the price of cottages in the home counties.

Similarly, when Dorothy Fields wrote:

> Gee, I'd like to see you looking swell, Baby,
> Diamond bracelets Woolworth doesn't sell, Baby . . .

she is immensely in touch both with the realities of modern life, and with the
aspirations of those who wish to break out of it.

This important aspect of the pop song—its contact with the ordinary person, which so much coterie art does not have—is surely a great strong point, and it is not surprisingly reflected also in the actual language of the songs. Here there is an increasing freedom with the traditional rules of syntax and of decorous expression. To my mind, it is flying in the face of reality not to admit that this does have and is likely to continue to have a greater impact than the highly formalised diction of the older style of song. This and the fact that the older folk songs have a fatal tendency to deal with bashful young maidens, knights in armour and pressganged sailors are, in fact, likely to be the insurmountable obstacles to a resurgence of this style of music.

In contrast to this, the use of a more colloquial idiom is not only likely to free one from nineteenth-century cliché and melodramatic language, but is likely to make available the full resources of spoken English, which is a highly flexible, highly accented and elided, and highly incisive language. It has found a vital point of contact with music in jazz, and the interaction between the two has already produced a greater subtlety in musical rhythm and in the musical interpretation. Clearly, the view that poetry of quality demands an elevated diction and heightened language which is not the language of ordinary speech cannot be dismissed lightly, much less the suggestion that though the diction may have changed, cliché is more prevalent than ever, both in ideas and in the expression of them. As I have indicated in the discussion of earlier periods, the creation of lyrics by the reshuffling of stock ideas and phrases can in itself be perfectly acceptable. But none of these periods was so limited in its range as the current period. It will in future years be seen as a great tragedy, I think, if our lyric writers do not exploit the possibilities which lie before them, especially in view of the tremendous musical advances which have taken place in the present century.

A few examples will illustrate how even the ungrammatical has been permitted to enter the lyric. From 1927 we have:

> I ain't got nobody,
> And there's nobody cares for me
> I'm so sad and lonely,
> Won't somebody come and take a chance with me?

In 1964, and 3,000 miles away, the language not only of ordinary men but even of uneducated ones is still used:

> I'm the kind of guy
> Who never used to cry;
> The world is treating me bad,
> Misery.

> I've lost her now for sure,
> I won't see her no more;
> It's going to be a drag,
> Misery.

Finally, a classic of piled-up negatives form from 1965:

> He don't want no hen in the barnyard
> Layin' eggs for nobody else . . .

The following line, though technically ungrammatical, has by its colloquialism and by the elimination of redundant syllables (*e.g.* the adverbial ending) a definite impact:

> It's awful hard to love someone when they don't care about you.

There are, of course, many faults in popular-lyric writing, especially when the authors are jumped-up as a result of high-pressure salesmanship, and thus, though professional in name, are still amateur in standard. Most common, perhaps, is the faulty handling of metre.

This is a common error among amateurs, who do not always realise that apart from the practical difficulties of fitting more than a certain number of syllables to a given number of notes, overloading with syllables is aesthetically unsatisfactory, since it is against the nature of the lyric. The best lyrics are short, snappy, and though not lacking in invention, easily comprehensible. They obviously have to be so if they are to make any impression on a mind which is at least half occupied with taking in the musical content of a song. Large numbers of syllables seem only to be usable generally for burlesque and facetious verse (*e.g.* Walton's *Façade*).

A well-known recent example will illustrate the type of fault under discussion:

> (Well she was) just seventeen
> (You) know what I mean
> (And the) way she looked was way beyond compare
> (So) how could I dance with another
> (When I) saw her standing there.

The second line of the above must surely be the most meaningless in all music!

> (Well) she looked at me
> (And) I, I could see
> (That be)fore too long I'd fall in love with her
> She wouldn't dance with another
> (When I) saw her standing there.

Again, the second line of the stanza is faulty—the author has felt the musical need to repeat a note, but has done so in a very ineffective way by repeating the word "I", which adds nothing to the sense. Apart from this I have bracketed the frequent anacruses so that the reader may more easily see where the first musical accent falls, since it is mainly in the handling of this that the real weakness of the lyric is felt. Anacrusis is a regular feature of all jazz-inspired lyrics, but in this case it is weak because it is used in a repetitive and unimaginative fashion. The words usually add nothing instead of mirroring in the sense of the words the feeling of a lead-up to a climax which is present in the melody. In the first line of the stanza there is also some lack of sympathy for accent in that this is thrown onto "she" instead of the more natural "looked".

The Beatles' tune "Anna" shows this inability to handle metre even more clearly. I have numbered the lines and lettered the stanzas A and B, so that they can be juxtaposed for easier comparison:

1. A Anna You come and ask me girl
   B Anna Girl before you go now

2. A To set you free girl
   B I want you to know now

3. A You say he loves you more than me
   B That I still love you so

4. A So I will set you free
   B But if he loves you mo'

5. A Go with him
   B Go with him

Here the commonest of all faults in amateur writing is to be seen. Given a tune of a standard type, the amateur will ruin one of its main virtues, a clear-cut, simple outline, by jigging from one foot to another as though he needed to urinate, but had to wait. The difference between this and the work of a jazz artist is that both have a realisation of the need for flexibility and motion in the rhythm, but only the latter is capable of keeping this and a sense of an organic development from one section to another.

Another fault of popular lyric writers which is quite often found is a lack of concord, without any real artistic justification for it, between metrical and musical rhythm.

This fault is not a new development; the following example dates from 1928:

(x heavy stress; – light stress; u unaccented)

Metrical Stress	x	u	–		x	u	–
Words	Dream	awhile,			scheme	awhile	
Musical rhythm	♩	♫♩			♩	♫♩	
Musical Stress	–	x			–	x	

Metrical Stress	u	x	u	–
Words	We're	sure	to	find
Musical rhythm	♩	♩	♫♩	
Musical Stress			x	

Metrical Stress	x	u	–	u	u	–
Words	Happiness		and	I	guess	
Musical rhythm	♩	♫♩	♩	♫♩		
Musical Stress	–	x	–	x		

Metrical Stress	x	u	x	u	–	u	x	u
Words	All	those	things	you've	always	pined	for	
Musical rhythm	♩.	♪	♩	♩	♩♩	♫♩	♩	
Musical Stress	x		x		x	x		

A couple of lines written in 1934 illustrate well the way that lyrics can be forced to fit an existent tune:

Metrical Stress	–	x	u	–	x	u
Words	Love	rules	you,	love	fools	you
Musical rhythm	♩ ♩	♩ ♩	♩. ♩.	♩. ♩		
Musical Stress	x	–	x	–		

Metrical Stress.	u	u	–	u	x
Words	Then	you	pay	the	price
Musical rhythm	♩. ♩	♩. ♪	♩.		
Musical Stress	x	–	x	x	

A present-day example shows that the lyric writer's sense of rhythm may not be developing as fast as that of the player and musician:

Metrical Stress	u x u –
Words	I think of you
Musical Stress	x

Metrical Stress	u x u – u – u x
Words	The things you do go round my head
Musical Stress	x x

Metrical Stress	u – u x u u – x u –
Words	The things you said, like 'I love only you'
Musical Stress	x x x

The last phrase is also weak in not conveying the meaning of the author in the most forceful manner; there is also considerable incongruity in the use of a sentence whose structure is poetic in an otherwise colloquial context.

On the other hand, popular writers can achieve a most happy union of the two. Where the rhythms of the language do not fit readily to iambic and trochaic formulae, or where the writer does not force the jog-trot of such a basic framework to influence his feeling for the accents as they are spoken, the songwriter can come much closer to that sensitivity to language and the ability to create poetic patterns which clearly suggest music, or are apt to already existing musical rhythms, which may be exemplified by such a phrase as T. S. Eliot's "Shakespahearean Rag". A couple of examples of such a happy union follow:

u   – u   –   u   u   – u   x u   u   x u
I'm flying high but I've got a feeling I'm falling

♩ ♪♩· ♫♩. ♩ | ♫   ♫♫   ♩ |♩ ♩

or from "Basin Street Blues":

x   u   u   – u   –   u   – u   x
Steam down the river down to New Orleans

♩   ♫   ♫   ♫ |♪·   ♩ ♫

u   x   u   u   –   u
The band's there to meet us

♪ | ♩   ♫   ♪ ♩.

In the last example, the real nature of the last syllable (ambivalent in that it is unstressed, but rising in pitch and with a long vowel) is well caught by the musical rhythm.

Rhyme is, of course, vital to the popular lyric, but in the present century the better writers have avoided mere jingle-making. They have often used internal rhymes, which have been very satisfying when used with suitable syncopations:

> For you're the lover I have waited for
> The mate that Fate had me created for . . .

or more recently:

> I don't wanna sound complainin'
> But you know there's always rain in my heart.
> I do all the pleasin' with you
> It's so hard to reason with you
> Oh yeah, why do you make me blue?

Both of these need to be heard, or at least seen in score in order to grasp their effectiveness.

The foregoing arguments can only be appreciated with a certain degree of training, but the sentiments expressed and the manner of their expression (subtlety of thought, images etc.) are available immediately to all. For this reason it is essential to be aware of the quality both of the sentiments expressed, and of the means of their expression, and to be on guard against the trivial, the undesirable and the second-rate.

Let us begin by looking at two types of song that have periodic popularity, beginning with the "religioso" song. As I have already commented on the purely musical construction of this song, I propose to look again at "You'll Never Walk Alone":

> When you walk through a storm hold your head up high,
> And don't be afraid of the dark.
> At the end of the storm is a golden sky
> And the sweet silver song of a lark.
> Walk on through the wind, walk on through the rain,
> Tho' your dreams be tossed and blown.
> Walk on, walk on, with Hope in your heart,
> And you'll never walk alone
> You'll never walk alone.

The reader is already aware of my general sentiments about this song, and so will not be surprised to find that I see my musical impression as entirely

borne out by the lyric. As in so many songs of this type, no specific religious
message is given—this would involve some degree of commitment, and might
offend sizeable minorities. The idea of "hope" is carefully left ambiguous,
and its source is vague. It is linked to a concept of trouble, which is left
equally vague so that each may attribute to it his own meaning, but which has
thus been pruned of any genuinely troubling elements. The writer attempts
to arouse some disquiet by reference to the most obvious childish fears
("don't be afraid of the dark"), and this helps to reinforce the whole impression of adolescence in the poem. The whole experience is, in fact, reminiscent
of a teenage girl's feelings upon walking in the rain, clearly not an atmosphere
which is congruous with a semi-religious topic. I need hardly comment on
the weakness of such phrases as a "golden sky" and a "silver song". One
might well ask how many city people could have ever seen a lark, or heard one,
or could recognise its song.

Another type of song which enjoys waves of popularity is the jolly, back-
slapping song. Though occasionally the humour is good and shows a realistic
eye; for example:

> Look at the florists, counting their profits
> Ain't it grand to be blooming well dead . . .

The same song is capable of the banal line:

> Look at the parson, collar on backwards . . .

However, even these flashes are lacking in a song such as Gracie Fields'
"Christmas in Killarney", a picture of unalloyed happiness in which "The
door is always open" (at Christmas?):

> The neighbours pay a call
> And Father John, before he's gone
> Will bless the house and all.

Songs at this season still take much the same form, except that they are now
sung first in November—the customers must be put into and kept in a state
of goodwill, so that this year's Christmas spending will establish a new
record.

The public like to be driven into happiness at any time though, as the
following shows:

> Grab your coat and get your hat,
> Leave your worry on the doorstep
> Just direct your feet
> To the sunny side of the street . . .

Two stanzas later the song closes:

> If I have never had a cent
> I'll be rich as Rockefeller
> Gold dust at my feet
> On the sunny side of the street.

Words of sublime optimism and comfort at the time of the Depression.

We are now left with the consideration of the large bulk of popular songs, which are on the subject of love. I am aware of having left out various minority types, such as occasional songs ("Twenty-one Today"), "In a Golden Coach" (the Coronation song), as well as nonsense songs ("Yes, We Have No Bananas", "The Purple People Eater"). Such songs appear to arise in every age and do not appear to alter much in standard or nature, but they do not, of course, constitute the main musical diet of the people.

Love songs do though, presumably because love is an eternally abiding interest, and the most enjoyable and easily accessible. The public seems to have turned away from other possible topics for a variety of reasons. Religion, for instance, needs depth of feeling, conviction, and often prejudice. Heroism and Patriotism have fallen out of fashion since people have been unable to contemplate them from the warmth of their beds. Death is a shunned topic, especially since the medieval knack of laughing in the face of it has disappeared:

> Is it not fine to dance and sing
> When the bells of death do ring?

Love, however, has the attraction of appealing to all except the very young, either through anticipation, present enjoyment, or reminiscence. Of late, the older group and songs typical of it have fallen out of favour, because we no longer get old. I mentioned this tendency when talking about dancing.

Let us begin by taking a love song and analysing it:

> You don't have to tell me I know,
> The touch of your lips told me so,
> And I know in my heart that we're drifting apart
> But if you love another then I'll let you go.

> But some day you'll find your mistake,
> And whose heart is going to break.
> When the new love forsakes you,
> It's the old love that takes you.
> It's no use pretending and so,
> You don't have to tell me I know.

In the above, there are a few clichés, "drifting apart", "whose heart is going to break", and the obsolescent "forsakes", but even with these the lyric is not offensive as a piece of writing. In fact, it is not anything, since its fault from a technical point of view is that it communicates too well what is to be said, and that it is too obvious and direct—in other words it lacks art. What we find unpleasing here is the rather petty, vindictive tone, and the ideas upon which the song is based. These can have a more distinct effect on the diction, as follows:

> Lovely Lady, I'm falling madly in love with you
> It's a feeling beyond concealing, what can I do?...

The vocabulary used here is directly linked with the attitude which the writer holds (or is assuming). The term "lady" with its social implications, the use of the now meaningless hyperbole of English middle-class origin "madly in love", and the contrived "feeling beyond concealing" all point to a distinct social ideal, and considerable insincerity, and unreality.

Another type of unreality, far more widespread, and to my mind far more insidious is the idealisation to the point of perfection of the circumstances (and particularly the first events) of love.

> It happened in Monterey a long time ago;
> I met her in Monterey where lights softly glow.
> Stars and steel guitars and luscious lips as red as wine
> Broke somebody's heart and I'm afraid that it was mine [sic].

This sounds like the background to a Technicolor advertisement inviting you to spend (all) your money on a magnificent holiday, love included for 7s 6d a day extra. The soft glowing lights (perhaps due to a lack of electricity), lips as red as wine (no anaemia here), steel guitars (Spanish guitars are, of course, gut stringed) and the ever-present stars (no clouds in Loveland) combine to present an illusion whose effect is made quite grotesque by the final rueful public school apology.

At this point readers may accuse me of wilful misinterpretation; the regular argument is, "It is not meant like that." To this the only reply of a thinking person must be that we have to interpret the meaning of any piece of communication according to the meanings which are actually present. The very best that could be said in the case of the above lyric and many others, is that they are unfortunately chosen, in that they are not accurate enough to prevent possible misreading by an average reader. In fact, I see any attempt to justify such lyrics as pin-pointing what I feel to be the real problem of present-day pop love lyrics. We are continually being asked to make such allowances and to "suspend our disbelief". We are expected to put reality aside in the cause of romance, and this is done a large number of occasions over a long period of time. While I am prepared to concede a possible need to do this at times, I maintain that to do so most of the time, without being fully aware of the escapist assumptions, is likely to lead to a situation in which we cease to be aware of these assumptions, and to accept a fantasy situation as being a real one. A conflict can thus arise between the idealised fantasy world and the world of reality. Consider, for instance, the amount of attention given to the courtship situation, and the comparative lack of stress of the nature of the difficulties of marriage: the lack of realistic expectation of what marriage is likely to involve is, as far as I can see from the comments of those who have to deal with the resultant problems, perhaps the biggest single contributory fact to our rising divorce rate.

The frequent criticism that popular culture has an increasing sexual element has, however, very limited validity in connection with popular lyrics. Our examination of earlier songs, even of the Victorian period, shows just how inhibited and formalised modern lyrics are. There is little else but the avowal of or regret for the lack of "eternal passion". This might be regarded as a formal expression of widely accepted modes of behaviour, analogous to the formalised behaviour at weddings, which though stylised is a social mechanism which gives us an acceptable way of expressing genuinely held and valued feelings.

But in the case of popular music there is a real danger of trivialisation, because of the cultivation of a habit of music as a background effect, together with a habit of very short periods of concentration. This in turn reduces the value of listening to songs as an experience, and to the words as a mode of communicating, so that they become little more than vocalese. The frequent utilisation of romantic stimuli for the purpose of advertising may also lead to a debasement of our responses.

The above should not be taken as approving the common statement about the songs of the present generation, that they lack coherence or even meaning.

This is doubtful—phrases of the "You know what I mean" type cited earlier are rare. But there are lyrics which have no meaning whatsoever, and raise periodic howls of disapproval from older listeners. I am thinking of the "Be-bop-a-lula", "Bop-bop-shuah" and "Sha-la-la" variety. One might add from an earlier period the "Boop-i-doop" and "Vo-do-deo-do" songs. I am always amazed at the vehemence of some critics about these songs as they are nothing more than vocalisations, or the fitting of meaningless syllables to a melody. This is a technique which has been used for effects (especially of exultant songs) throughout musical history. This type of song is, therefore, as valuable or otherwise as the Elizabethan "Fa-la-la", the Hanoverian "Tol-dilly-rol-dilly-ri-do", or the Gregorian "Gloria" for that matter. The only grounds upon which criticism may validly be made are those of the suitability of the vocalisation to the musical line and to the expression required.

As I have previously suggested, the exact extent of the influence of any popular form is hard to define. Victorian sensational ballads were produced in response to a public demand, as Mayhew's interviews show. Deficiencies in our art may be nothing more than a reflection of deficiencies in ourselves. But all who are concerned for the welfare of the society they live in will see here a parallel to the much debated problem of pornographic books. Clearly they are unlikely to affect the sexual morality of the Archbishop of Canterbury, but many of us have a suspicion that there may be people upon whom their effects are socially undesirable. In neither case would I advocate censorship: I see the censor's function as only justifiable when he represents the generally held view of the population—in which case he is redundant. There is little need to ban Communist texts in the United States, because the climate of opinion is against their acceptance. Perhaps the only thing one can do is to restrict one's patronage to that which one approves, and to encourage others to do the same. In view of the modern economic structure of popular music, this is likely to be by far the most effective sanction, if it is at all widely applied.

16 Conclusion

This unpopular art which cannot be turned
into a background noise for study.
W. H. AUDEN

The urge to discuss art in general terms is widespread, and for many people very strong; but it is, perhaps, the most futile of intellectual pursuits. One of the most important lessons to be learned from artistic studies is that, however great the relationships between any two works, even by the same creator, they must, if of real worth, be approached frequently, with great attention to detail, and always as totally separate entities; each work must be separately experienced and evaluated, and must stand upon its own merits, or not at all. Even when a composer of the highest quality has created a work, this may be no guarantee of its quality, or of its content—witness the vast difference between the Ninth Symphony and the Variations on "God Save the Queen".

Nevertheless, every musical work must have its final statement of the theme, and it would seem that the same is true of books. I hope that what is to be said below will only reflect correctly on what has already been said. But a literary background makes one very prone to rhapsodise, and I strongly urge the reader to check anything with which he disagrees against the facts given earlier—and, for that matter, to do the same with what he finds unexceptionable.

Our examination began with the Anglo-Saxon period. Here it was suggested that perhaps the greatest interest lay in the fact that this was a society to which we are united by the strongest biological ties, yet which created a cultural world as different from our own as anything we know of, in Europe, at least. We have noted the limited range of topics, the rigid formulaic treatment, and have considered the idea that such a homogeneous culture, and even such topics (e.g. the heroic), can never be repeated, since they belong to an earlier phase of social evolution. Perhaps not irrelevant, in a chapter concerned with prediction, is the fact that a society apparently so stable was transformed in a comparatively short space of time.

The medieval period showed the emergence of a lyric form based on stress, fixed numbers of feet, and rhyme, which is little different technically from anything which followed. The first known popular melodies are found, and though many of them have a kind of remoteness, caused by their being modally conceived, the "major" mode was rapidly rising to dominance. A striking difference from our own time is the extent to which and the freedom with which religion is used as a subject. Again this seems to be a situation which is not likely to be repeated.

In the Tudor and Stuart period, the violence of the upheavals caused by religious disputes brought about the removal of religious topics from the range covered by popular poets. Despite occasional attempts to alter this, the separation of function has continued, and even been extended. In the sixteenth and seventeenth centuries, the theatre took on a different character. Instead of being a rare and communal event, involving a large proportion of a town's citizens, at religious festivals, it became a form of entertainment, in the modern sense, produced regularly by professionals. The increasing specialisation of the actor's job, the secularisation, and the fact that the audience had to pay, gave rise to a different concept of the theatre. The professional wished to show his skill, by increasingly subtle means, and the audience dictated content to a fair degree, because of their new economic power.

The popular styles of the seventeenth century were still very direct and often boisterous, but in the eighteenth century the desire of the more advanced artists for a certain type of beauty, involving adornment, and delicacy of language, began to find expression in the popular world. A musical concomitant of this was the beginning of the rejection of the modal style as being archaic, and uncouth. Music also started to move indoors: domestic music increased in popularity, and street entertainers, other than ballad sellers, began to disappear. Another stream of taste began, to satisfy the needs of the middle class: the characteristics of this were the avoidance of coarseness (especially of a sexual type), and sentimentality.

In the nineteenth century, the long tradition of street singing came to an end, as did the vital period of communal folk song; the phase of adaptation of this to the needs of a new industrial society seems not to have had any permanent influence. The most important event seems to have happened in the "serious" artistic world however. The Romantic image of the artist, as a man with a social and spiritual duty to perform, took hold and gave rise to at alienation of the artist from his society, both on account of his content, and of his techniques. Even in mid-century it was possible for a composer to be like Balfe, and to dabble successfully in both worlds. But it is well known that one of the causes of the break between Gilbert and Sullivan was Sullivan's fear that his artistic integrity and ability was in doubt: by the end of the century, a serious artist was obliged to make his choice. This must, in part at least, account for the increasing move towards pure forms. In the middle of the century, the serious drama moved away from music, so that today we get playwriting, on the one hand, and musical entertainment, on the other.

In the present century (the developments of the past five years being for the moment excluded), we can see that lyrics have become, if anything, much more restricted in form and range, though the music has reached a degree of complexity hitherto unparalleled. A new element has come into popular music in the form of a greatly increased interest in rhythm; this has taken not only the more traditional form of cross-rhythm in the melodic line, but also the demand for a kind of regular beat, which goes far beyond a regular pulse for keeping dancers together. In it the physical excitement which rhythm can arouse is consciously sought out, as in African cultures. In this sense, the traditional complaints of young people leaping around like savages are entirely correct. The middle-class culture has sought out sweetness ever since it evolved, in contrast to the high artist's intensity. A similar thing has happened in the new rhythmic music, which may still be divided, in the slang of the twenties, into "sweet" (emphasis on melody) and "hot" (emphasis on rhythmic excitement). Both sorts of music have become enjoyed increasingly as entertainment, because the idea of musical evenings has largely disappeared. A subculture of popular groups has arisen, though, since the First World War, and these may be said to be the only point at which there is direct contact between the people and culture: they are the main form in which any working-class man can express himself, without having to go through processes which alienate him from his class, and change his perspective.

At the beginning of the foregoing paragraph I excluded temporarily the music of the past few years. There were two reasons for this: the first, the obvious one, is that it is always immensely difficult for us to evaluate the trends of the moment. The second is that there are grounds for believing that we are moving into a new phase of popular music. Professor Mellers' article summarises very well the type of feeling which has been increasingly voiced since the first success of the Beatles. As a consequence, it is very difficult to assess trends. What I am attempting to do in this chapter is to view the period 1917–67 as a whole, so as not to be too misled by the pressures of fashions, no matter how desirable these may be. The comments below, therefore, must be taken as relating to the fifty years of American influence; they may thus at times conflict with works currently popular. But I am attempting to extrapolate from past evidence what is essential in modern popular taste, and thus assume that whatever conflicts there are will not be of permanent influence. This is a risky procedure, however, and if the interpretations of the better newspapers and magazines over the past year or so are correct, these lines may make very ironic or ridiculous reading, even while the print is still fresh.

In attempting to isolate and evaluate current trends, critics seem to be asking two questions. The first is, what technical features the next wave of popular music will have. The other is, what value its essential message will have. As in earlier chapters, I propose to look at the technical first.

Until now, the popular lyric has been growing increasingly weak: its range and mode of expression have become limited even since Victorian times. There are now a few signs that lyric writers are paying less attention to rhyme and strict metre, and there has been a small amount of experiment in setting lyrics in ways which until now would have been considered "ungrammatical". There has been an increasing interest in unconventional imagery, often of an elusive, almost apocalyptic nature. This is making quite a wide impact, as the following, written by an ex-Secondary modern, pre-O level student, will demonstrate:

> Mother gives birth to a son,
> Its father is dying for his freedom,
> No winners, just losers,
> Most will not see a daughter or a son.
>
> Mud, sickening, colour of blood,
> Cluttered with unwanted corpses,
> Bird songs cannot bring back sweet memories.
>
> No politician lays rotting
> They have no haunting black shadows of death,
> They may lend a spare moment for the forgotten.
>
> Honour for some,
> Coffins for others,
> Good old days say the rest.

Now a button is pushed,
Hell lets loose,
No pain will penetrate the body,
Just a feeling of eternal slumber.

The above lines demonstrate well the strengths and weaknesses of this style. Clearly, even allowing for the subject-matter, there is a vitality not to be found in the stereotyped lyrics of earlier decades: the freedom of the form seems to allow the writer to roam freely in a world of image which is certainly not even hinted at in his everyday language. It is this element which has attracted educationists such as David Holbrook, and has moved them to encourage this kind of writing in schools.

But the rejection of form and conscious working which has become an increasing element in some modern poetry has the very dangerous tendency to eliminate the element of discipline from art altogether. And though Shakespeare is said never to have blotted out a line, he is typical only of a very small number of artists. Few artists have rejected discipline and succeeded. The above lines show this clearly: the writer has not learned to eliminate cliché, and it is arguable whether the formlessness adds anything to the poem: it certainly makes the work of the composer very difficult. Furthermore, even in the work of well-known writers, the image is often pursued for its own sake, although it may have little or no meaning, and add not at all to the central theme; Jonathan King's "Everyone's Gone to the Moon" or Donovan's early songs illustrate this well.

As we have already seen, the melody and harmony of popular music made rapid advances, but only until the end of the war. The complaint that "They don't write tunes like they used to" has a foundation in truth, for the great tunes of this century were written during a period of (popular) musical expansion, whereas since the war writers have, by and large, only gone over old ground: their work thus inevitably lacks the vitality of the earlier compositions. We have also seen that the current wave of popular music is trying to revitalise by using folk techniques. Historical study would suggest, however, that the scope here must be very limited; certainly a fair degree of harmonic resource has to be ignored. I have already suggested that this trend is a form of musical escapism—an unwillingness to move on to the next logical stage to which conventional harmony has brought us.

The rhythmic element in modern popular music will be, I believe, with us for a long time yet. From time to time, some authorities predict a return to sweetness or to strict tempo. Unfortunately, such predictions only seem to come from teachers of dancing and traditional musicians. But the graph seems to be moving upwards: popular rhythms continue to increase in complexity, and the analysis of other cultures suggests that we are as yet nowhere near the limits which even the least musically educated societies can take as a matter of course. Jazz, for instance, has shown what can be done in the way of subtlety: its popular rejection has been largely due to complexity of melody and harmony.

The recent experiments with Indian music also point in this direction. At present there have only been the crudest of results, but this is inevitable. Again, difficulties can be expected to occur when melody and form are involved, these being far more complex than their Western popular equivalents. But these things illustrate the fact that the trend in all modern art is increasingly towards the international: the popularity of the Beatles abroad is not only due to good publicity. In this way, our study is involved not only with English popular culture, but with that of the world. But there will be a limit to the extent to which other cultures can be utilised, since their music is based upon radically different philosophies—this is especially true of India. Moreover, in most cases these philosophies are on the wane: the trend in India and Africa is to reject the traditional, despite the efforts of minorities to the contrary, in favour of an international and predominantly Western culture. Lagos daily becomes more like London. But whatever its form, the influence of complex rhythm will, I think, continue: popular music without it would be like meat without salt.

Constant exposure to this must result in the creation of an expectation of a distinct texture in popular music, and of a distinct effect. The dominant interest in jazz and in allied forms of popular music has always been in the creation of the particular type of rhythmic excitement described earlier. To the Classical musician, such effects are of little or no importance. In fact, it may well be that such rhythmic emphasis is inherently opposed to the creation of the type of mood in which the European composer is interested. The comments which I quoted in Chapter 12 do express something which is vital, however extreme or senseless they may be, in some respects. The jazz type of music seems to seek the release of different aspects of the personality by different methods. It may be that, from the psychological point of view, these are merely different manifestations of the same human emotions —the need for social relationships, metaphysical frames of thought and so forth. No one would suggest that the African tribesman is, for instance, any less in touch with God than the European. But the mode of release is different: it is active, physical, and excitable, whereas classical music is calm, mental, and meditative. The different modes of worship of the tribesman and the

European illustrate this. The tribesman sings and dances: through physical release he finds religious ecstasy and social expression. The European's religion might well be said, without much distortion, to be the antithesis of this: his release is mental, his communion is essentially a personal thing. Such a viewpoint may be a little startling, but its existence is well enough attested. It also explains the many clichés about racial difference: these are clearly based on different forms of social expression. In times such as these, it is perhaps necessary to reiterate that this is not a social *judgement*: I do not imply superiority on either side.

The musical relevance of this is that such experiences are, at present, mutually exclusive: whatever the potentialities of humankind in this respect, there seems to be a division between the two at the moment. I think it would be difficult to find many people who feel equally drawn to both types of response, and who can accept each in the way it is generally accepted. It would seem that a true coexistence is impossible, in that one form must be enjoyed less, and experienced with an attitude of mind which is to some extent mildly patronising. If this is not in the nature of things, our young people's attraction to popular music may well, in time, produce a race capable of accepting the merits of both: this I would see as a most important move in human spiritual development, for we have been too long under a Pauline cloud, in which there is something innately to be rejected and despised in the physical. But if the two are irreconcilable the future for serious culture is in some ways bleak: the effects of constant rhythmic stimulation will combine with the almost inevitable loss of power which time gives to any work of art, to produce an inability in many people to find interest in earlier masterpieces. There are many persons of intelligence who, brought up in a world in which even popular music has, by eighteenth-century standards, an intolerable degree of discord, find the rhythms and harmonies of that period unexciting: they tend not to admit it for fear of ridicule.

The direction in which the above considerations have taken us shows how difficult it is, even in a purely technical discussion, to avoid for long the second interest of the critic: values. It seems to be pretty well universally felt that the landmarks of serious art have qualities which make them more valuable than any other form of artistic expression, and that they are thus worthy of a special place when we are considering the nature of things. A recent example of this situation is the debate which arose over the use of money at the time of the Italian floods. The values which are asserted are firstly those of greater technical command, and technical subtlety, and secondly of greater moral insight and moral worth. The listener to art music thus requires subtlety of performance and a complex use of techniques: the composer in turn demands from his listener a willingness to give repeated and attentive listenings, and even to study, to find out the qualities of the music.

At the present, this is not to be hoped for from popular music in anything like the intensity which great works have led us to expect. Much blame for this situation has been laid at the feet of the commercial enterprises; certainly it is unlikely any great changes will be made as long as cash return is so important and alluring a feature of the popular music world as it is at present. But this element can be overstressed, since, as I have said previously, the salesman can only sell that for which there is a market. And there is a very large market for music which is not demanding, and which entertains: we have seen that this situation has become increasingly important since the eighteenth century. In this area of music, a very high degree of attention is not required. When at its maximum, as when an audience goes to a performance by a star singer, the attention seems to be centred on personality, and a kind of emotional indulgence is the aim. But the music itself is easily understood, and almost without importance: the singer and not the song is the centre of attraction. To some extent we can find a parallel to this in the stereotyped plots of the eighteenth-century Italian opera, which were meant only to provide a framework for the appearance of greatly admired star singers. A further comparison from that period illustrates the other main attitude of a popular listener: music was very often, even when written by a composer as great as Haydn, an ancillary to other pursuits. In modern times, with the advent of transistorised radio, these may be either work or leisure; the attitude of the listener is, as Wesker's Mrs Bryant put it, "Blast gel, it ent a laxative."

Not surprisingly, music which occupies a utilitarian function is regarded in much the same way as any object is which is designed for use. Rapid obsolescence is not only accepted but expected. In part, the reason for this is the value placed upon changing fashion: a change will always be for the better, is a sign of youthful vitality, gives life the illusion of pace and purpose. Music is only required to be attractive *now*, whereas the art listener and the art composer are thinking about future value: art must have such depth that it will be valued by posterity. Thus, the popular musician can only take superficial elements from the art composer. The Beach Boys may use a little fugato, but they may not write a fugue. Similarly, their idiom must be immediately accessible, to a wide range of musical intelligence and experience, and their language must be suitably restricted to achieve this. The serious artist must not restrict himself; in fact, the development of modern music has been such that the idiom even of the great composers of the last century is denied to him—it is in constant danger of triteness, or even lightness. For instance, I recently heard for the first time, the *Rumanian Rhapsody* of Enesco, which was announced as being his best and most well-known work. Its traditional idiom made it dangerously close to light music.

The shunning of lightness again illustrates the increasing categorisation to which our century has been prone, and is linked with the whole movement which has been concerned with giving a liberal education. The thought of this movement is that art has high qualities, but also has value as a formative influence. Technical education, specialisation in schools, and the pressures of commerce both in the form of advertising and in their influence upon mass media, are seen as detrimental to human development. It is felt that many children are denied access to the best art, or are even turned against it by such pressures. Most of us could find examples which would substantiate such beliefs.

The solution offered to this situation is to utilise the arts as an educative medium. Thus Irene Armitage recently wrote a pamphlet, which was rightly well reviewed, called *Does Music Matter?*, and expressing the view that music was a vital element in the formation of minds: only by exposure to the most excellent music could people be made aware of and given the moral sensitivity which is vital in assessing the direction in which our society will move. The development of Music Schools in Hungary, under Kodály, is based on a similar attitude. A system is being organised in which all children will do at least an hour's music a day: it is felt that this increases not only their sensitivity, but also their all-round ability. My own college has a similar attitude, but with a slant which might not meet with the whole-hearted approval of the above authorities: it is felt that "the discriminating use of words is part and parcel of the business of coming to terms with life", and that as a consequence "as a Liberal Study, English is preferable to any other subject". Naturally, I quote the institution best known to me, but the viewpoint is generally held, even if the insistence upon literature is not always so great.

The results which the education system has achieved are not easily obtainable: few authorities, if any, would be prepared to admit failure on any scale. Nevertheless, those who have to teach are, in my experience, in general very dubious of the value of their work, and especially if it is suggested that any more than a minority of students can be affected. Rationalisations for this vary according to philosophical standpoint. Some people feel that the fault lies in the system, which warps minds beyond the help of the teacher. Others feel that the lack of response is due to innate deficiencies, that art will always be for an elite, and that there are people who will never be able to come to grips with the greatest artistic works. The experience of Centre 42 is much the same. Arnold Wesker, believing that the lack of a thriving popular tradition was to be deplored, and that if the popular tradition was revitalised people would become far more sympathetic to the serious arts, started this movement a few years ago. The aim was to put on a series of festivals, followed by the building of cultural centres in suitable places. Some festivals were put on, but reading between the lines one finds that they had little impact. The Round House in Camden Town was bought, and converted: it has already been used for various events. But the movement seems to be in great difficulties, through a lack of money. The amounts required are not as much as is spent on one Beatles record, and certainly only a fraction of the total annual expenditure on popular music, yet they are not forthcoming. Several problems thus emerge. The first of these is the fact that in the immediate future there is a limit to what any authority can spend on reversing these trends; such amounts may well be beyond their means at present. Such an argument is not final, however, since clearly money could and would be found if it were felt that the role of the arts was important enough. One therefore has to ask whether the social value of the arts is as great as it is made out: unless the arts can show themselves to have a special value in the development of personality which is not found in gardening, or amateur electronics, there is no reason why they should be given preference over other activities of comparable popularity.

To this must be added the consideration that by current artistic standards popular art forms can never be considered as doing more than showing talent and potential. Their language is too light, their structure too simple. The dice would thus have to be loaded against the popular: there would be a need for what would, according to one's standpoint, be either a "rescue operation" or "brainwashing". In the case of popular music, the gulf is so great that it would be difficult to avoid a conscious displacement of it. The essential nature of a popular record is by and large opposed to those values which are respected in serious art. This is even true of the difference between popular music and jazz. As I have shown, formally there are very close links between the two, but in spirit they are worlds apart: the subtlety of approach and avoidance of sentimentality which is a prerequisite of any jazz work of quality is the very antithesis of the aims of the popular creator. The best that popular music could be, in such a system, would be a separate form of creation, a musical equivalent of the car or the washing machine, a musical amenity for use on special occasions, not seeking to edify or to uplift, and not to be judged by such standards. The folk-music lover often believes this to be so at present, but he feels that it should not be so, that it should be to a certain degree linked to and reflective of serious artistic values. But I wonder if any artist can set out to write to second-class standards without courting failure; it is surely likely to be fatal to attempt to create minor art. No matter how limited the form, or the subject, I would suggest that if it does not have that suggestion of a more embracing picture, it can only be light, in the worst sense. Folk art, like fine art, must surely always have a touch of the noble, or even of the tragic, in it.

We have thus been led to raise problems of very great moment: what is the value of art, has it an educative function, can all people benefit from this, should society be changed to permit this benefit to be felt? And, if the answer to these questions is yes, how should this be done? Clearly these are very big questions, and are out of the scope of this book—they are, ultimately, philosophical problems. But the fact that they have arisen is, I believe, a justification of this book, and in particular the second half. Too often in the past our attitude has been to avert our eyes from the horror before us; perhaps this is still the attitude of most "art" musicians. Yet the great contrast between current popular and art music is in itself valuable: to examine one gives us a new perspective on the other. It also reflects the extent and the nature of popular ideals. These may not be acceptable, but they have to be taken into account in any reckoning. Most important, as I said a moment ago, are the questions the topic raises. In essence they are aspects of the way we interpret the meaning of life: I think the reader will agree that nothing is more important to us.

Some Suggestions for Further Reading

PRE-CONQUEST PERIOD

BEARE, W. *Latin Verse and European Song* (Methuen, 1958). A lucid account of the nature and style of Old English verse.

GORDON, R. K. *Anglo-Saxon Poetry* (Dent, Everyman Series). Prose translations of the bulk of Old English verse.

POUND, E. "The Seafarer" (in *Ripostes*, Faber and Faber, 1912), offers an interesting reworking which catches some of the spirit of the original.

More technical articles have been written by Baum on "The Harp in Old English Poetry" (*Modern Philology* 46), and Rankin on "Rhyme in Old English Poetry" (*P.M.L.A.* 36).

MEDIEVAL PERIOD

NETTEL, R. *Seven Centuries of Popular Song* (Harrap), gives a general picture of the period, and is in fact of some interest over the whole range of song up to 1900.

Original lyrics may be studied in:

ROBBINS, R. H. *Secular Lyrics of the Fourteenth and Fifteenth Centuries* (London, 1952).

GREENE, R. L. *The Early English Carols* (Oxford University Press).

GREEN, C. *English Secular Lyrics* (Oxford University Press).

SISAM, K. *Fourteenth Century Verse and Prose* (Oxford University Press).

STONE, B. *Medieval English Verse* (Penguin Classics), provides adequate translations of many of the lyrics.

More detail about particular topics may be found in:

BRIDGE, J. C. "Town Waits" (*Proceedings of the Royal Musical Association* (1928)).

OAKDEN, J. *Alliterative Poetry in Middle English* (Oxford University Press).

MARTIAL, R. *The Wakefield Mystery Plays* (Evans Bros., 1961).

STEVENS, J. *Poetry and Music in the Early Tudor Court*. A scholarly book, which has interesting sections on minstrels.

THE PERIOD 1500–1660

At this point, material becomes more easily accessible and comprehensible: there is a steady stream of editions or arrangements of the better-known Elizabethan songs. The reader's best plan is to go to a reputable music shop and to ask what is currently available. Historical background may be acquired in the first instance from *Shakespeare's England* (ed. Barclay, Pelican), especially the chapters by W. Berkely Squire (XVII) on music, A. Forbes-Sieveking (XXVIII) on dancing, and C. H. Firth (XXIX) on ballads and broadsides. There is an article by E. J. Dent in *A Companion to Shakespeare Studies* specifically on "Shakespeare and Music" and more detailed work on music in the theatre of this period may be found in Professor Sternfield's *Shakespeare and Music*.

Two interesting articles are:
WESTRUP, PROF. SIR J. "Amateurs in Seventeenth-Century England" (*Monthly Musical Record*, vol. 69, 1939).
PULVER, J. "Music in England During the Commonwealth" (*Acta Musicologica* VI–VII, 1934–5).

SCHOLES, P. *The Puritans and Music* (Oxford University Press), gives the fullest treatment of the Commonwealth period.

THE PERIOD 1660–1900

Material specifically about the eighteenth century seems to be rather diffused, but Reginald Nettel's book (*op. cit.*) is very valuable. However, a good picture of the Victorian situation can be obtained from:
DISHER, M. W. *Victorian Song: From Dive to Drawing Room* (Phoenix House).
PULLING, C. *They Were Singing* (Harrap).
Both these books go into the origins of the Victorian song in the eighteenth century.
NETTEL, R. *Music In The Five Towns* (Oxford University Press), gives a most valuable insight into urban working-class musical life in late Victorian England.
THOMPSON, F. *Lark Rise* (Oxford University Press), includes a selection of eyewitness accounts of life in the country.

ENGLISH FOLK SONG

Much work has now been done on the English folk song, and some recommended texts are:
LLOYD, A. L. *The Singing Englishman* (Workers' Music Association).
            Folksong In England (Lawrence and Wishart).
            Come All Ye Bold Miners (Lawrence and Wishart).
SHEPARD, L. *The Broadside Ballad* (Herbert Jenkins).
SHARP, C. *English Folksong: Some Conclusions* (Methuen).

Useful anthologies of songs are:
The Penguin Book of English Folksong.
Marrow Bones (English Folk Dance and Song Society).
The Seeds of Love (English Folk Dance and Song Society).
Coaldust Ballads (Workers' Music Association), mining songs.
Songs of the 60's (Workers' Music Association), protest songs.
The Common Muse, ed. da Sola Pinto and Rodway (Penguin). An anthology of ballads.
The English and Scottish Popular Ballads, ed. F. J. Child (Dover Publications).

THE TWENTIETH CENTURY

If there were many books to recommend about this period, this present book would not have been written.

SPAETH, S. *History of Popular Music in America*, a useful book of reference.
HOGGART, R. *Uses of Literacy* (Penguin), contains some generalised and rather personal comment.
Discrimination and Popular Culture, ed. Denys Thomson (Penguin). The relevant article is by Donald Hughes.
NETTEL, R. *Seven Centuries of Popular Song* (Harrap). Though the author mentions the twentieth century, he is very biased and at times inaccurate.
SIMS, L. *Piano Method*. The technicalities of popular music are to some extent covered in the introduction.
GARCIA, R. *Arranging Method*, covers much the same ground.

There is no book, to my knowledge, on the lyrics. The reader's best plan is to go to a music shop, and buy the thickest album he can, and judge from there.

MABEY, RICHARD. *Connexions* (Penguin Educational Books). A short, but useful insight into the business structure of popular music. It is a book designed for schools.

For some idea of the critical standards which apply to all American-style rhythm music, the classically trained reader will be obliged to turn to books on related subjects; inadequate though this must clearly be, some useful texts in this respect are:
LAMBERT, C. *Music Ho* (Faber and Faber). The section on jazz.
HODEIR, A. *Jazz: Its Evolution and Essence* (Secker and Warburg). *Towards Jazz* (Grove Press). A less technical study than the first book.
GREEN, B. *The Reluctant Art* (MacGibbon and Kee).
SCHULLER, G. *Early Jazz* (Oxford University Press). A very technical book.
KEIL, C. *Urban Blues* (University of Chicago Press). This work has a sociological slant.

The books in the last group are at times very technical, and may often refer to artists whose names the reader will not know, but they are at least written by trained and articulate men, and may point the way for a classically educated musician or listener.

Indices

INDEX OF MUSICAL EXAMPLES

INDEX OF FIRST LINES OF SONGS (including extracts)

INDEX OF SONGS, COMPOSITIONS AND MUSICAL DRAMA

INDEX OF COMPOSERS AND ARTISTS

GENERAL INDEX